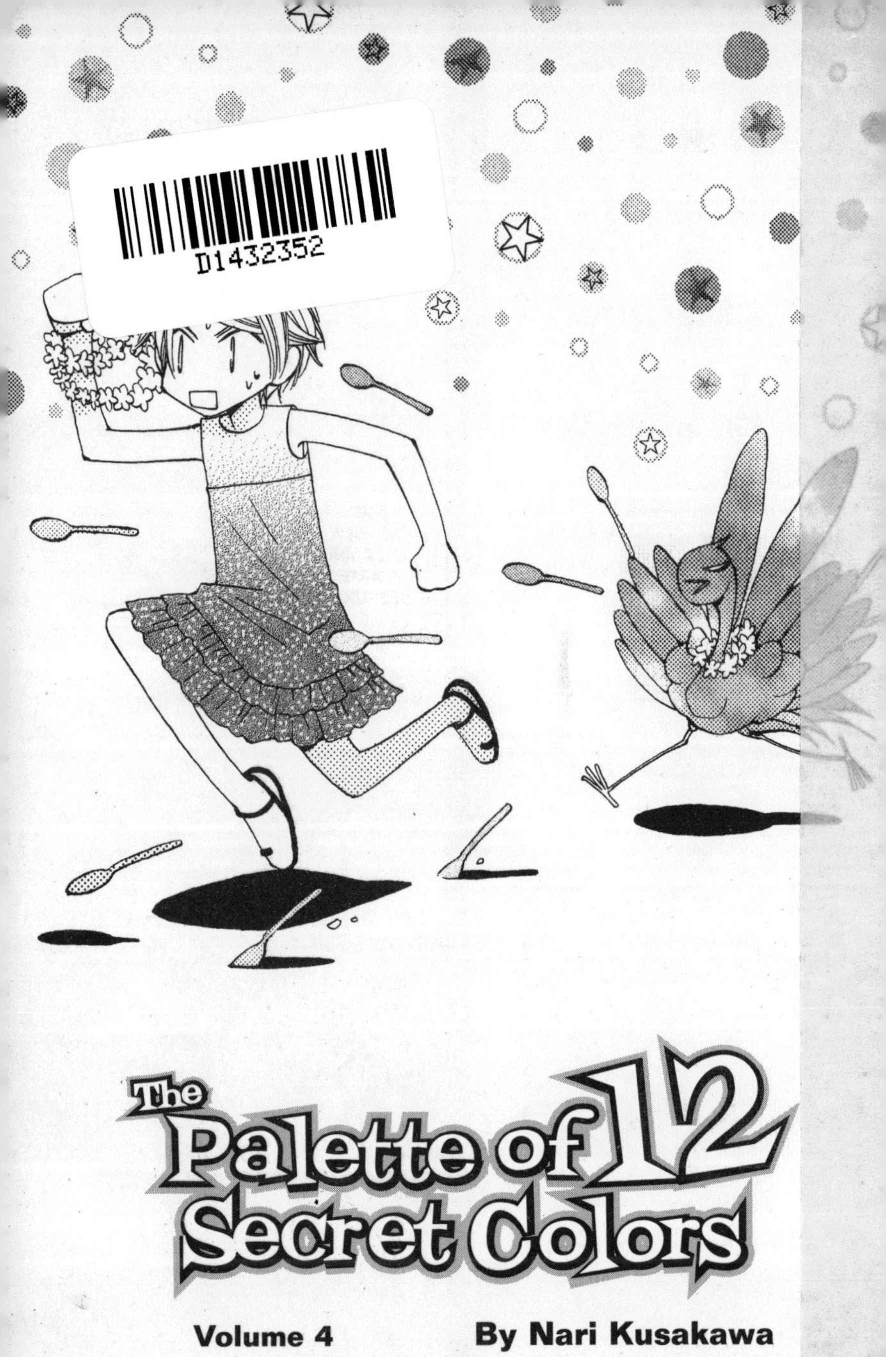

The Palette of 12 Secret Colors

Volume 4

By Nari Kusakawa

CONTENTS

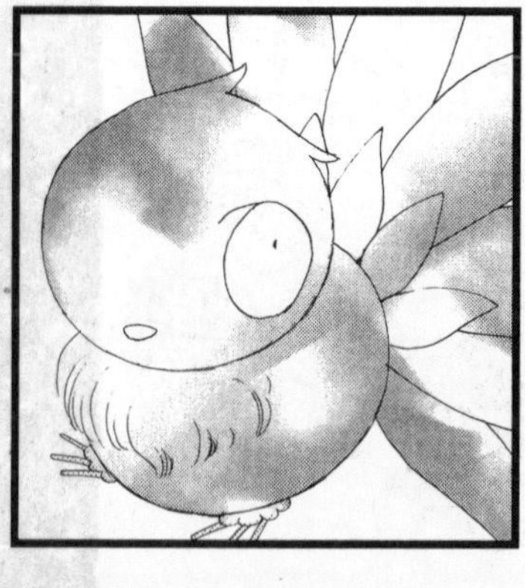

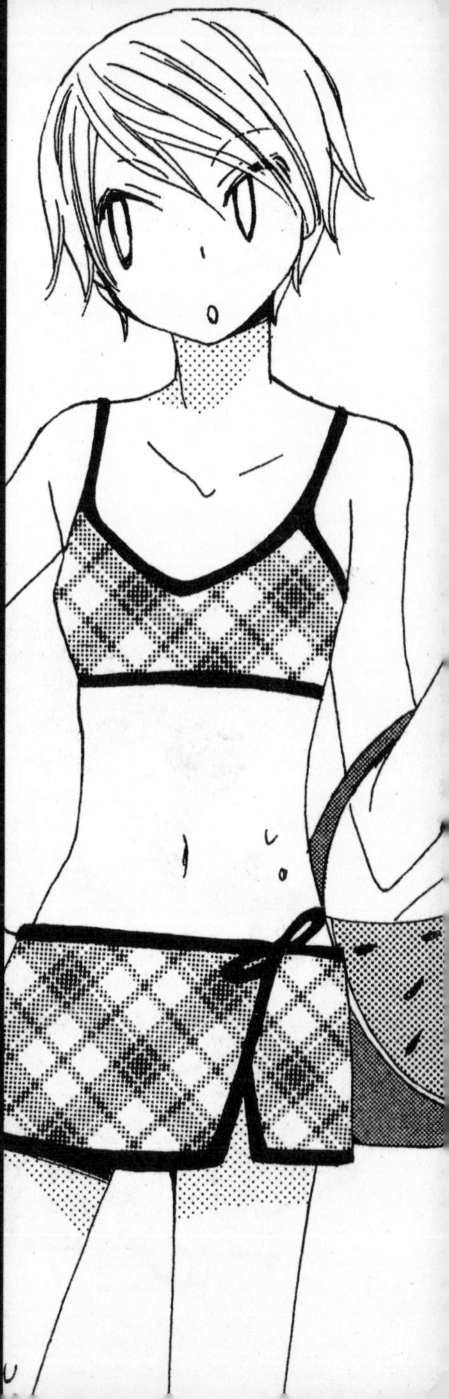

Episode 12 Preview Cut

Cello relaxes by stretching out on the hammock with Yoyo

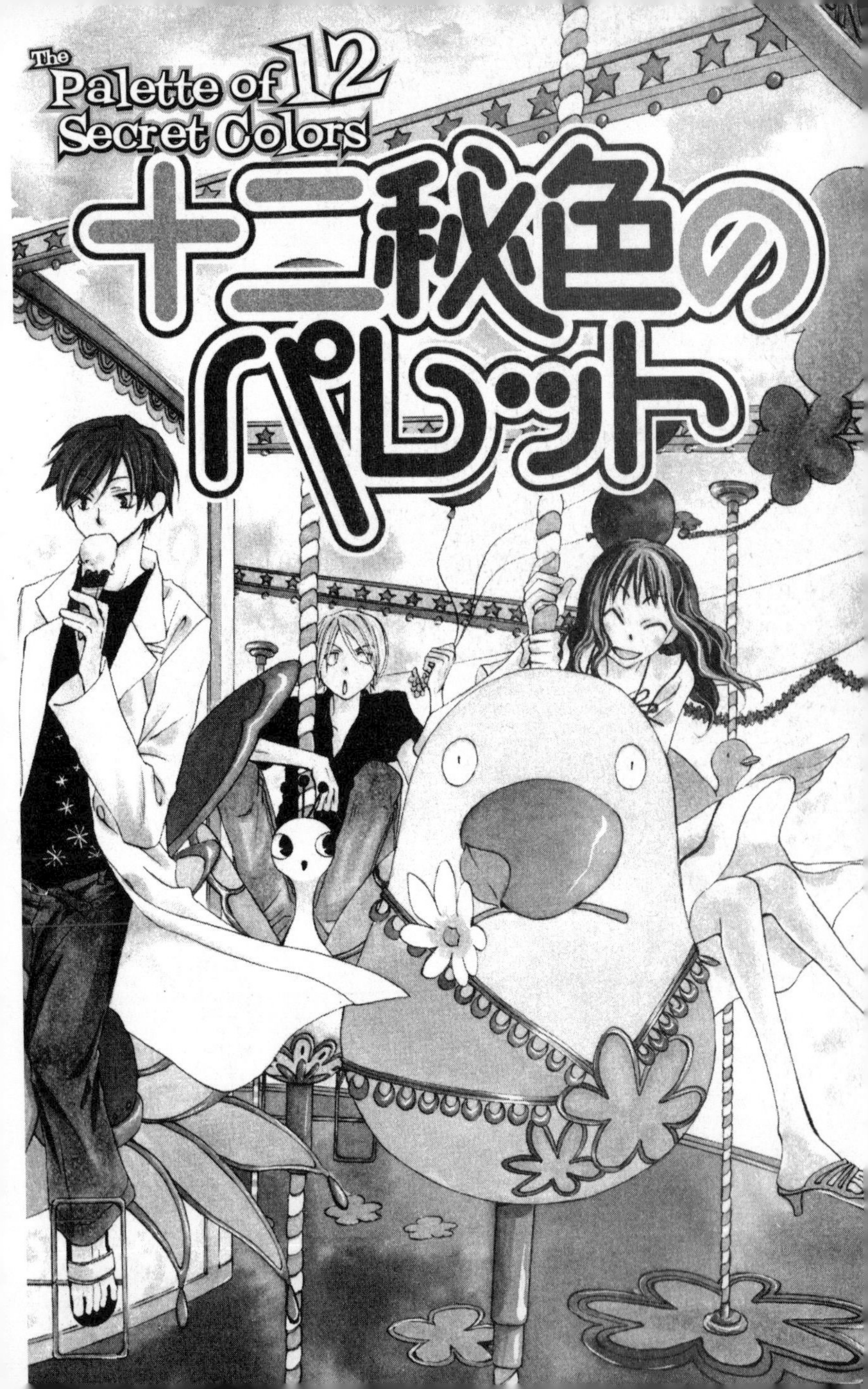
The Palette of 12 Secret Colors
十二秘色のパレット

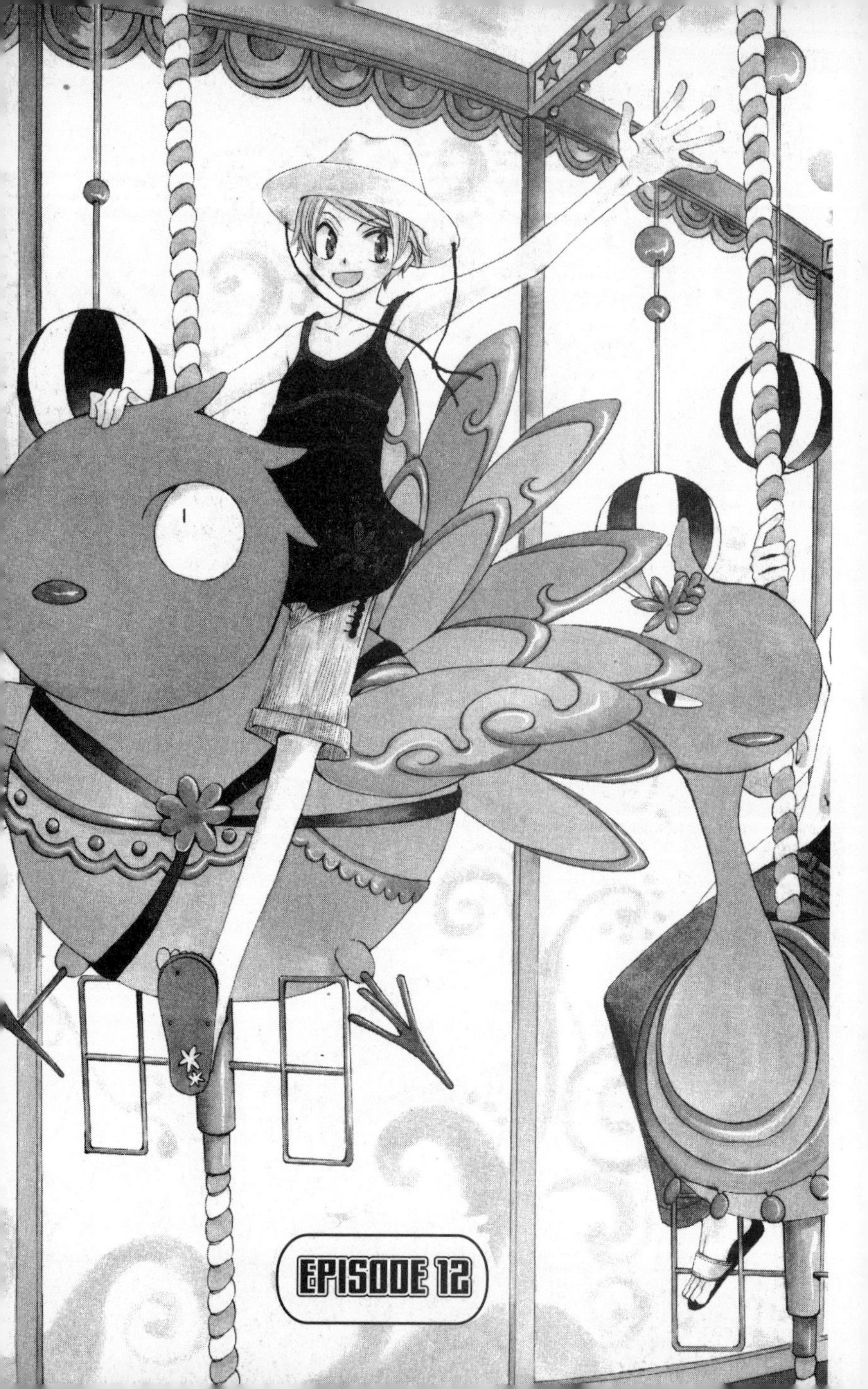
EPISODE 12

Episode 13 Preview Cut

Shaved ice in the shape of Olga. It's grape-flavored. However, I slipped with the eyes part; they have a calm look that Olga's would never have. I can see the Doctor arguing with the shaved ice seller: "Olga doesn't have these eyes. Give me a discount for my disappointment."

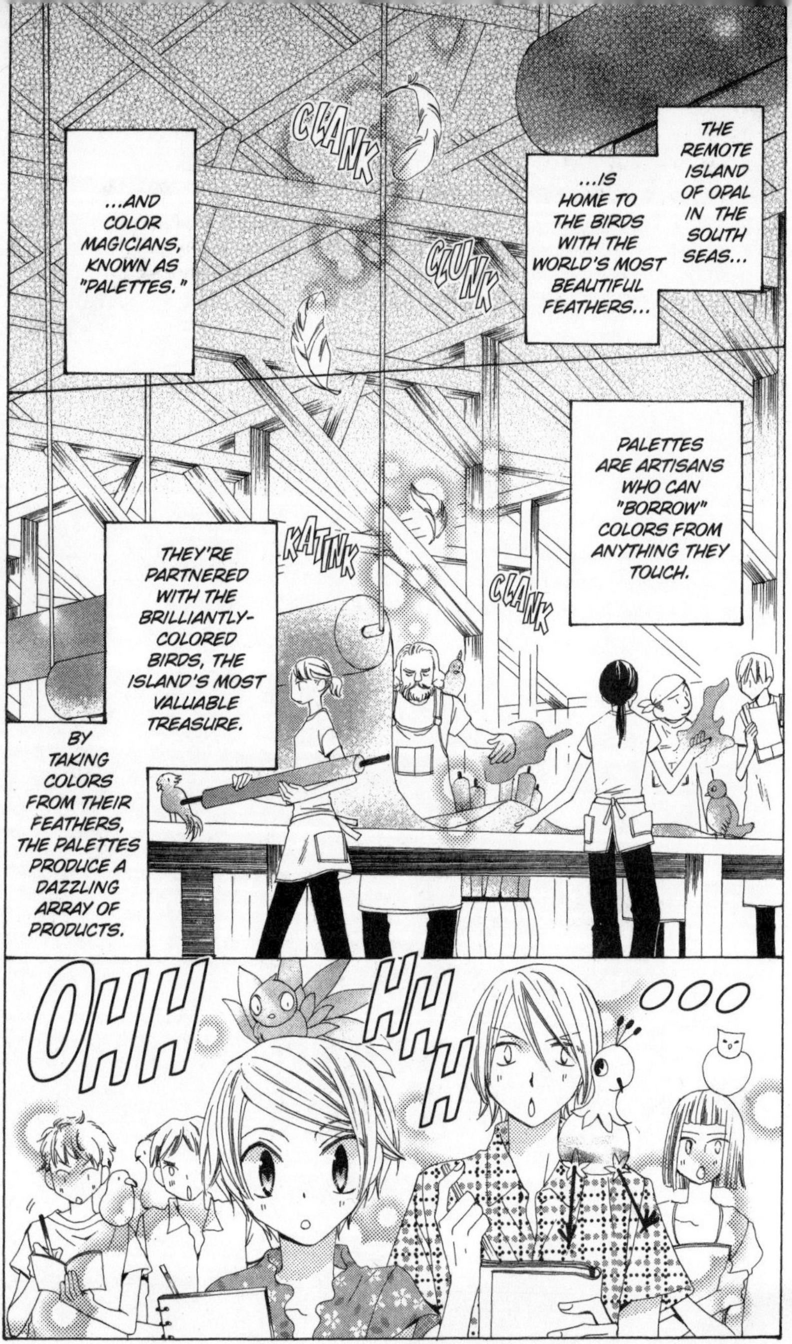
THE REMOTE ISLAND OF OPAL IN THE SOUTH SEAS...
...IS HOME TO THE BIRDS WITH THE WORLD'S MOST BEAUTIFUL FEATHERS...
CLUNK
CLANK
...AND COLOR MAGICIANS, KNOWN AS "PALETTES."
PALETTES ARE ARTISANS WHO CAN "BORROW" COLORS FROM ANYTHING THEY TOUCH.
CLANK
KATINK
THEY'RE PARTNERED WITH THE BRILLIANTLY-COLORED BIRDS, THE ISLAND'S MOST VALUABLE TREASURE.
BY TAKING COLORS FROM THEIR FEATHERS, THE PALETTES PRODUCE A DAZZLING ARRAY OF PRODUCTS.
OHH
HHH
OOO

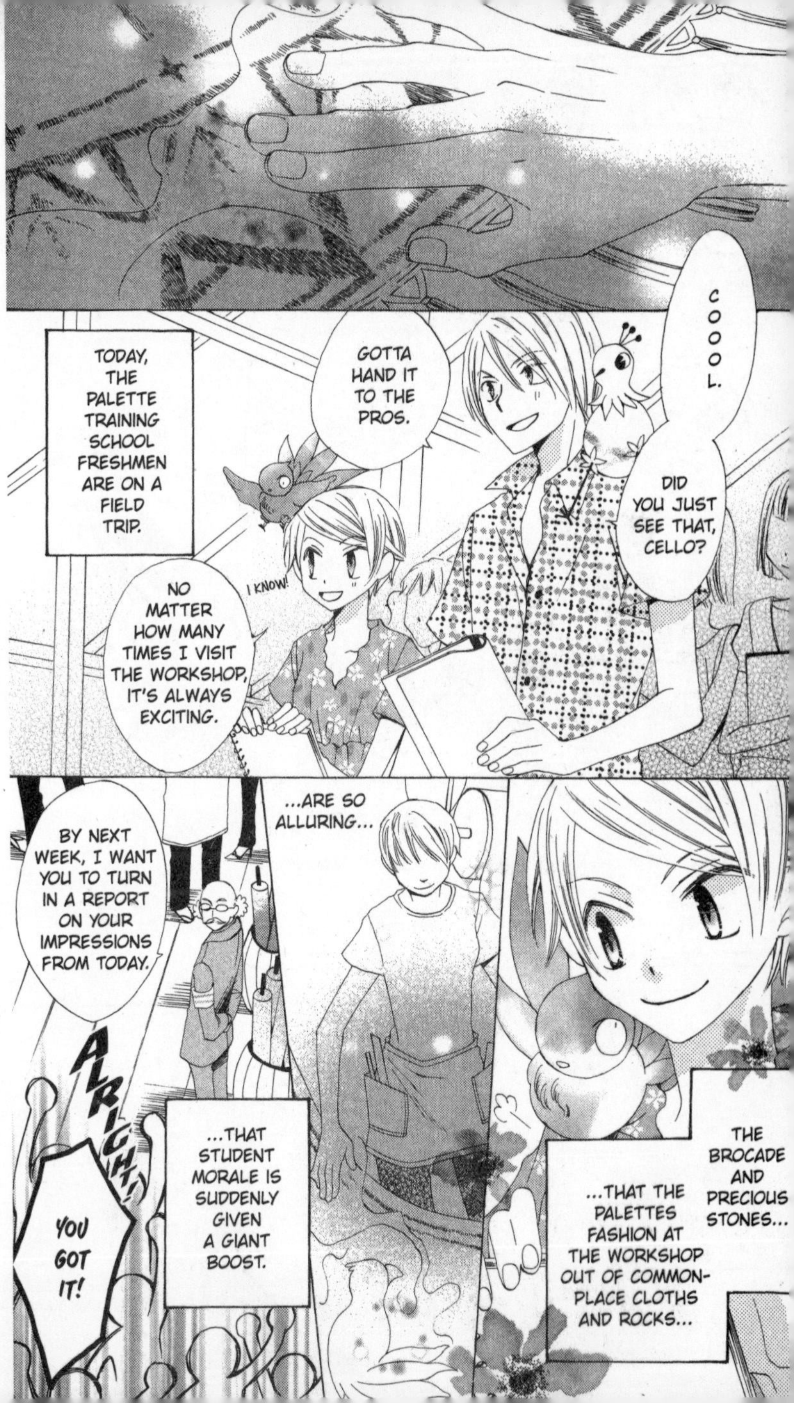
COOOL.
DID YOU JUST SEE THAT, CELLO?
GOTTA HAND IT TO THE PROS.
TODAY, THE PALETTE TRAINING SCHOOL FRESHMEN ARE ON A FIELD TRIP.
I KNOW!
NO MATTER HOW MANY TIMES I VISIT THE WORKSHOP, IT'S ALWAYS EXCITING.
THE BROCADE AND PRECIOUS STONES...
...THAT THE PALETTES FASHION AT THE WORKSHOP OUT OF COMMON-PLACE CLOTHS AND ROCKS...
...ARE SO ALLURING...
...THAT STUDENT MORALE IS SUDDENLY GIVEN A GIANT BOOST.
BY NEXT WEEK, I WANT YOU TO TURN IN A REPORT ON YOUR IMPRESSIONS FROM TODAY.
ALRIGHT!
YOU GOT IT!

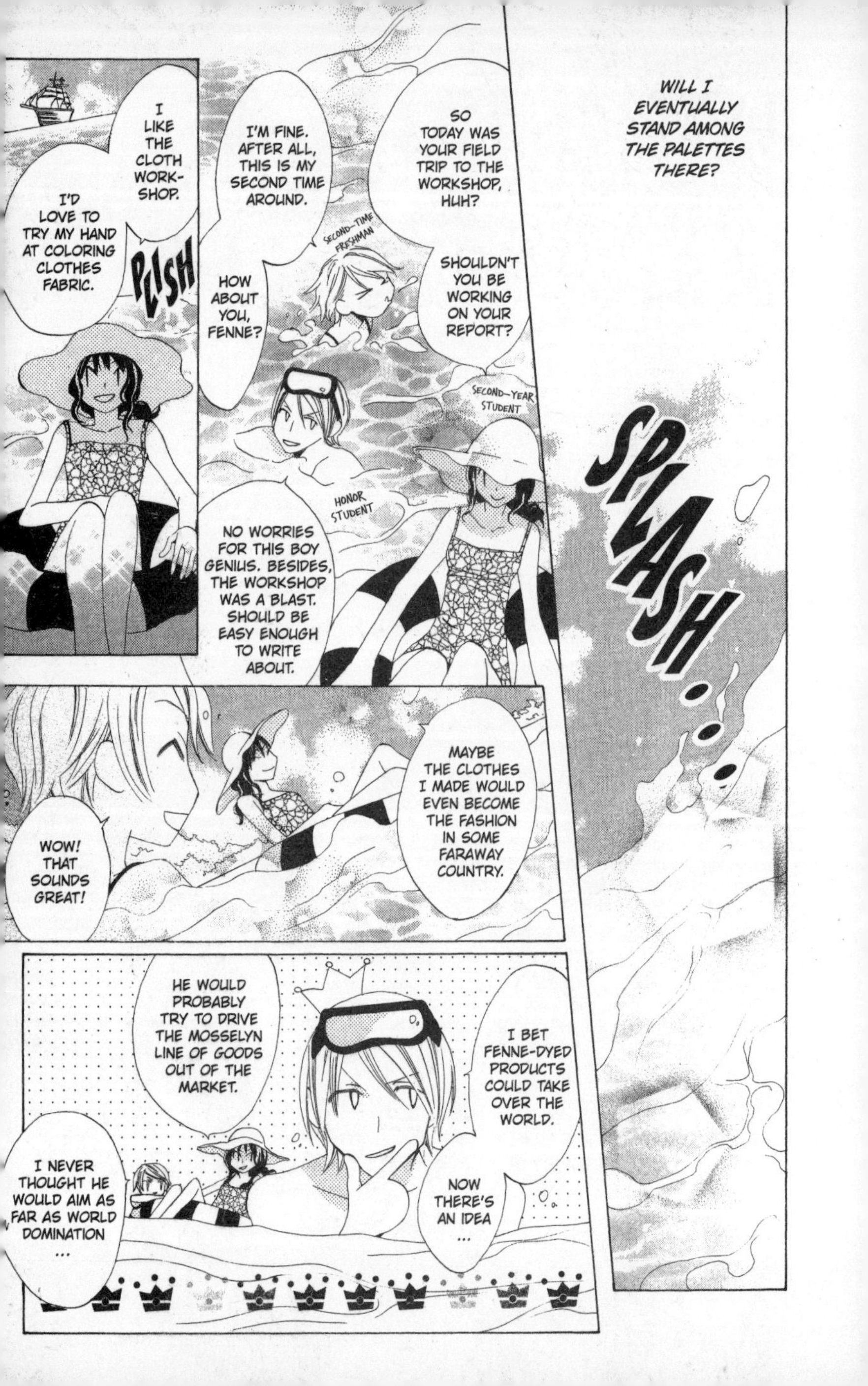
WILL I EVENTUALLY STAND AMONG THE PALETTES THERE?
SPLASH...
SO TODAY WAS YOUR FIELD TRIP TO THE WORKSHOP, HUH?
SHOULDN'T YOU BE WORKING ON YOUR REPORT?
SECOND-YEAR STUDENT
I'M FINE. AFTER ALL, THIS IS MY SECOND TIME AROUND.
SECOND-TIME FRESHMAN
HOW ABOUT YOU, FENNE?
HONOR STUDENT
NO WORRIES FOR THIS BOY GENIUS. BESIDES, THE WORKSHOP WAS A BLAST. SHOULD BE EASY ENOUGH TO WRITE ABOUT.
I LIKE THE CLOTH WORK-SHOP.
I'D LOVE TO TRY MY HAND AT COLORING CLOTHES FABRIC.
PLISH
MAYBE THE CLOTHES I MADE WOULD EVEN BECOME THE FASHION IN SOME FARAWAY COUNTRY.
WOW! THAT SOUNDS GREAT!
I BET FENNE-DYED PRODUCTS COULD TAKE OVER THE WORLD.
HE WOULD PROBABLY TRY TO DRIVE THE MOSSELYN LINE OF GOODS OUT OF THE MARKET.
NOW THERE'S AN IDEA ...
I NEVER THOUGHT HE WOULD AIM AS FAR AS WORLD DOMINATION ...

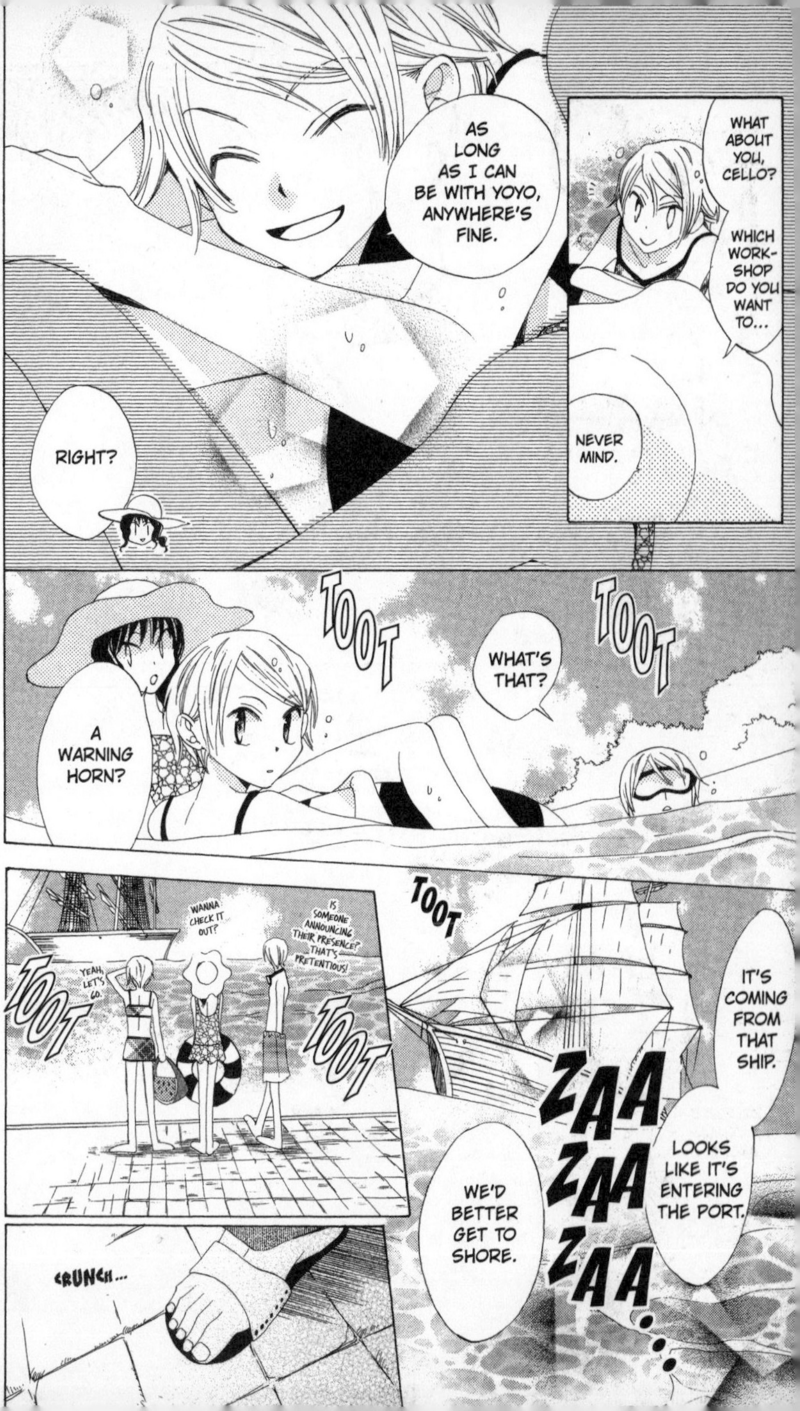
AS LONG AS I CAN BE WITH YOYO, ANYWHERE'S FINE.
WHAT ABOUT YOU, CELLO?
WHICH WORKSHOP DO YOU WANT TO...
NEVER MIND.
RIGHT?
TOOT
TOOT
WHAT'S THAT?
A WARNING HORN?
TOOT
IT'S COMING FROM THAT SHIP.
LOOKS LIKE IT'S ENTERING THE PORT.
ZAA
ZAA
ZAA...
WE'D BETTER GET TO SHORE.
TOOT
TOOT
IS SOMEONE ANNOUNCING THEIR PRESENCE? THAT'S PRETENTIOUS!
WANNA CHECK IT OUT?
YEAH, LET'S GO.
CRUNCH...

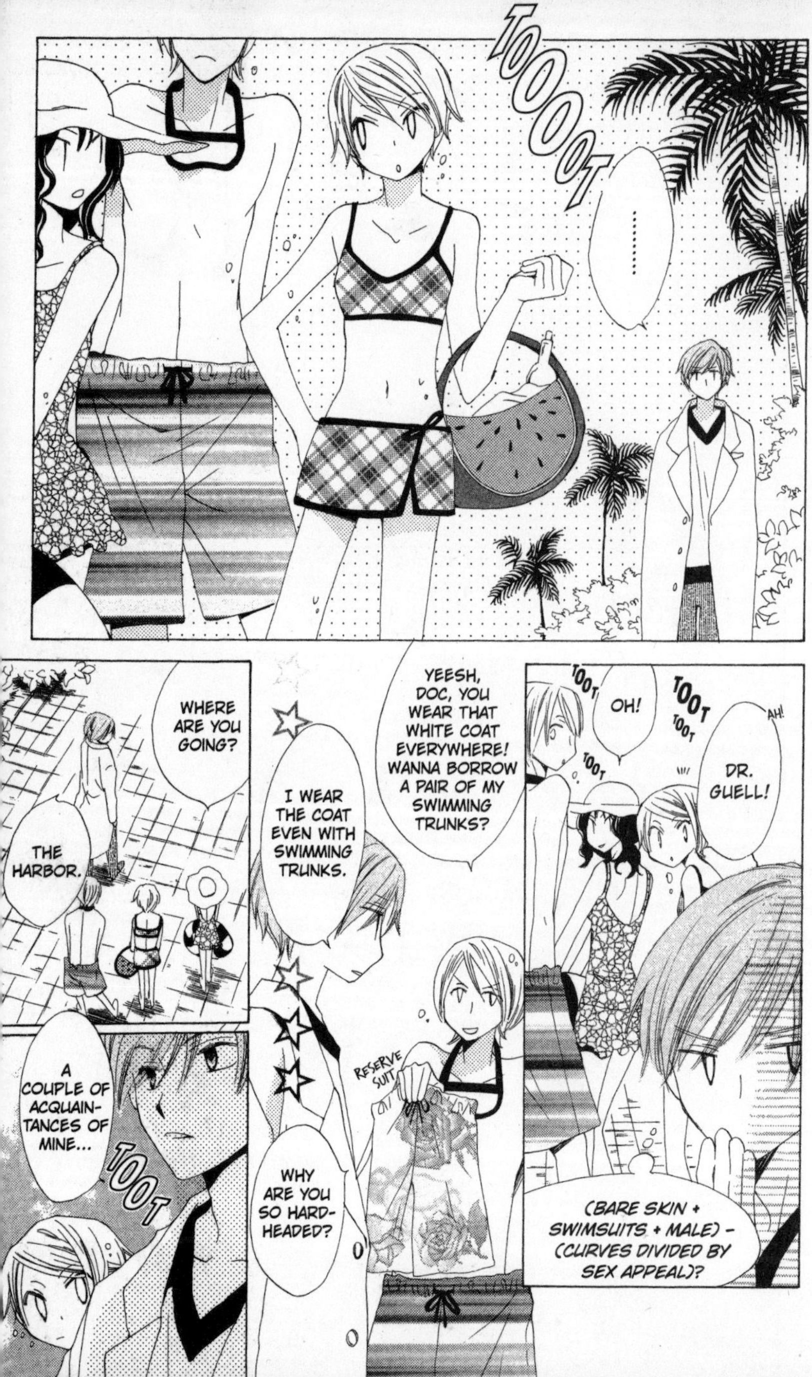
TOOOOT
......
TOOT
OH!
TOOT
TOOT
AH!
DR. GUELL!
TOOT
(BARE SKIN + SWIMSUITS + MALE) - (CURVES DIVIDED BY SEX APPEAL)?
YEESH, DOC, YOU WEAR THAT WHITE COAT EVERYWHERE! WANNA BORROW A PAIR OF MY SWIMMING TRUNKS?
I WEAR THE COAT EVEN WITH SWIMMING TRUNKS.
RESERVE SUIT
WHY ARE YOU SO HARD-HEADED?
WHERE ARE YOU GOING?
THE HARBOR.
A COUPLE OF ACQUAINTANCES OF MINE...
TOOT

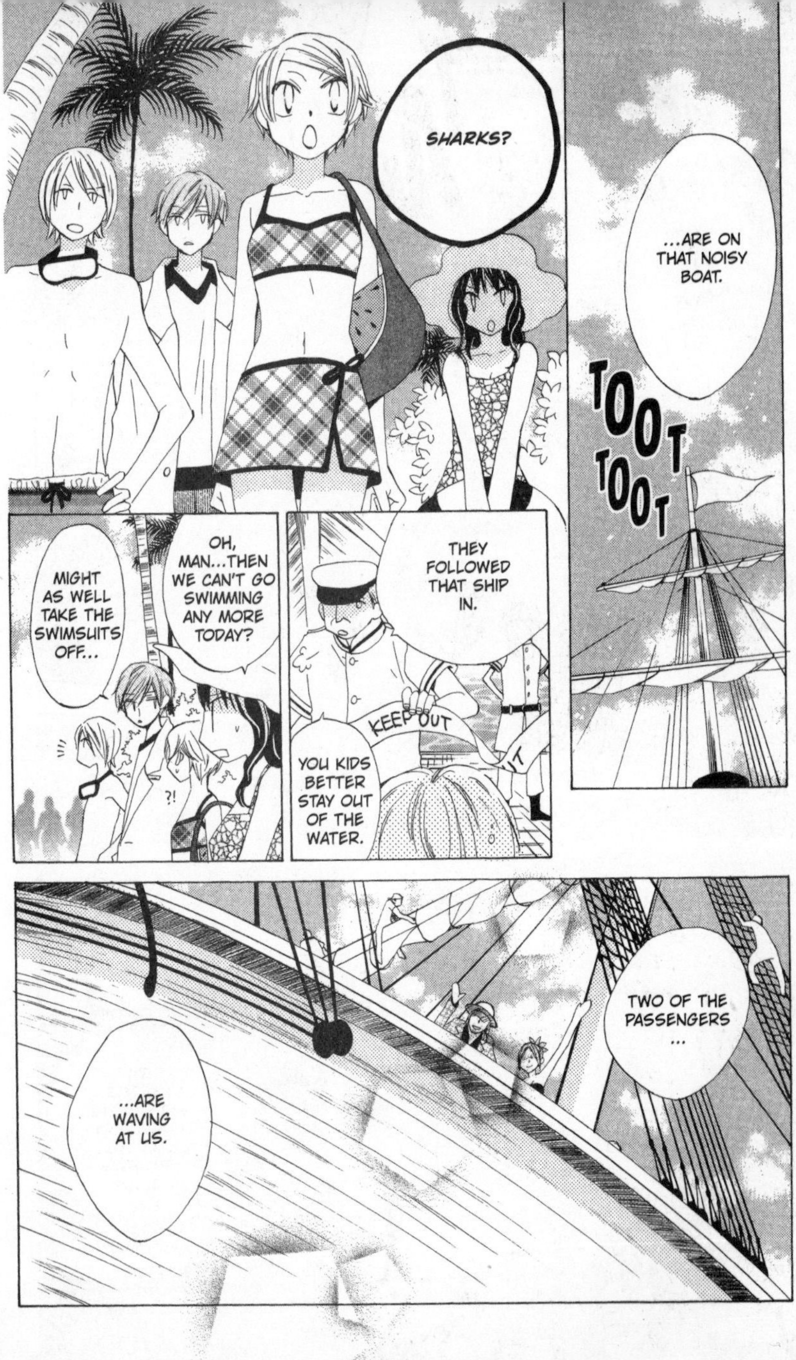
...ARE ON THAT NOISY BOAT.
TOOT TOOT
SHARKS?
THEY FOLLOWED THAT SHIP IN.
KEEP OUT
YOU KIDS BETTER STAY OUT OF THE WATER.
OH, MAN...THEN WE CAN'T GO SWIMMING ANY MORE TODAY?
MIGHT AS WELL TAKE THE SWIMSUITS OFF...
?!
TWO OF THE PASSENGERS ...
...ARE WAVING AT US.

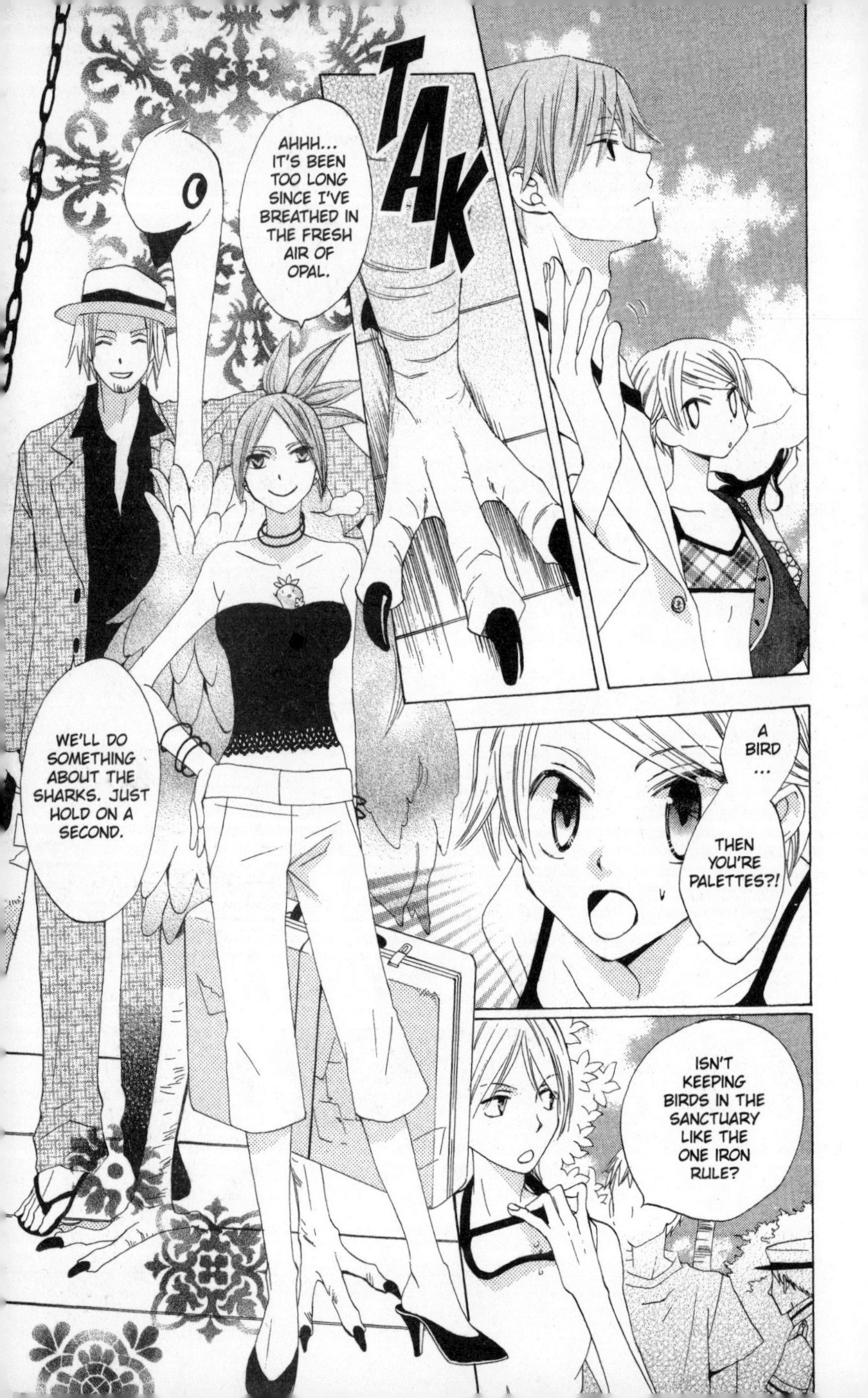
TAK
A BIRD ...
THEN YOU'RE PALETTES?!
ISN'T KEEPING BIRDS IN THE SANCTUARY LIKE THE ONE IRON RULE?
AHHH... IT'S BEEN TOO LONG SINCE I'VE BREATHED IN THE FRESH AIR OF OPAL.
WE'LL DO SOMETHING ABOUT THE SHARKS. JUST HOLD ON A SECOND.

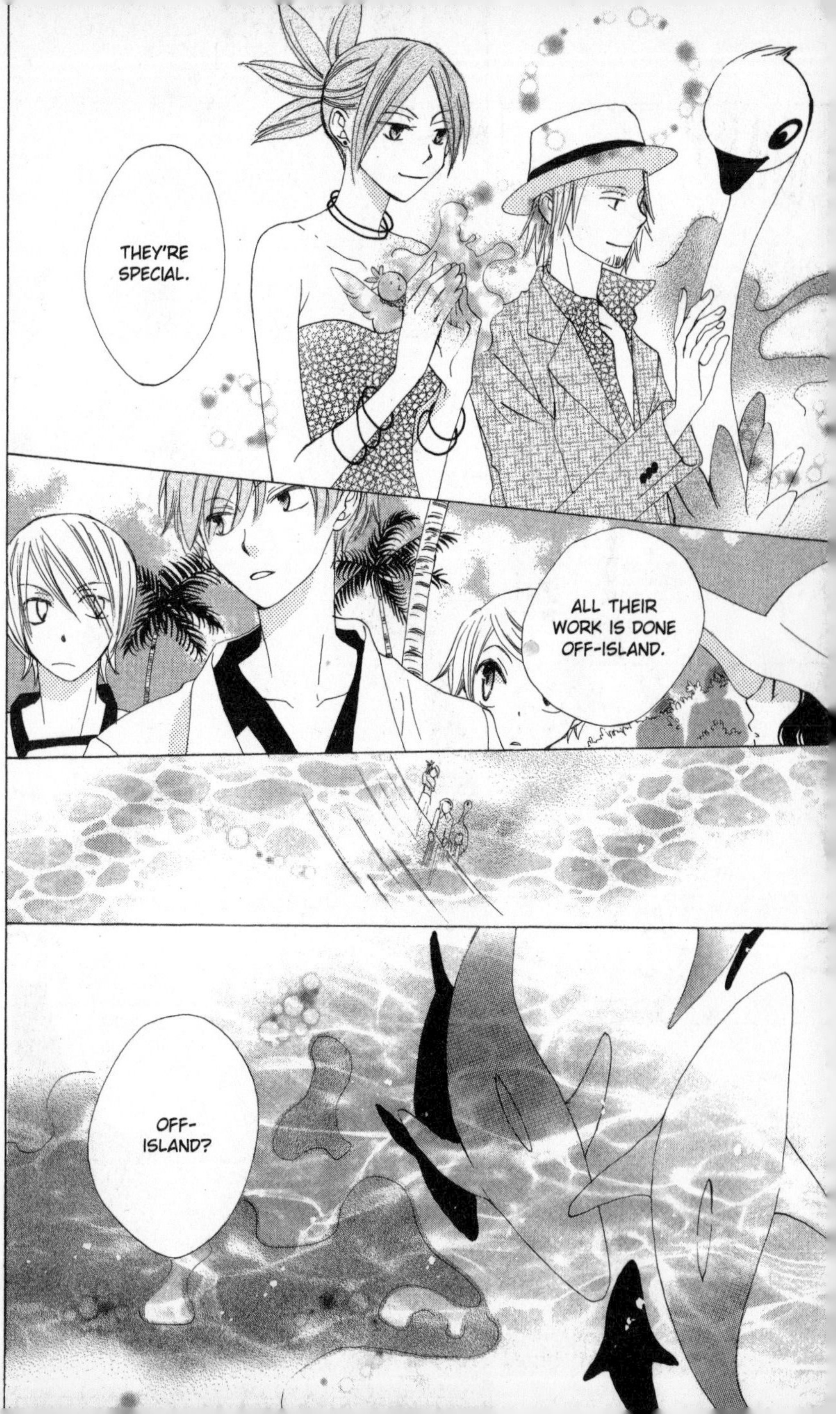
THEY'RE SPECIAL.
ALL THEIR WORK IS DONE OFF-ISLAND.
OFF-ISLAND?

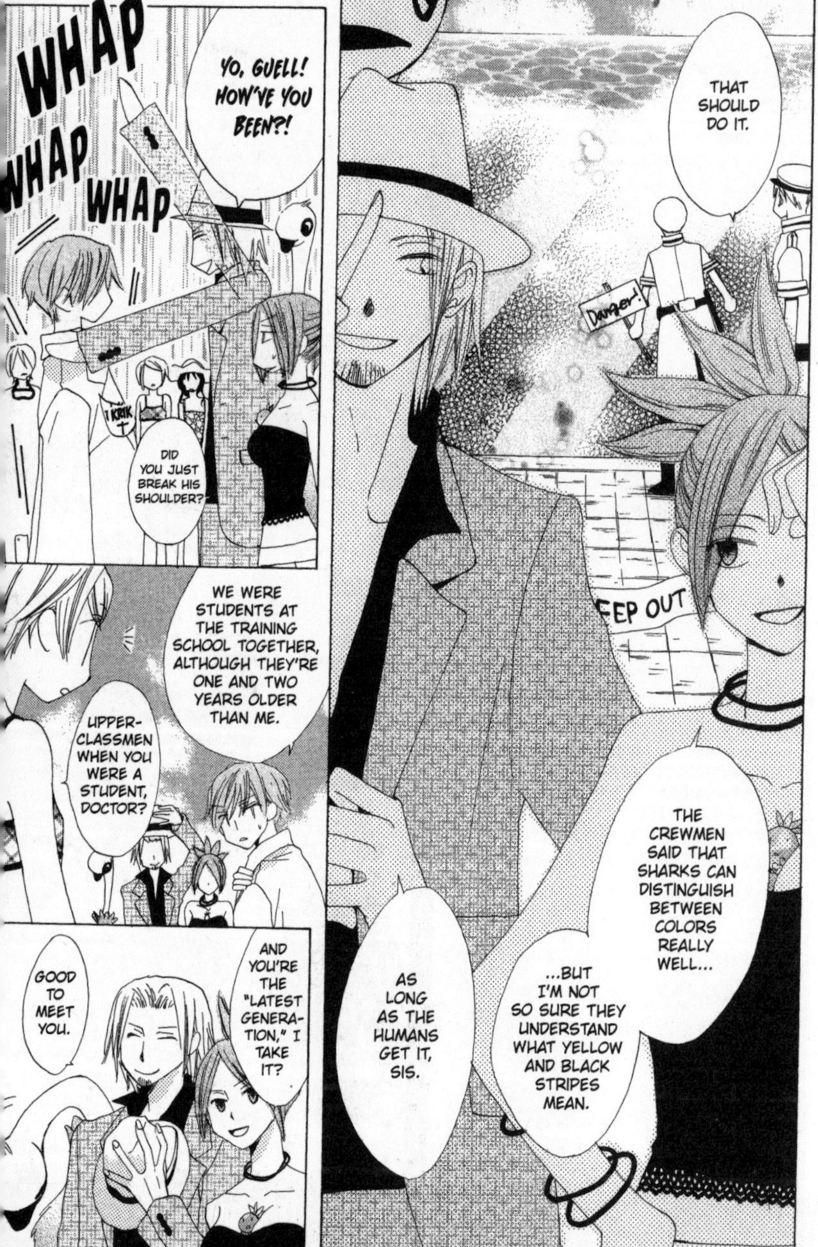
THAT SHOULD DO IT.
Danger!
THE CREWMEN SAID THAT SHARKS CAN DISTINGUISH BETWEEN COLORS REALLY WELL...
...BUT I'M NOT SO SURE THEY UNDERSTAND WHAT YELLOW AND BLACK STRIPES MEAN.
AS LONG AS THE HUMANS GET IT, SIS.
WHAP WHAP WHAP
YO, GUELL! HOW'VE YOU BEEN?!
KRIK
DID YOU JUST BREAK HIS SHOULDER?
WE WERE STUDENTS AT THE TRAINING SCHOOL TOGETHER, ALTHOUGH THEY'RE ONE AND TWO YEARS OLDER THAN ME.
UPPER-CLASSMEN WHEN YOU WERE A STUDENT, DOCTOR?
AND YOU'RE THE "LATEST GENERA-TION," I TAKE IT?
GOOD TO MEET YOU.

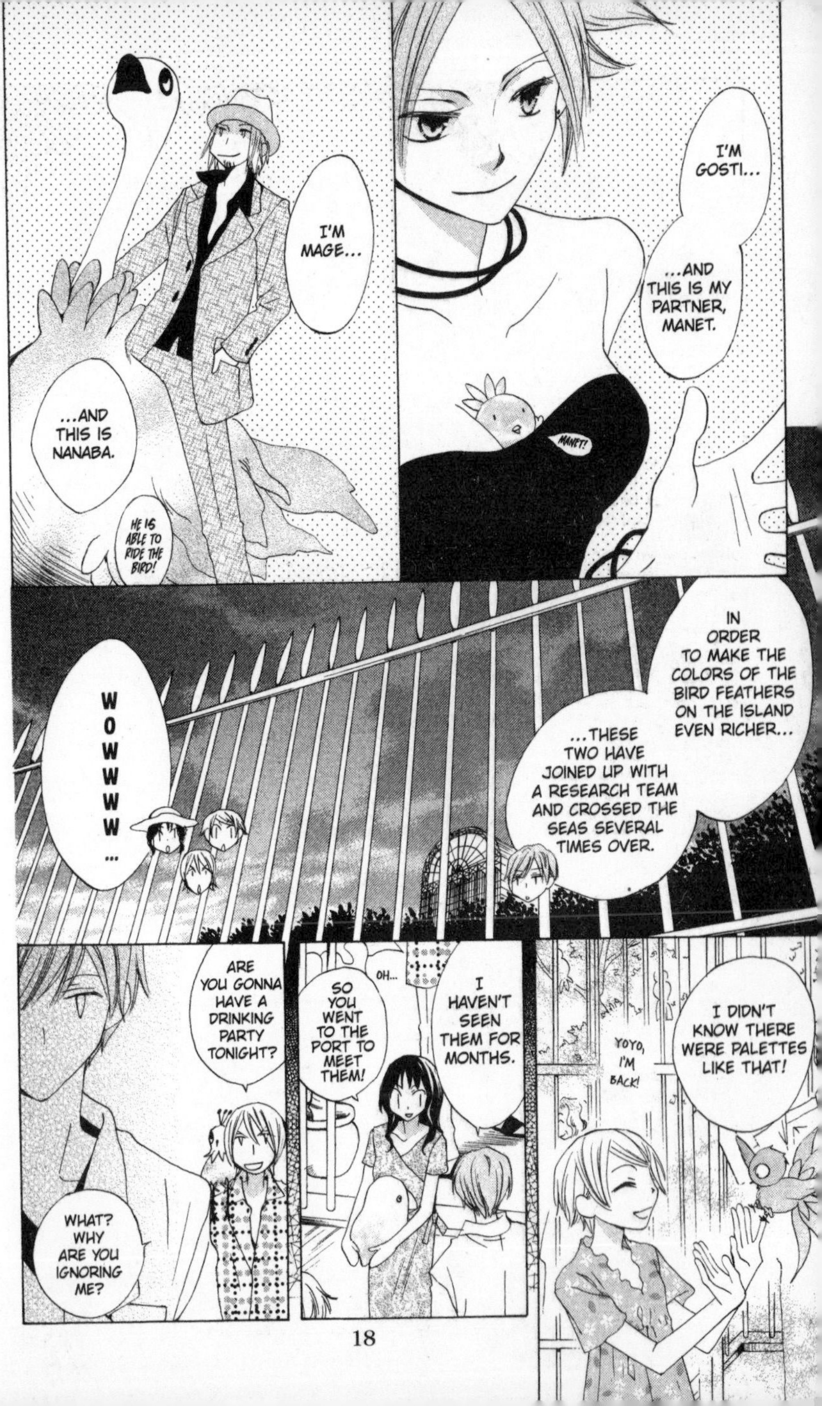
I'M GOSTI...
...AND THIS IS MY PARTNER, MANET.
MANET!
I'M MAGE...
...AND THIS IS NANABA.
HE IS ABLE TO RIDE THE BIRD!
IN ORDER TO MAKE THE COLORS OF THE BIRD FEATHERS ON THE ISLAND EVEN RICHER...
...THESE TWO HAVE JOINED UP WITH A RESEARCH TEAM AND CROSSED THE SEAS SEVERAL TIMES OVER.
WOWWWW...
I DIDN'T KNOW THERE WERE PALETTES LIKE THAT!
YOYO, I'M BACK!
I HAVEN'T SEEN THEM FOR MONTHS.
OH...
SO YOU WENT TO THE PORT TO MEET THEM!
ARE YOU GONNA HAVE A DRINKING PARTY TONIGHT?
WHAT? WHY ARE YOU IGNORING ME?

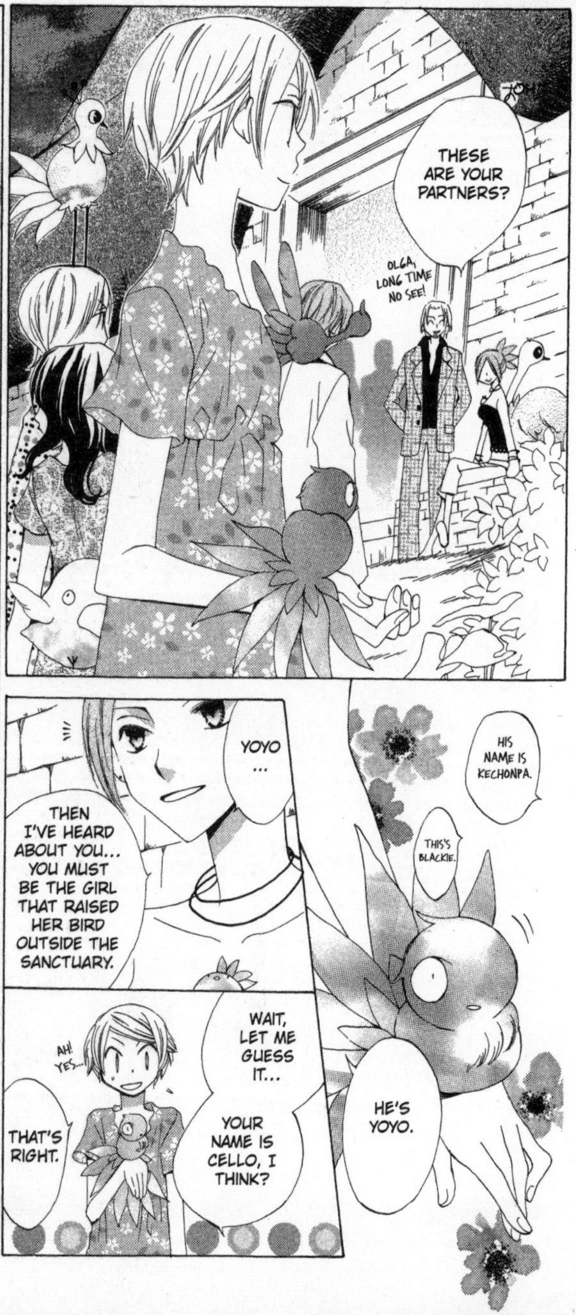
THESE ARE YOUR PARTNERS?
OLGA, LONG TIME NO SEE!
HIS NAME IS KECHONPA.
THIS'S BLACKIE.
HE'S YOYO.
YOYO...
THEN I'VE HEARD ABOUT YOU... YOU MUST BE THE GIRL THAT RAISED HER BIRD OUTSIDE THE SANCTUARY.
WAIT, LET ME GUESS IT...
YOUR NAME IS CELLO, I THINK?
AH! YES...
THAT'S RIGHT.

1

HELLO.
THANK YOU FOR GETTING VOLUME 4 OF "*PALETTE.*" VOLUME 4...WOW, THAT WAS FAST. OF COURSE, NOT NEARLY AS FAST AS THE EPISODES PUBLISHED IN THE MAGAZINE. USING MY FIRST PUBLISHED SERIES, THE FIVE-VOLUME "*RECIPE FOR GERTRUDE*" AS A YARDSTICK, GETTING TO VOLUME 4 MEANS I SHOULD BE TRYING TO WIND THE WHOLE STORY UP, BUT I THINK I'LL LET "*PALETTE*" GO AT A LITTLE MORE LEISURELY PACE.
AS I WRITE THIS, IT'S JUST AFTER NEW YEAR'S, 2007. ON A CERTAIN TV STATION WEBSITE, I SAW THAT MY LUCK FOR THE YEAR WILL BE 6 OUT OF 576 (ON A SCALE WITH ONE BEING PERFECT, 576 THE VERY WORST)! FANTASTIC!, I THOUGHT...UNTIL I SAW THAT THAT WAS FOR 2006. THE '07 FORECAST PUT ME AT 442 OUT OF 576. DOESN'T MAKE FOR A VERY GOOD STORY SINCE "442" IS NEITHER GREAT NOR TERRIBLE. AH, WELL, I'M GONNA FORGET ABOUT THAT CRUMMY PREDICTION AND DO MY BEST THIS YEAR.

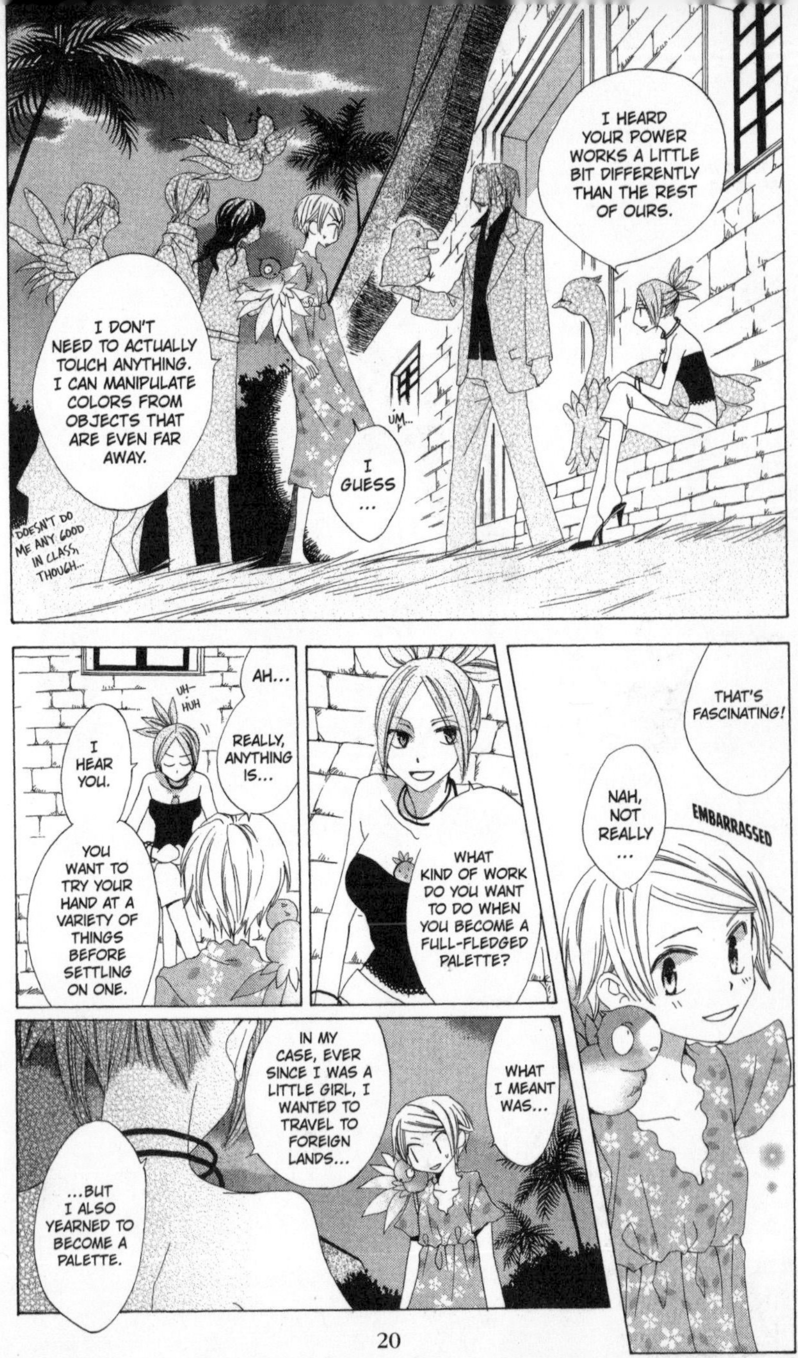
I HEARD YOUR POWER WORKS A LITTLE BIT DIFFERENTLY THAN THE REST OF OURS.
UM...
I GUESS...
I DON'T NEED TO ACTUALLY TOUCH ANYTHING. I CAN MANIPULATE COLORS FROM OBJECTS THAT ARE EVEN FAR AWAY.
DOESN'T DO ME ANY GOOD IN CLASS, THOUGH...
THAT'S FASCINATING!
NAH, NOT REALLY...
EMBARRASSED
WHAT KIND OF WORK DO YOU WANT TO DO WHEN YOU BECOME A FULL-FLEDGED PALETTE?
AH...
REALLY, ANYTHING IS...
UH-HUH
I HEAR YOU.
YOU WANT TO TRY YOUR HAND AT A VARIETY OF THINGS BEFORE SETTLING ON ONE.
WHAT I MEANT WAS...
IN MY CASE, EVER SINCE I WAS A LITTLE GIRL, I WANTED TO TRAVEL TO FOREIGN LANDS...
...BUT I ALSO YEARNED TO BECOME A PALETTE.

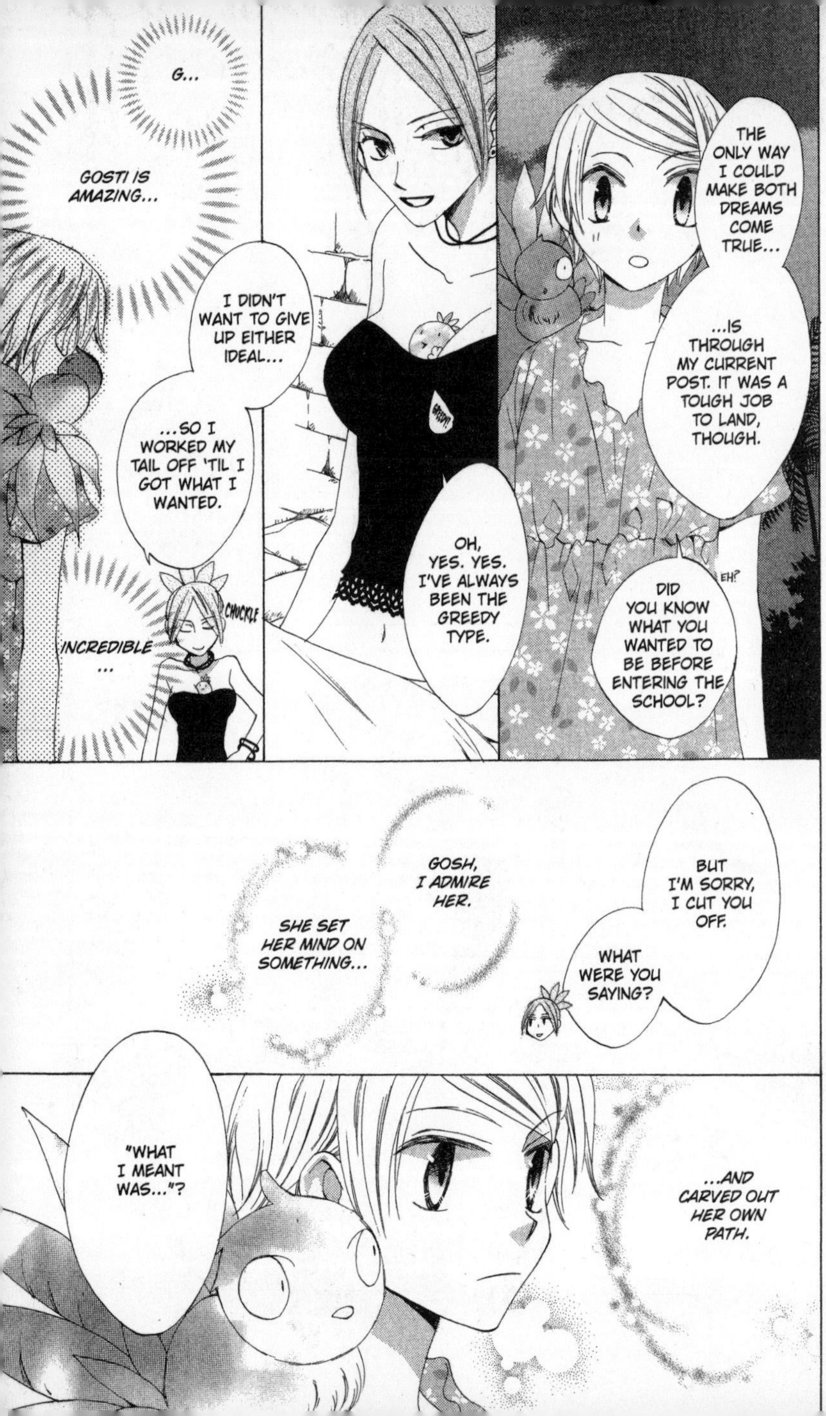
THE ONLY WAY I COULD MAKE BOTH DREAMS COME TRUE...
...IS THROUGH MY CURRENT POST. IT WAS A TOUGH JOB TO LAND, THOUGH.
EH?
DID YOU KNOW WHAT YOU WANTED TO BE BEFORE ENTERING THE SCHOOL?
I DIDN'T WANT TO GIVE UP EITHER IDEAL...
...SO I WORKED MY TAIL OFF 'TIL I GOT WHAT I WANTED.
OH, YES. YES. I'VE ALWAYS BEEN THE GREEDY TYPE.
GREEDY!
G...
GOSTI IS AMAZING...
CHUCKLE
INCREDIBLE...
BUT I'M SORRY, I CUT YOU OFF.
WHAT WERE YOU SAYING?
GOSH, I ADMIRE HER.
SHE SET HER MIND ON SOMETHING...
...AND CARVED OUT HER OWN PATH.
"WHAT I MEANT WAS..."?

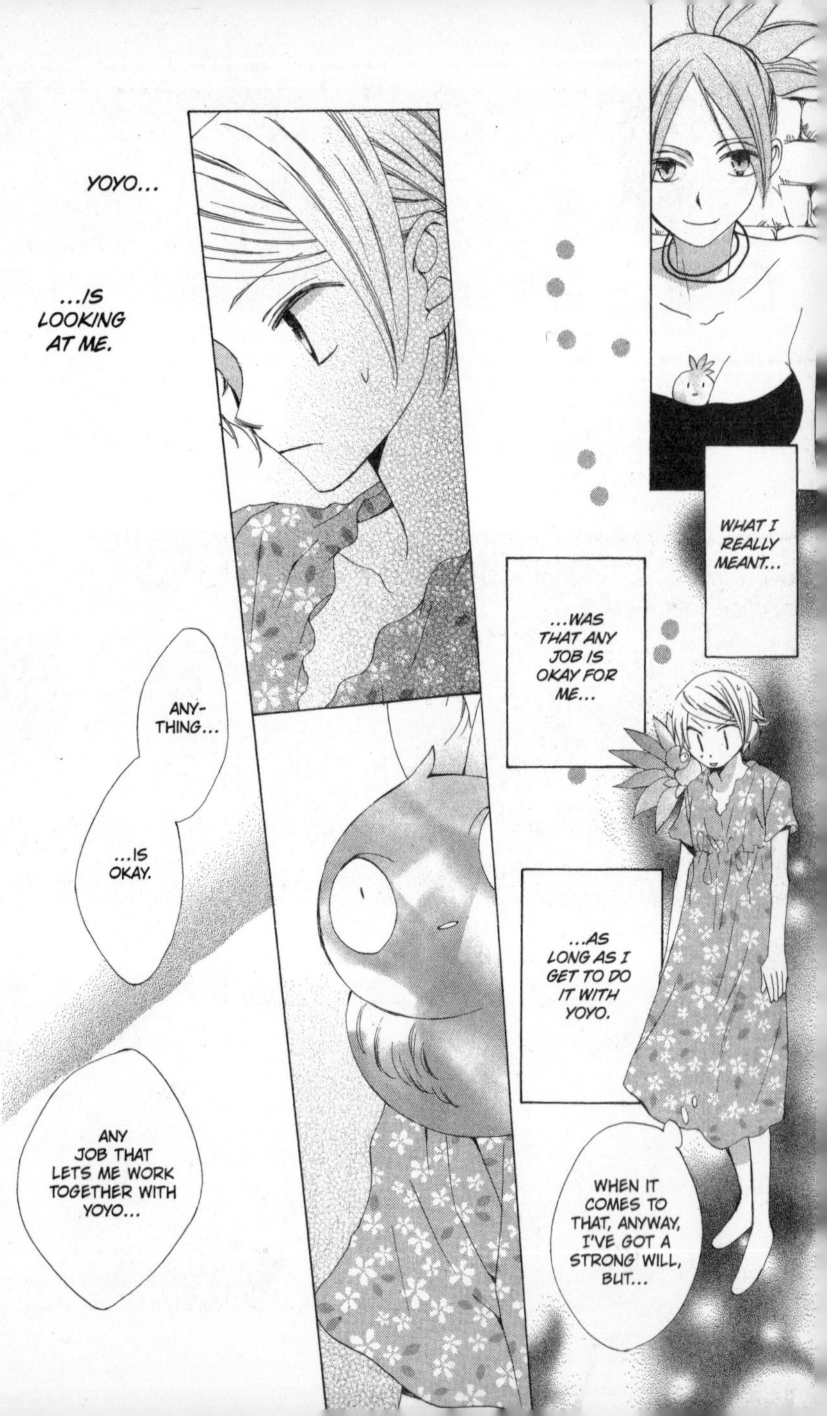
WHAT I REALLY MEANT...
...WAS THAT ANY JOB IS OKAY FOR ME...
...AS LONG AS I GET TO DO IT WITH YOYO.
WHEN IT COMES TO THAT, ANYWAY, I'VE GOT A STRONG WILL, BUT...
YOYO...
...IS LOOKING AT ME.
ANY-THING...
...IS OKAY.
ANY JOB THAT LETS ME WORK TOGETHER WITH YOYO...

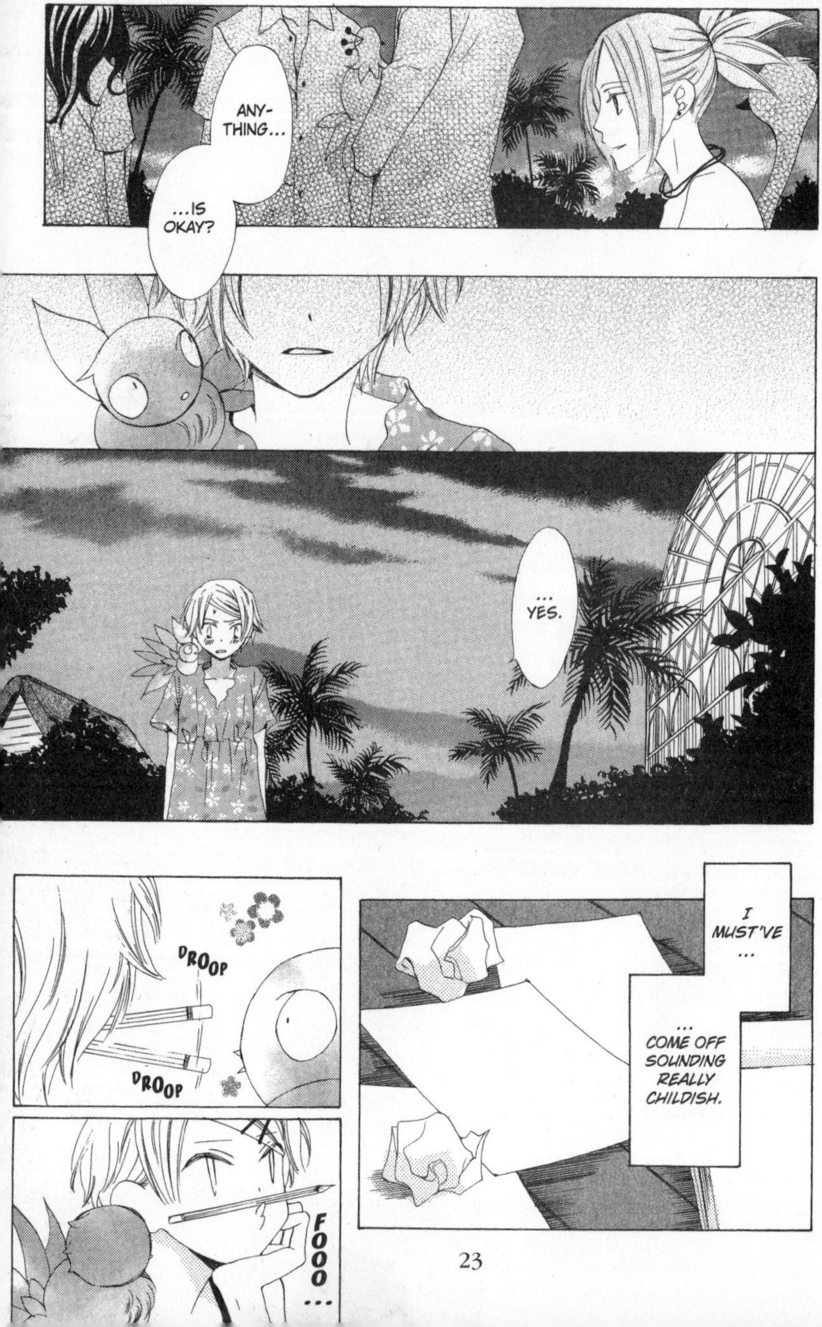
ANY-
THING...
...IS
OKAY?
...
YES.
I
MUST'VE
...
...
COME OFF
SOUNDING
REALLY
CHILDISH.
DROOP
DROOP
FOOO
...

MY WORKSHOP REPORT...

...IS GOING NOWHERE.

BUT NOW...

I THOUGHT IT'D BE A BREEZE...

...SINCE I HAD TO DO THE SAME THING LAST YEAR.

...WHEN IT'S TIME TO PUT PENCIL TO PAPER...

...I DON'T HAVE A SINGLE IDEA.

ROLLooo

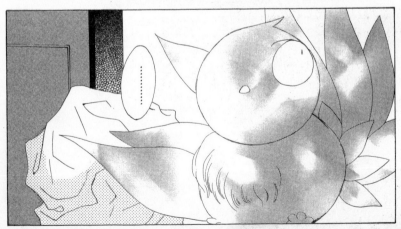

・・・・・

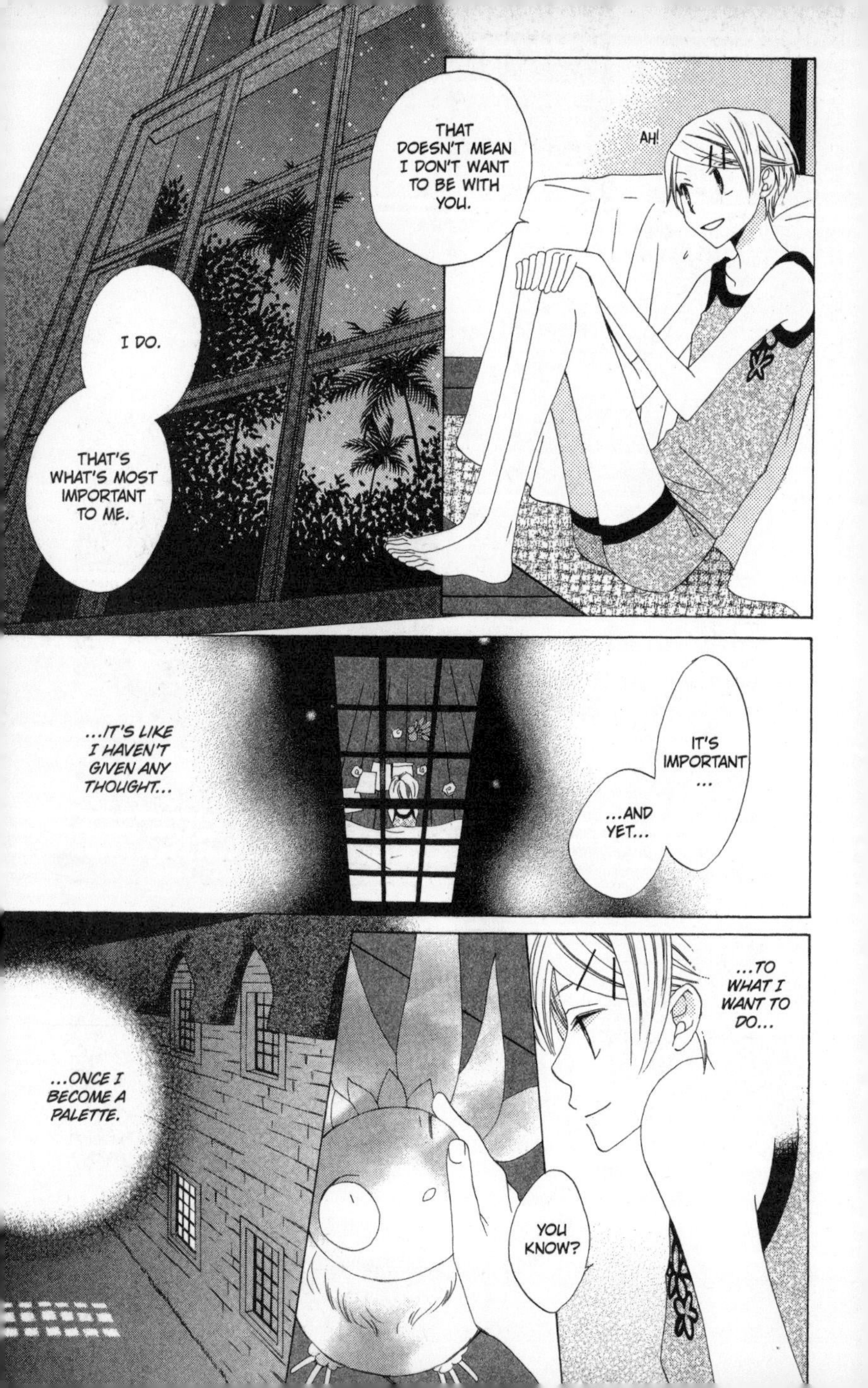
AH!
THAT DOESN'T MEAN I DON'T WANT TO BE WITH YOU.
I DO.
THAT'S WHAT'S MOST IMPORTANT TO ME.
IT'S IMPORTANT...
...AND YET...
...IT'S LIKE I HAVEN'T GIVEN ANY THOUGHT...
...TO WHAT I WANT TO DO...
YOU KNOW?
...ONCE I BECOME A PALETTE.

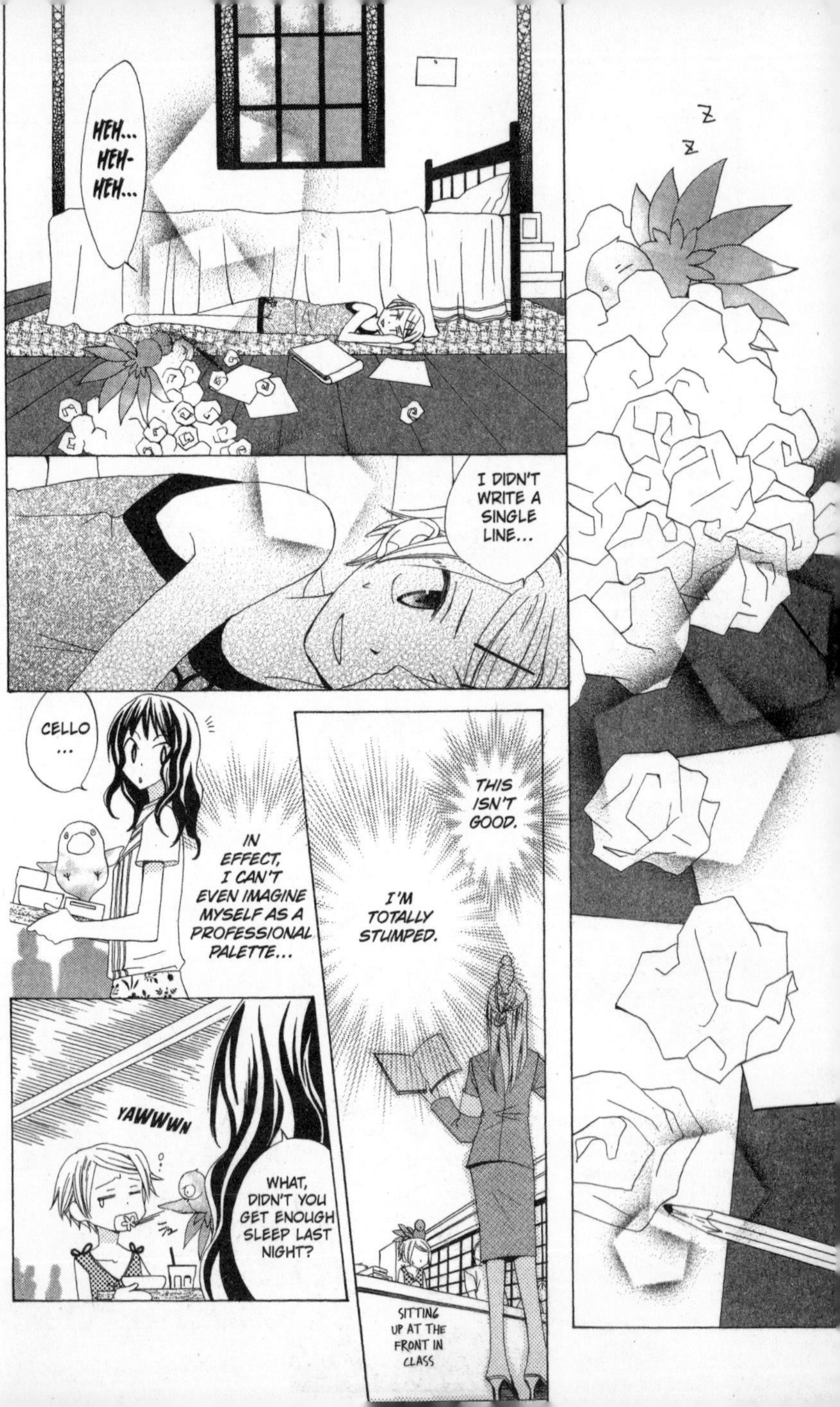
Z
Z
HEH... HEH-HEH...
I DIDN'T WRITE A SINGLE LINE...
THIS ISN'T GOOD.
I'M TOTALLY STUMPED.
SITTING UP AT THE FRONT IN CLASS
CELLO ...
IN EFFECT, I CAN'T EVEN IMAGINE MYSELF AS A PROFESSIONAL PALETTE...
YAWWWN
WHAT, DIDN'T YOU GET ENOUGH SLEEP LAST NIGHT?

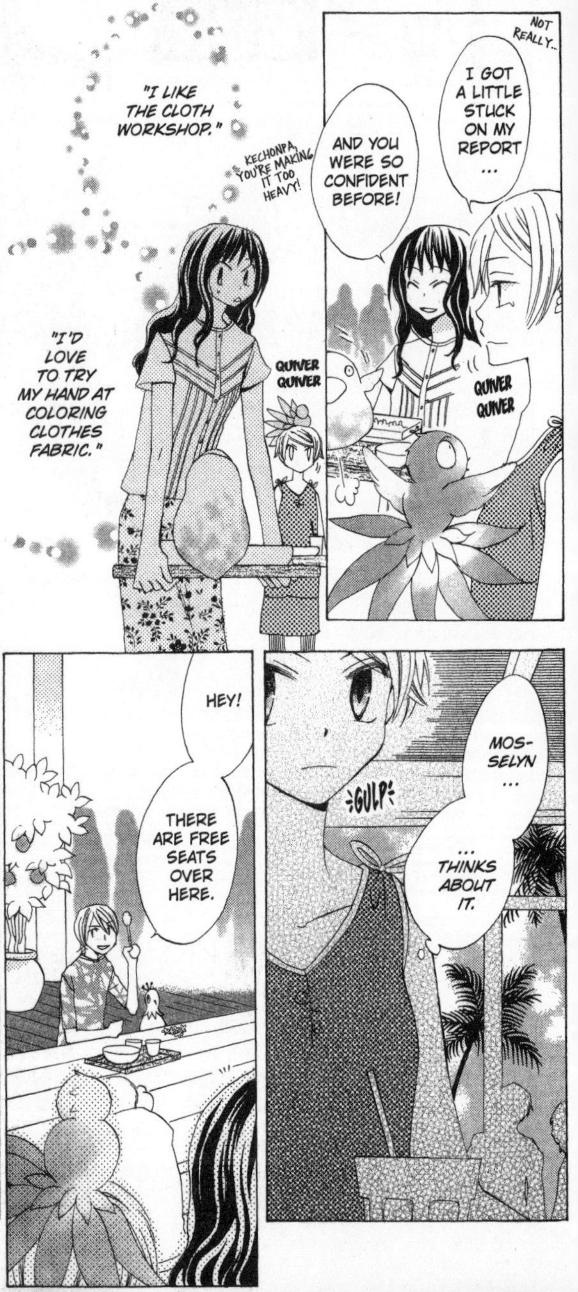
NOT REALLY...
I GOT A LITTLE STUCK ON MY REPORT...
AND YOU WERE SO CONFIDENT BEFORE!
QUIVER QUIVER
"I LIKE THE CLOTH WORKSHOP."
KECHONPA, YOU'RE MAKING IT TOO HEAVY!
"I'D LOVE TO TRY MY HAND AT COLORING CLOTHES FABRIC."
QUIVER QUIVER
MOS-SELYN...
...THINKS ABOUT IT.
GULP
HEY!
THERE ARE FREE SEATS OVER HERE.

2

MERRY-GO-ROUND IN AN AMUSEMENT PARK, THAT'S THE SOLE ATTRACTION I CAN FEEL COMFORTABLE ON. I HATE ROLLER COASTERS AND OTHER THRILL RIDES, SO EVEN IF I GO TO AN AMUSEMENT PARK WITH THREE OTHER PEOPLE AND THE ROLLER COASTER HAS TWO-BY-TWO SEATS, I'LL STILL BE THE ONE THAT STAYS ON THE GROUND. GO AHEAD, CALL ME HEARTLESS, I DON'T CARE. REALLY, I'M SO SCARED BY THOSE RIDES THAT IT'S NOT ANY FUN. I HATE THE FEELING OF BEING IMPRISONED WHILE ON THOSE RIDES, LIKE NO MATTER HOW MUCH I SCREAM FOR IT TO STOP, THE OPERATOR IGNORES ME. I HAVE A FEAR OF HEIGHTS IN THE FIRST PLACE, SO THAT LEAVES OUT THE FERRIS WHEEL AS WELL. WHEN I WAS A KID, THERE WAS THIS LITTLE RIDE WHERE, IF YOU PUT IN ONE HUNDRED YEN, THE FIGURE WOULD MOVE.

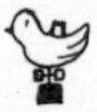 <--LIKE THIS

WELL, I PLEADED WITH MY PARENTS NOT TO PUT IN ONE HUNDRED YEN, AND TOLD THEM I'D RATHER JUST SIT ON THE THING WITHOUT HAVING IT WOBBLE AROUND. GOES TO SHOW THAT RIDES JUST AREN'T MEANT FOR ME.

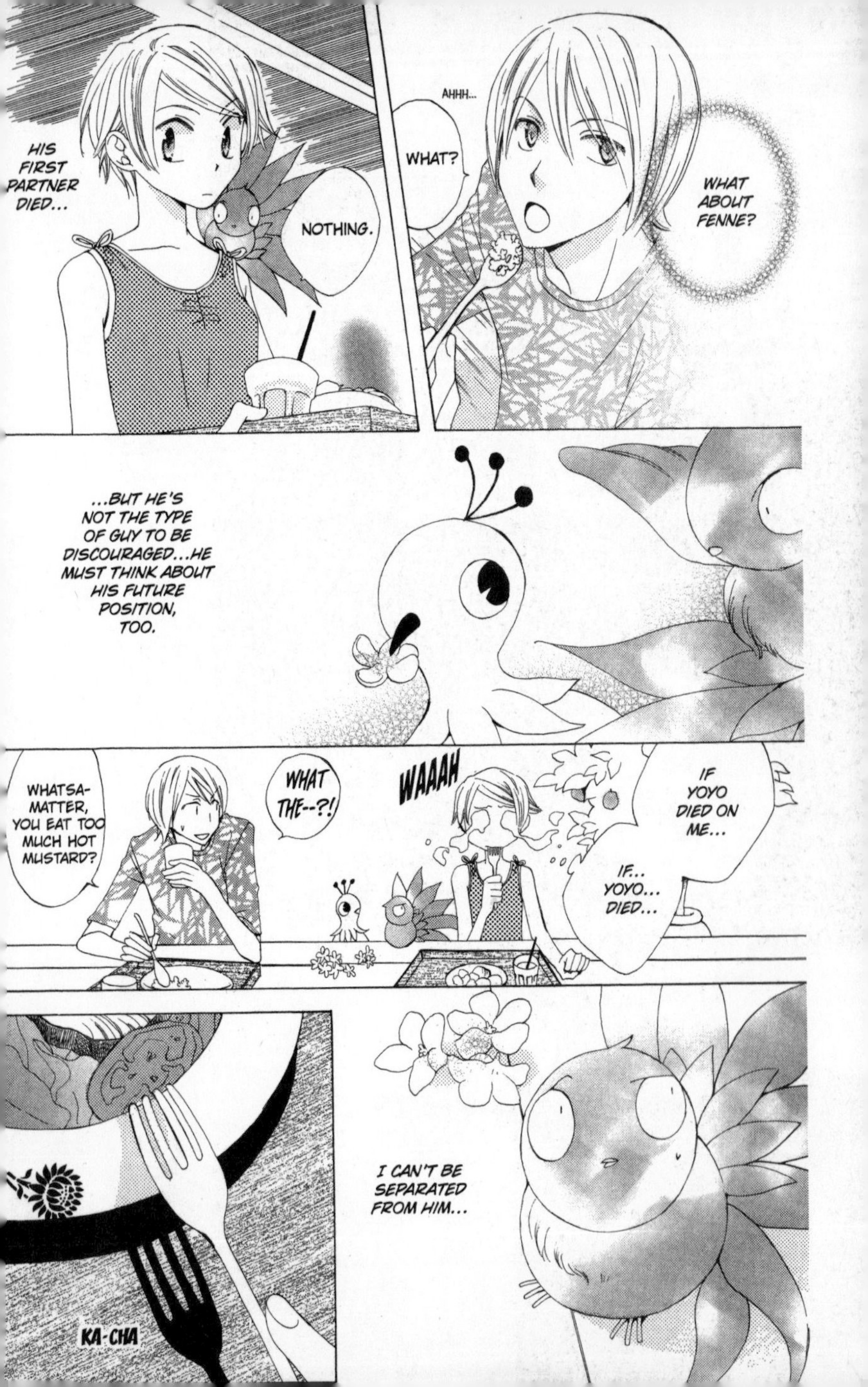
WHAT ABOUT FENNE?
AHHH...
WHAT?
NOTHING.
HIS FIRST PARTNER DIED...
...BUT HE'S NOT THE TYPE OF GUY TO BE DISCOURAGED...HE MUST THINK ABOUT HIS FUTURE POSITION, TOO.
IF YOYO DIED ON ME...
IF... YOYO... DIED...
WAAAH
WHAT THE--?!
WHATSA-MATTER, YOU EAT TOO MUCH HOT MUSTARD?
I CAN'T BE SEPARATED FROM HIM...
KA-CHA

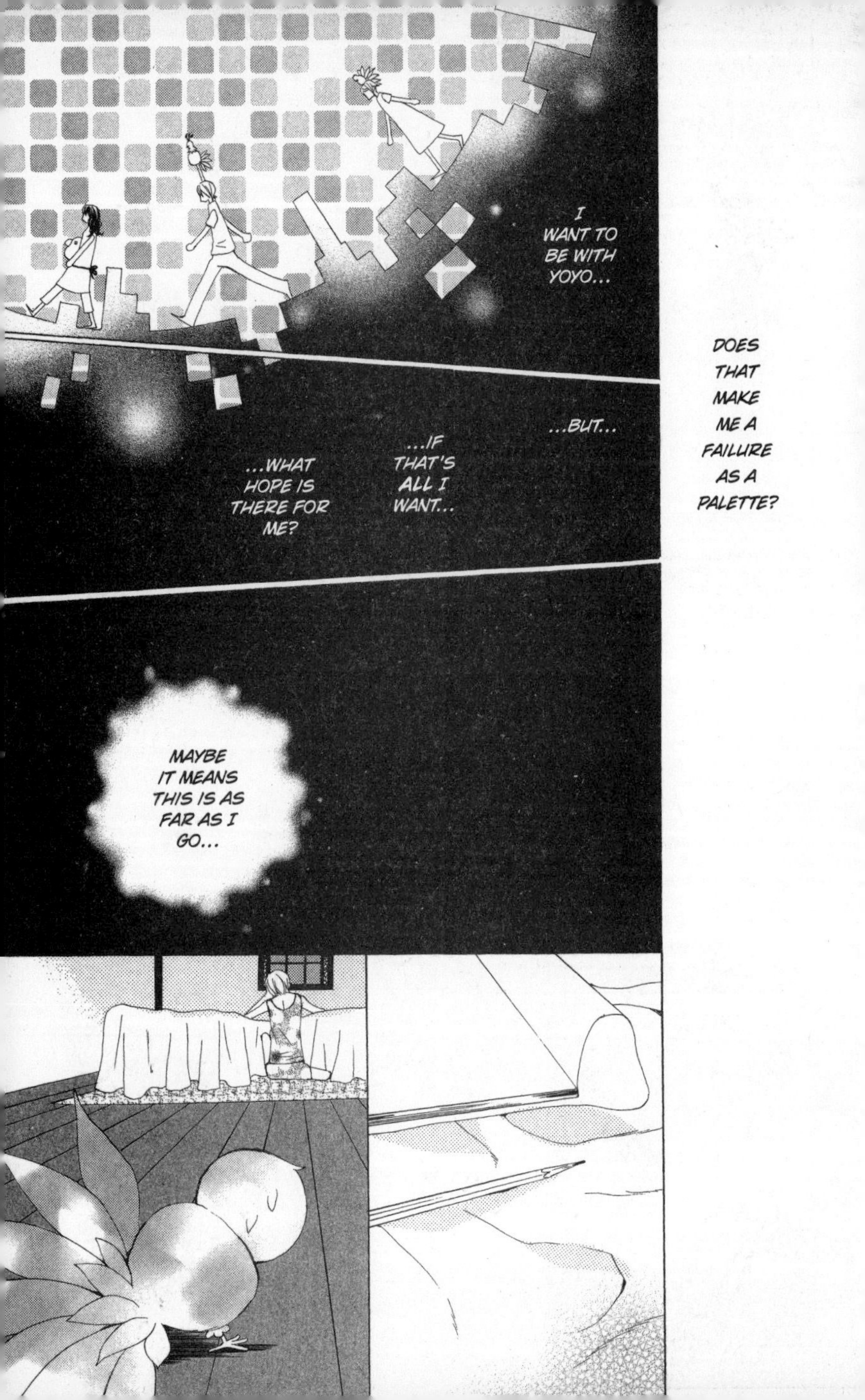
I WANT TO BE WITH YOYO...
DOES THAT MAKE ME A FAILURE AS A PALETTE?
...BUT...
...IF THAT'S ALL I WANT...
...WHAT HOPE IS THERE FOR ME?
MAYBE IT MEANS THIS IS AS FAR AS I GO...

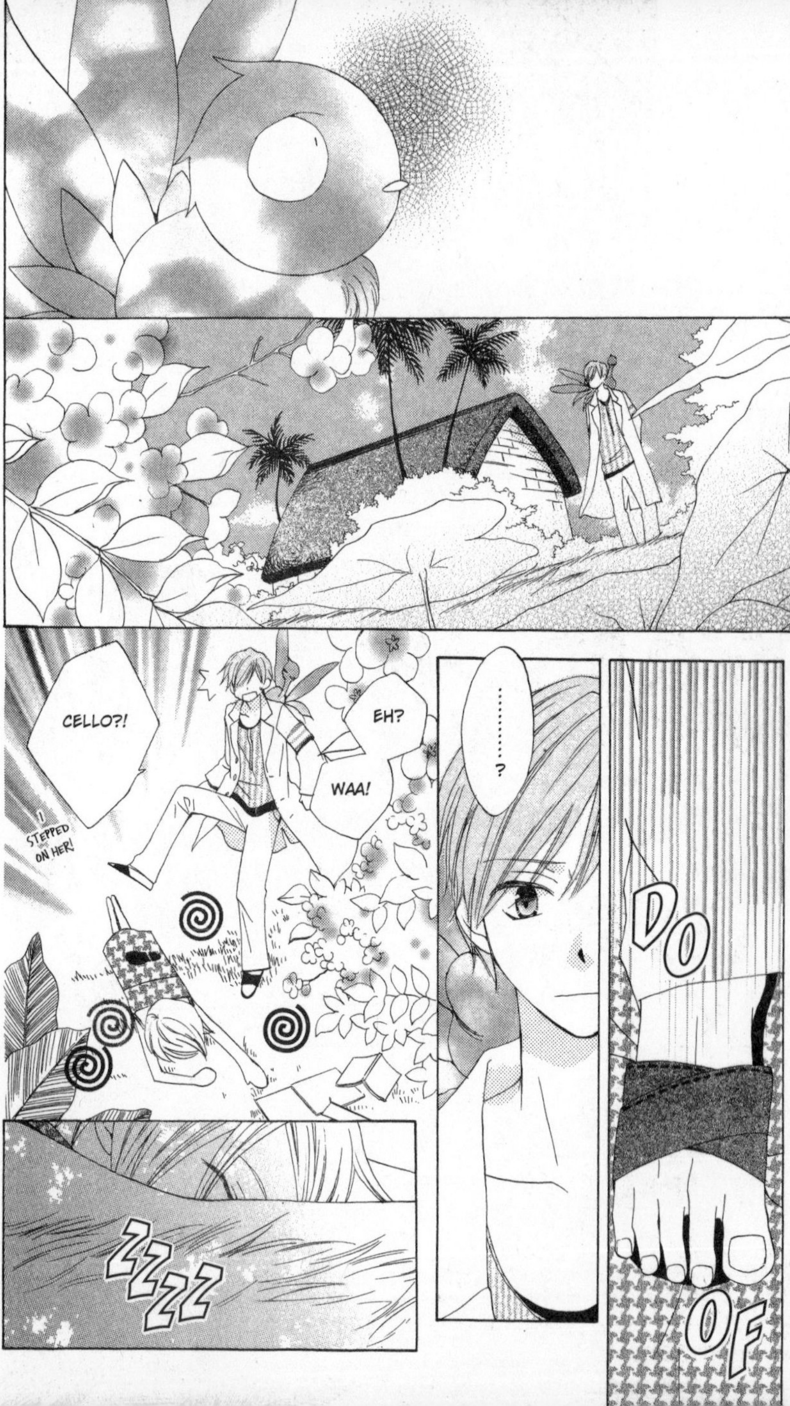
DO
OF
......?
EH?
WAA!
CELLO?!
I STEPPED ON HER!
ZZZZ

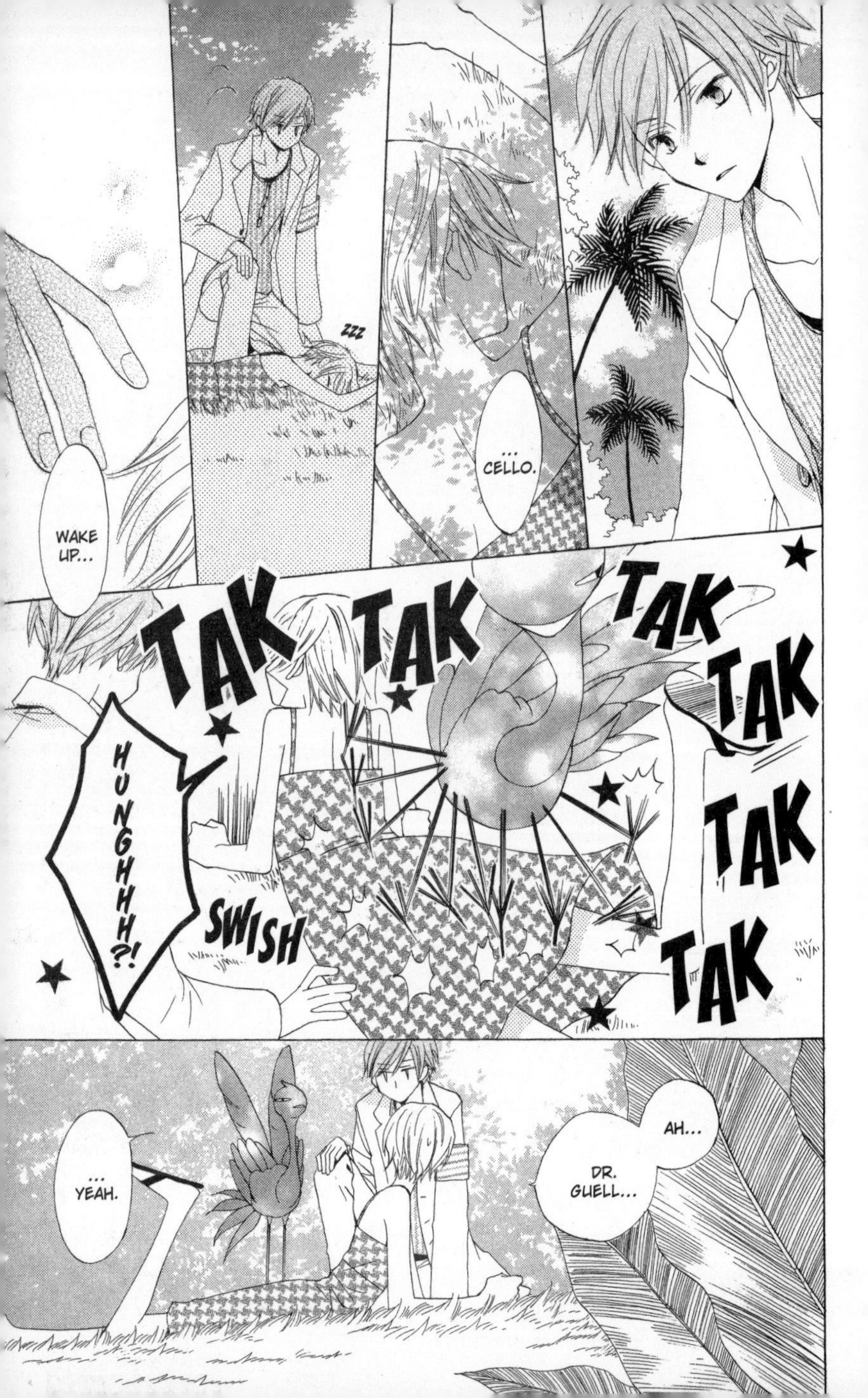

... CELLO.
ZZZ
WAKE UP...
TAK
TAK
TAK
TAK
TAK
TAK
SWISH
HUNGHHHH?!
AH...
DR. GUELL...
... YEAH.

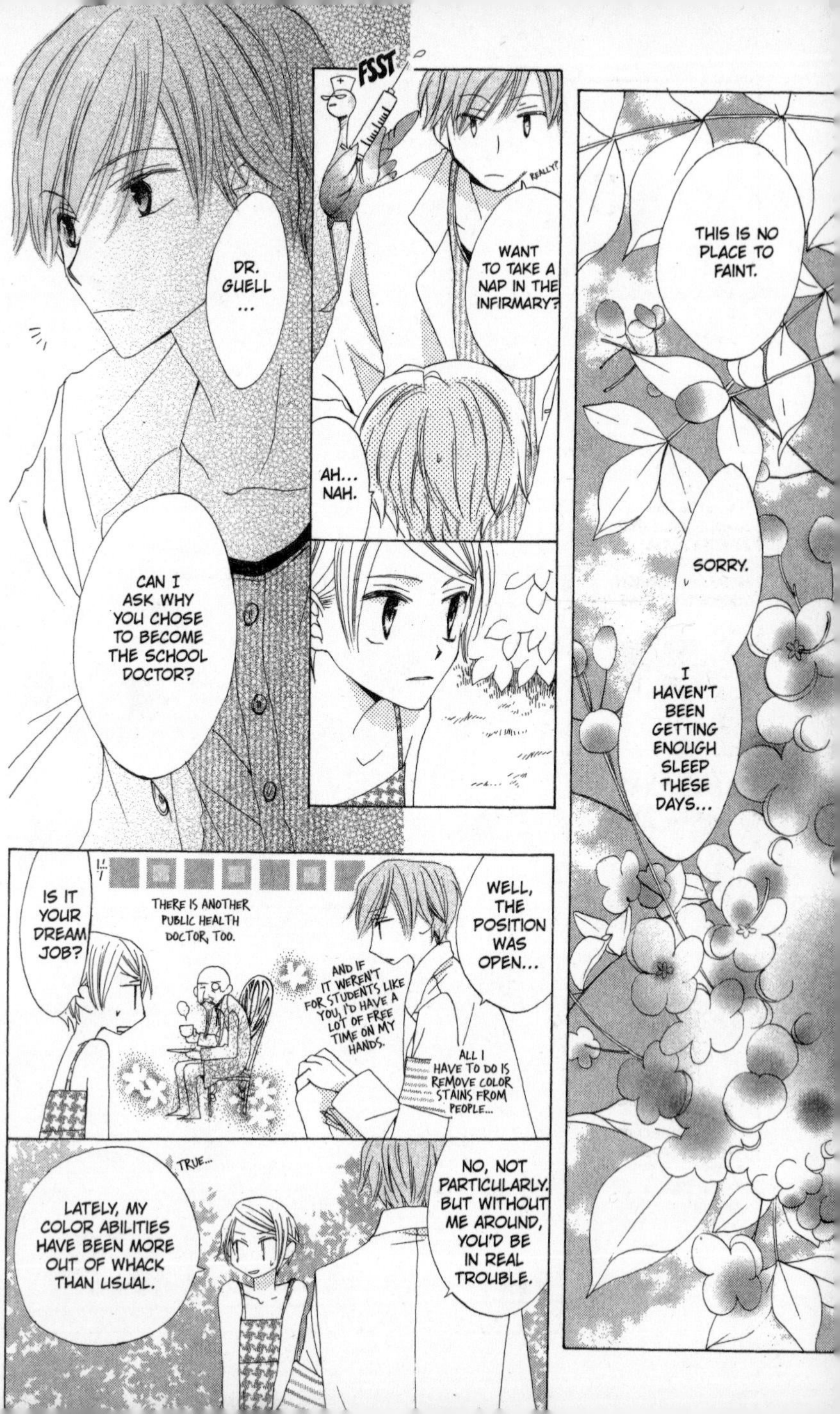
THIS IS NO PLACE TO FAINT.
SORRY.
I HAVEN'T BEEN GETTING ENOUGH SLEEP THESE DAYS...
FSST
REALLY?
WANT TO TAKE A NAP IN THE INFIRMARY?
AH... NAH.
DR. GUELL...
CAN I ASK WHY YOU CHOSE TO BECOME THE SCHOOL DOCTOR?
WELL, THE POSITION WAS OPEN...
ALL I HAVE TO DO IS REMOVE COLOR STAINS FROM PEOPLE...
AND IF IT WEREN'T FOR STUDENTS LIKE YOU, I'D HAVE A LOT OF FREE TIME ON MY HANDS.
THERE IS ANOTHER PUBLIC HEALTH DOCTOR, TOO.
IS IT YOUR DREAM JOB?
NO, NOT PARTICULARLY. BUT WITHOUT ME AROUND, YOU'D BE IN REAL TROUBLE.
TRUE...
LATELY, MY COLOR ABILITIES HAVE BEEN MORE OUT OF WHACK THAN USUAL.

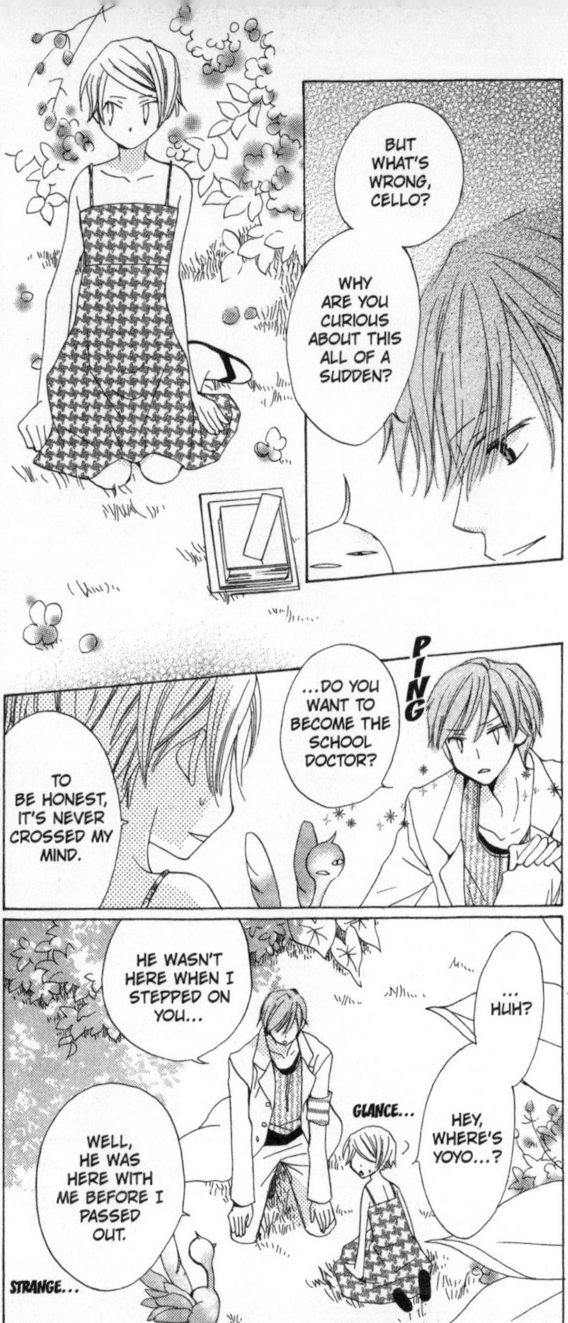
BUT WHAT'S WRONG, CELLO?
WHY ARE YOU CURIOUS ABOUT THIS ALL OF A SUDDEN?
PING
...DO YOU WANT TO BECOME THE SCHOOL DOCTOR?
TO BE HONEST, IT'S NEVER CROSSED MY MIND.
... HUH?
HEY, WHERE'S YOYO...?
GLANCE...
HE WASN'T HERE WHEN I STEPPED ON YOU...
WELL, HE WAS HERE WITH ME BEFORE I PASSED OUT.
STRANGE...

3

OTHER COUNTRIES (1)

I'M ALWAYS SHUT UP IN MY HOUSE, BUT THANKS TO MY WORK, I GET TO TRAVEL TO OTHER COUNTRIES. AT PRESENT, "PALETTE" IS ALSO PUBLISHED IN KOREA AND TAIWAN. THE KOREAN VERSION LOOKS LIKE THIS:

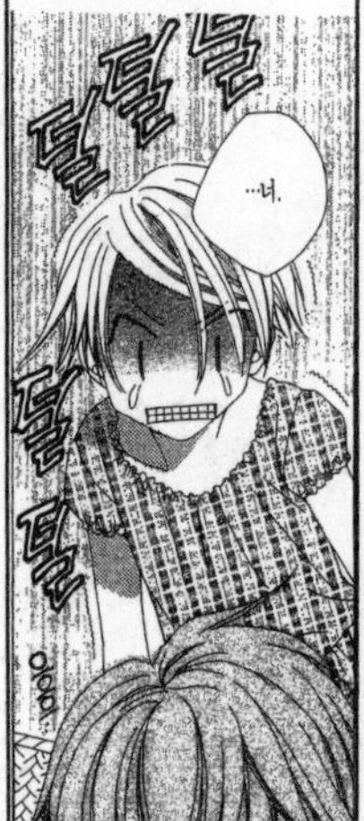
...너.

EVEN THE SOUND EFFECTS ARE IN KOREAN. I BET IT WAS A TOUGH JOB REPLACING ALL OF THE SFX.

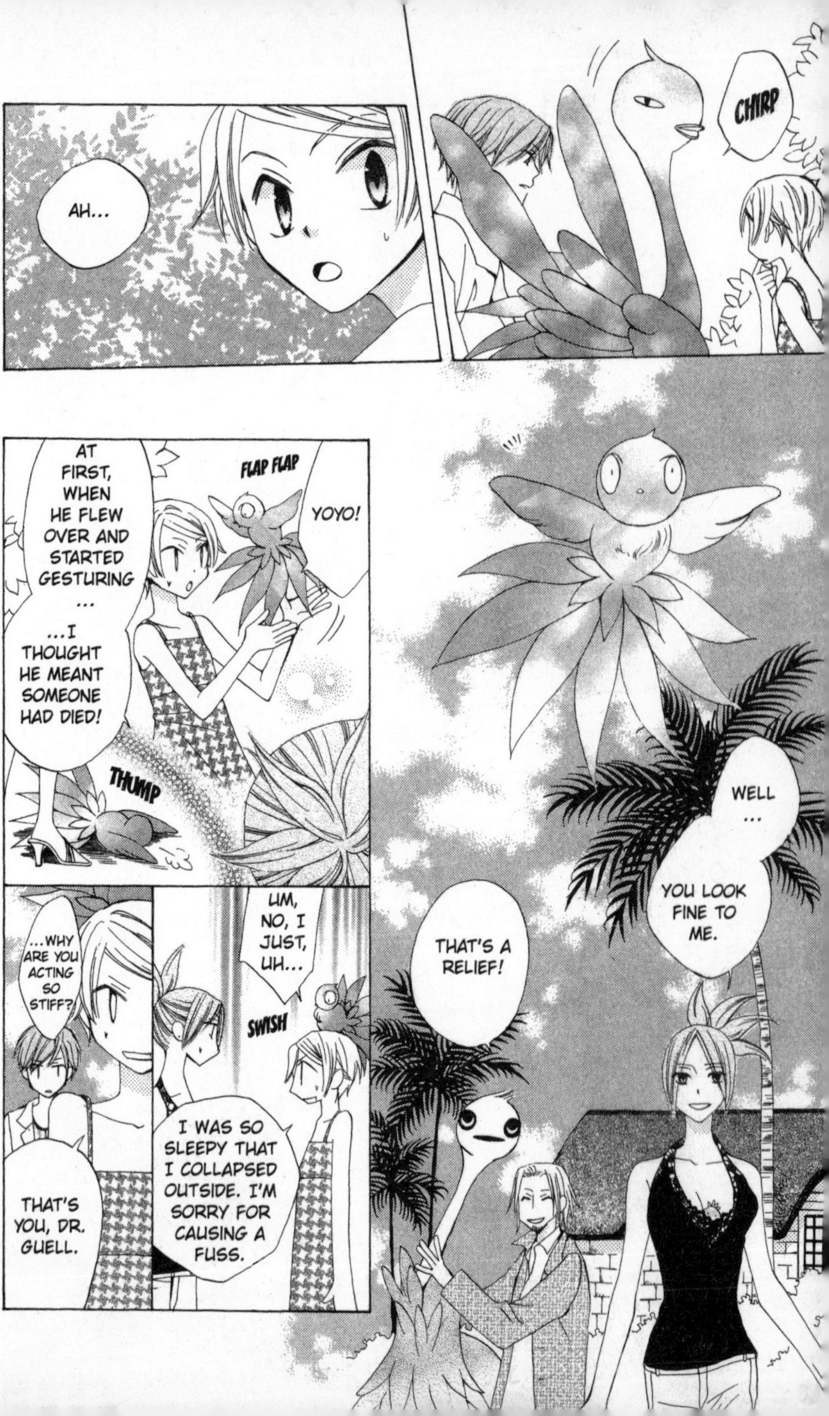
CHIRP
AH...
WELL...
YOU LOOK FINE TO ME.
THAT'S A RELIEF!
YOYO!
FLAP FLAP
AT FIRST, WHEN HE FLEW OVER AND STARTED GESTURING...
...I THOUGHT HE MEANT SOMEONE HAD DIED!
THUMP
UM, NO, I JUST, UH...
SWISH
I WAS SO SLEEPY THAT I COLLAPSED OUTSIDE. I'M SORRY FOR CAUSING A FUSS.
...WHY ARE YOU ACTING SO STIFF?
THAT'S YOU, DR. GUELL.

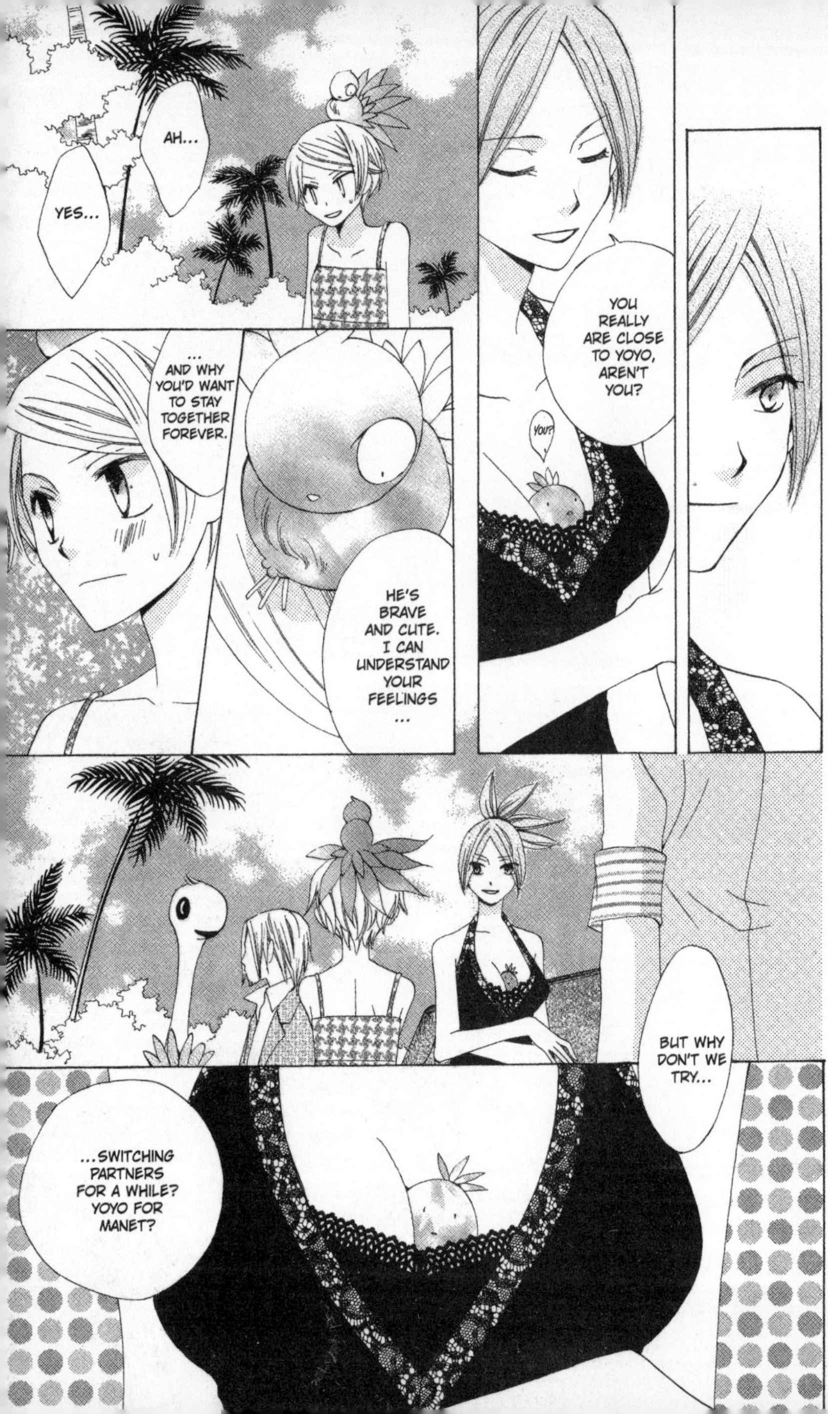
YOU REALLY ARE CLOSE TO YOYO, AREN'T YOU?
YOU?
AH...
YES...
HE'S BRAVE AND CUTE. I CAN UNDERSTAND YOUR FEELINGS ...
... AND WHY YOU'D WANT TO STAY TOGETHER FOREVER.
BUT WHY DON'T WE TRY...
...SWITCHING PARTNERS FOR A WHILE? YOYO FOR MANET?

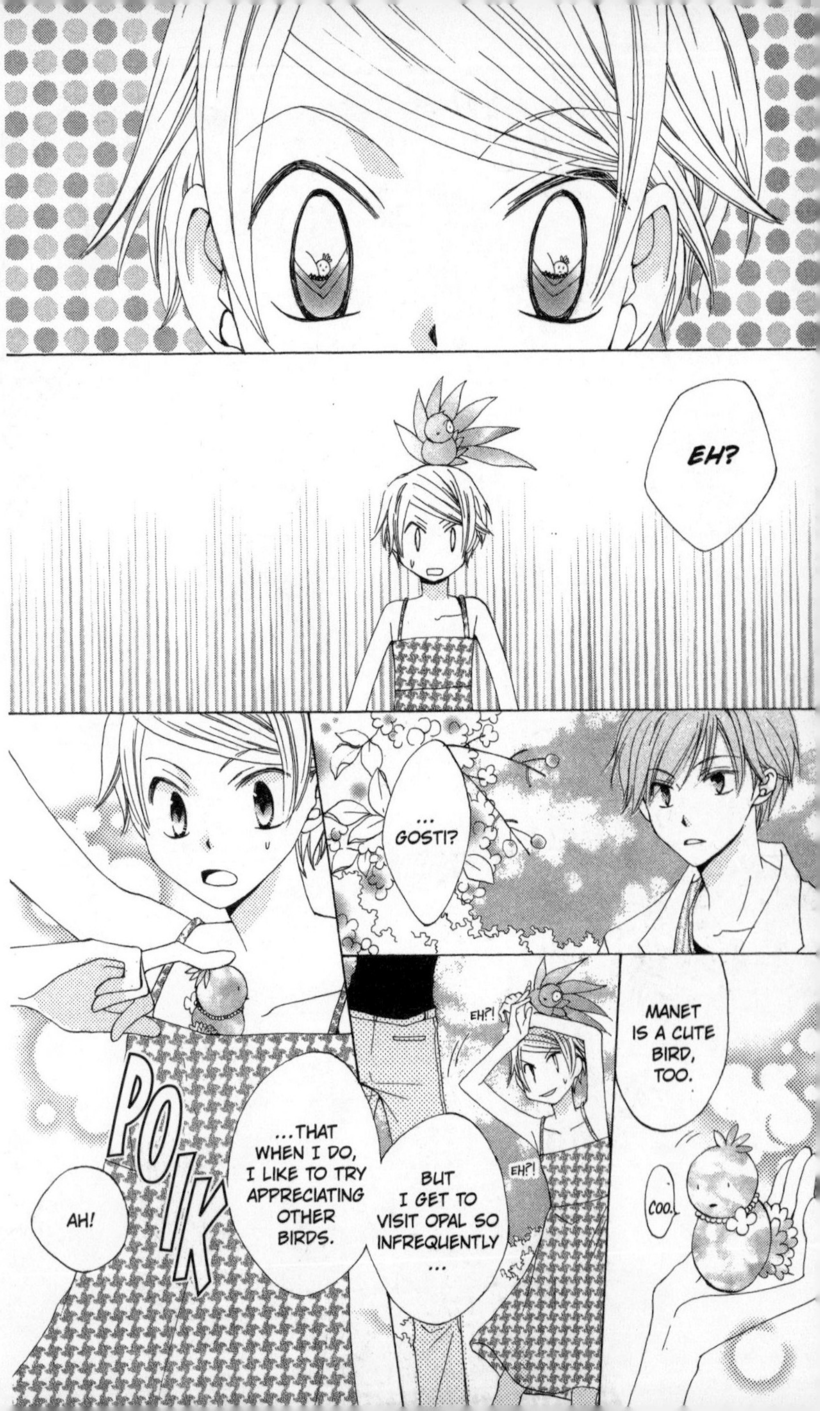
EH?
...GOSTI?
MANET IS A CUTE BIRD, TOO.
COO.
EH?!
EH?!
BUT I GET TO VISIT OPAL SO INFREQUENTLY ...
...THAT WHEN I DO, I LIKE TO TRY APPRECIATING OTHER BIRDS.
POIK
AH!

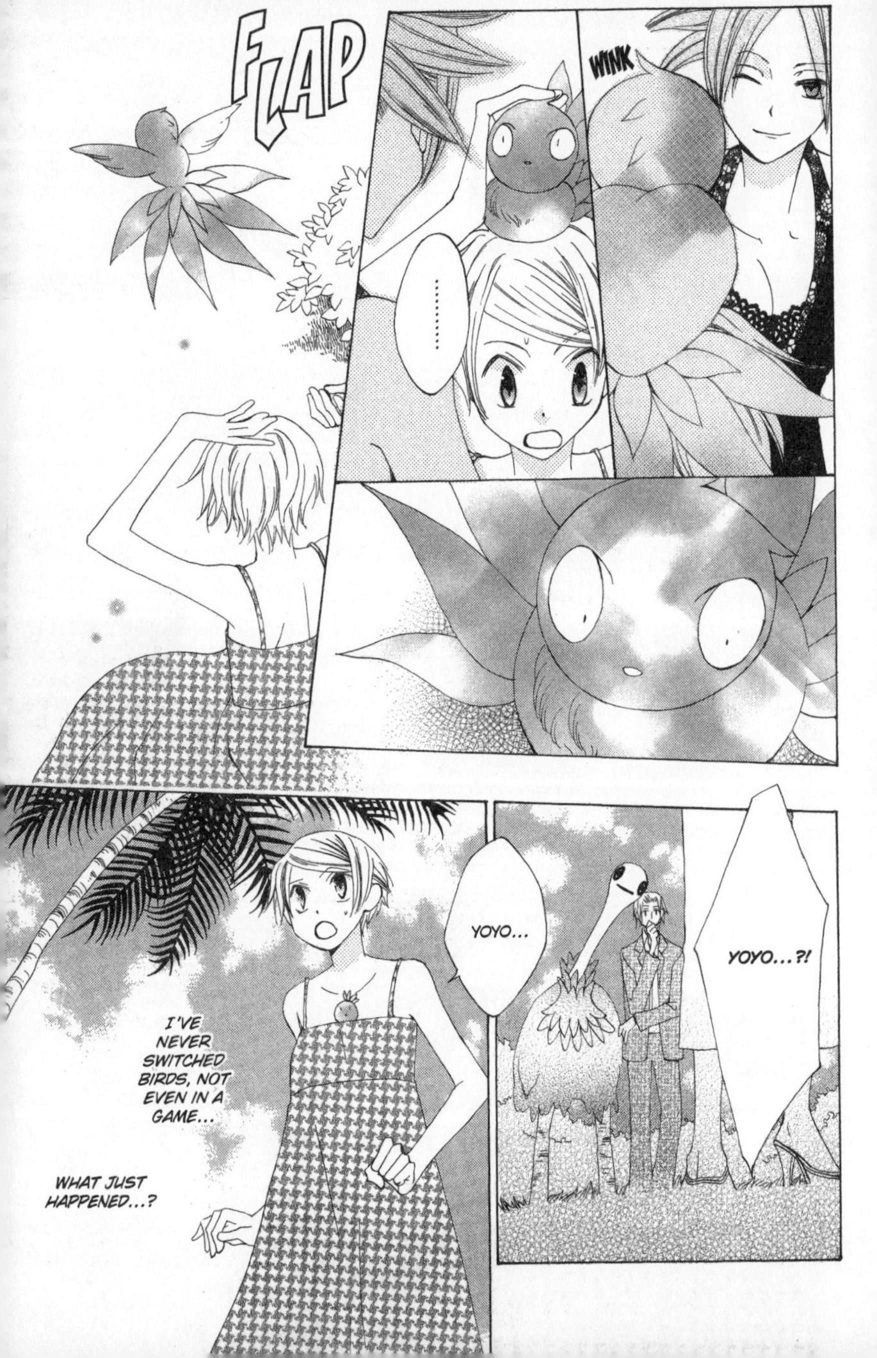
WINK
......
FLAP
YOYO...?!
YOYO...
I'VE NEVER SWITCHED BIRDS, NOT EVEN IN A GAME...
WHAT JUST HAPPENED...?

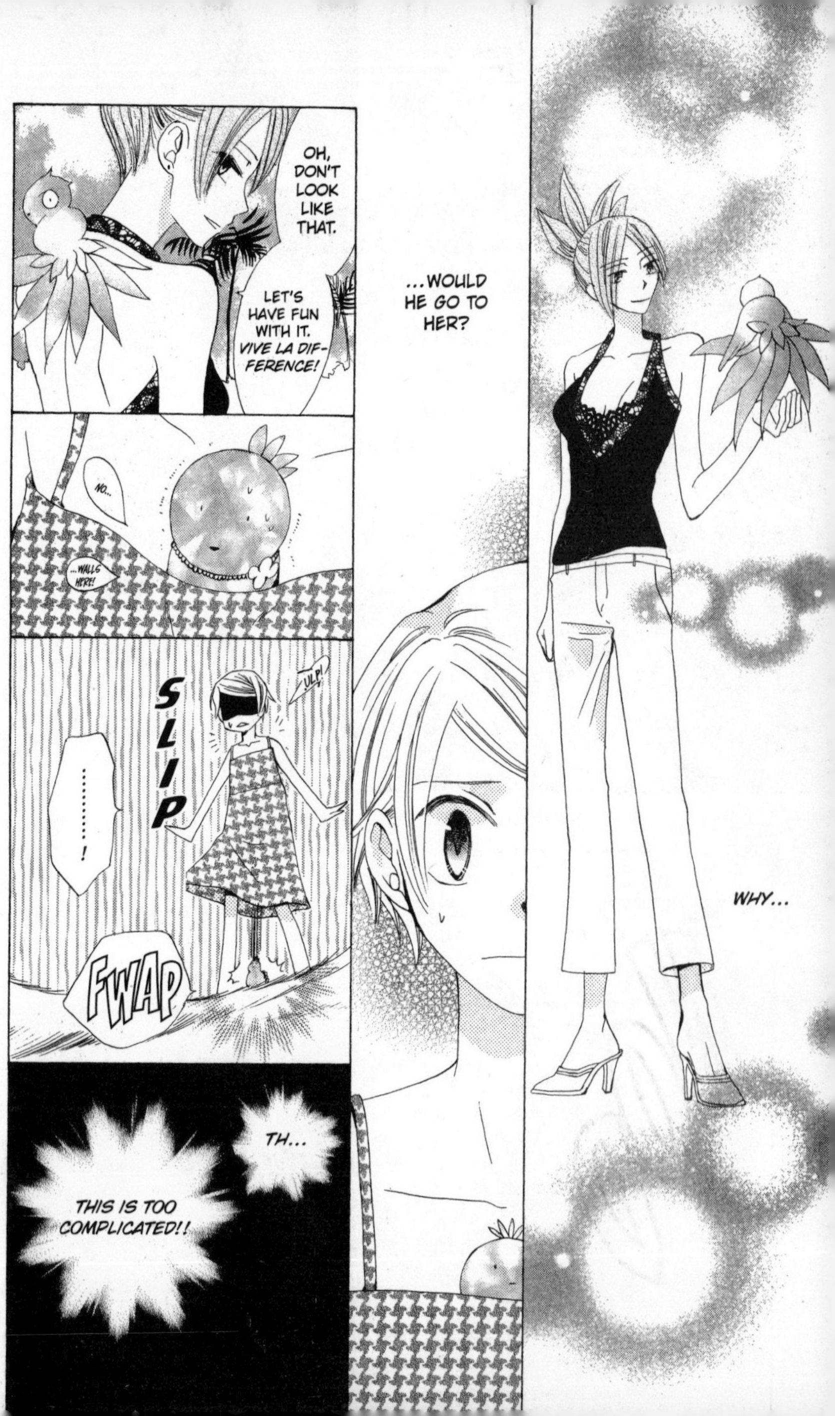
WHY...
...WOULD HE GO TO HER?
OH, DON'T LOOK LIKE THAT.
LET'S HAVE FUN WITH IT. VIVE LA DIFFERENCE!
NO...
...WALLS HERE!
ULP!
SLIP
......!
FWAP
TH...
THIS IS TOO COMPLICATED!!

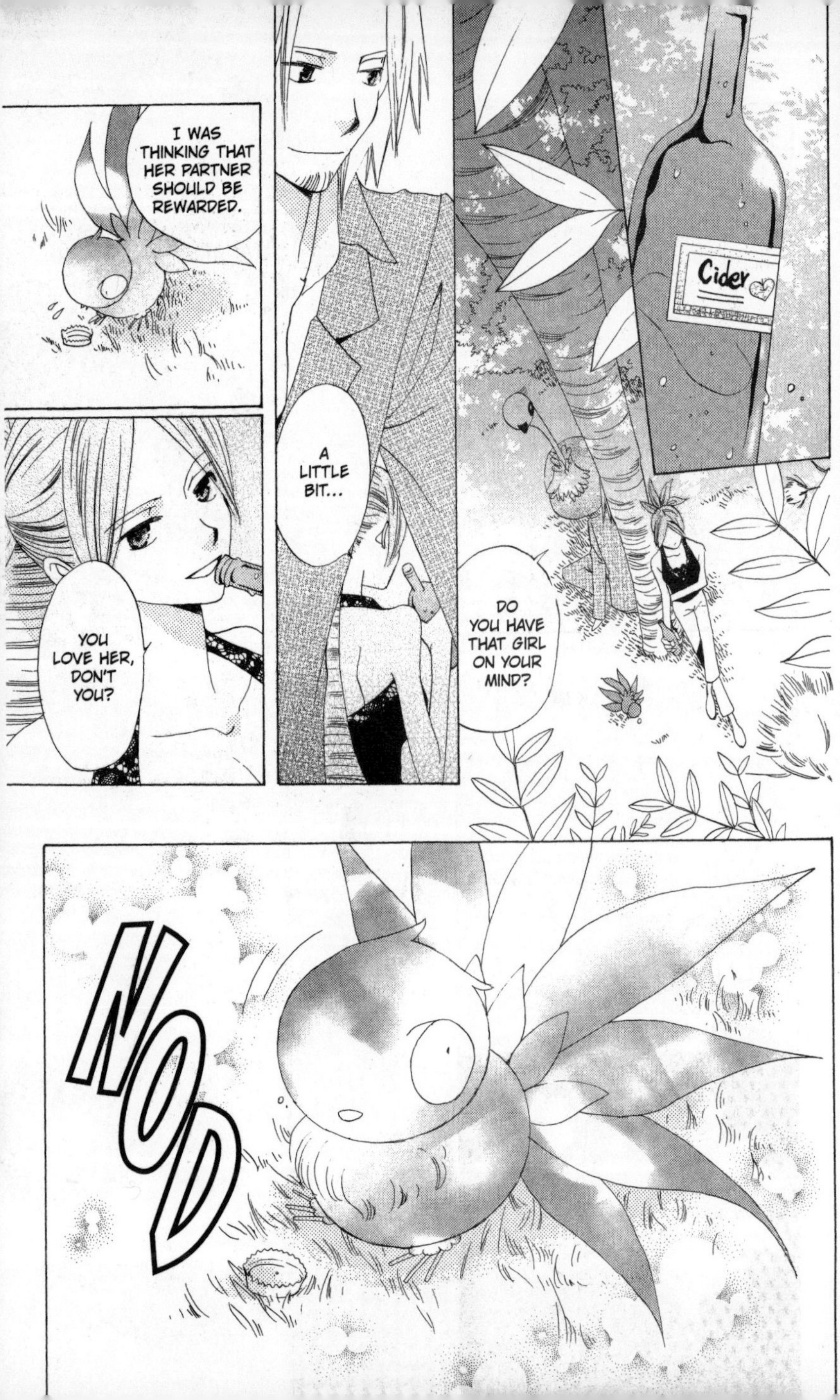
Cider
DO YOU HAVE THAT GIRL ON YOUR MIND?
A LITTLE BIT...
I WAS THINKING THAT HER PARTNER SHOULD BE REWARDED.
YOU LOVE HER, DON'T YOU?
NOD

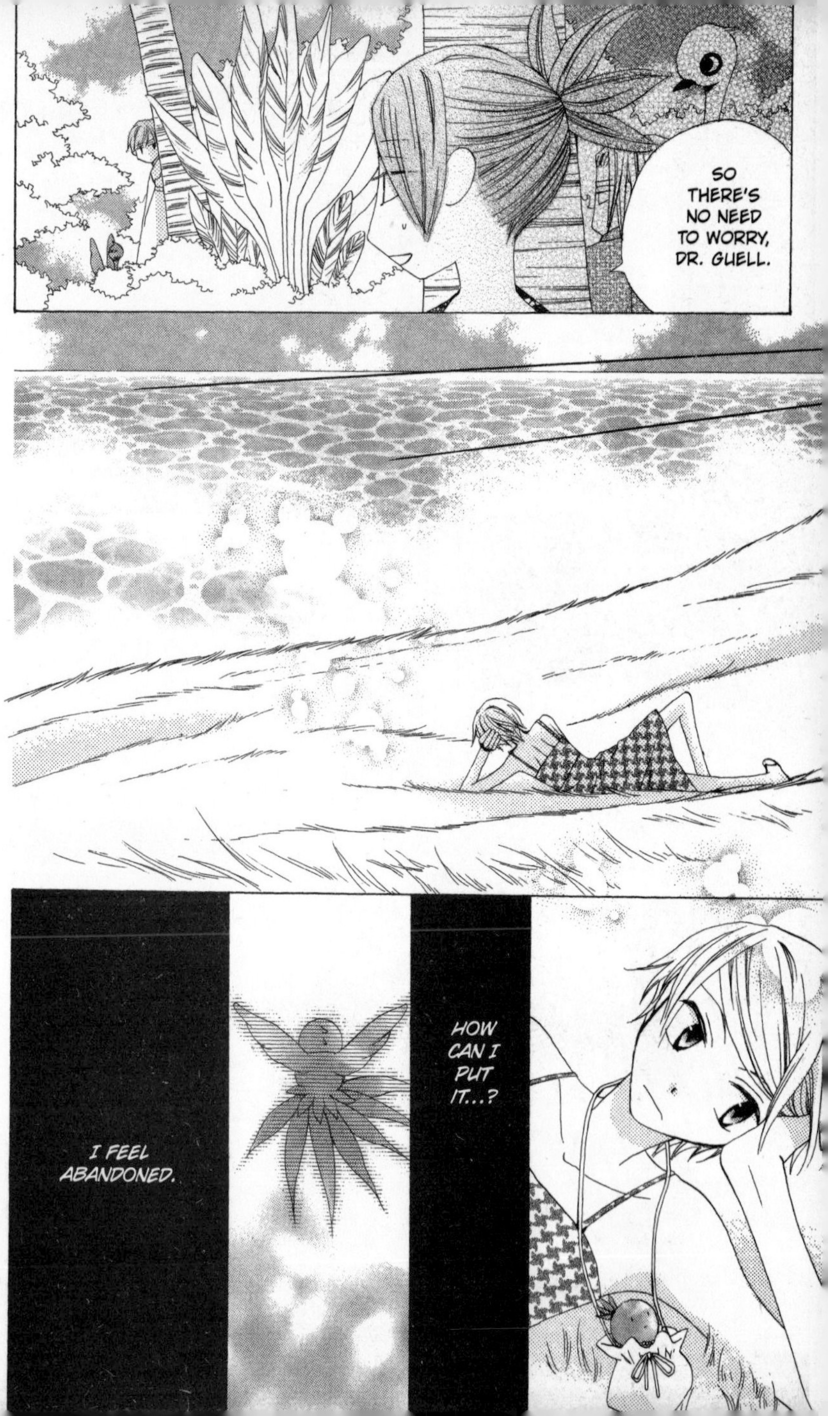
SO THERE'S NO NEED TO WORRY, DR. GUELL.
HOW CAN I PUT IT...?
I FEEL ABANDONED.

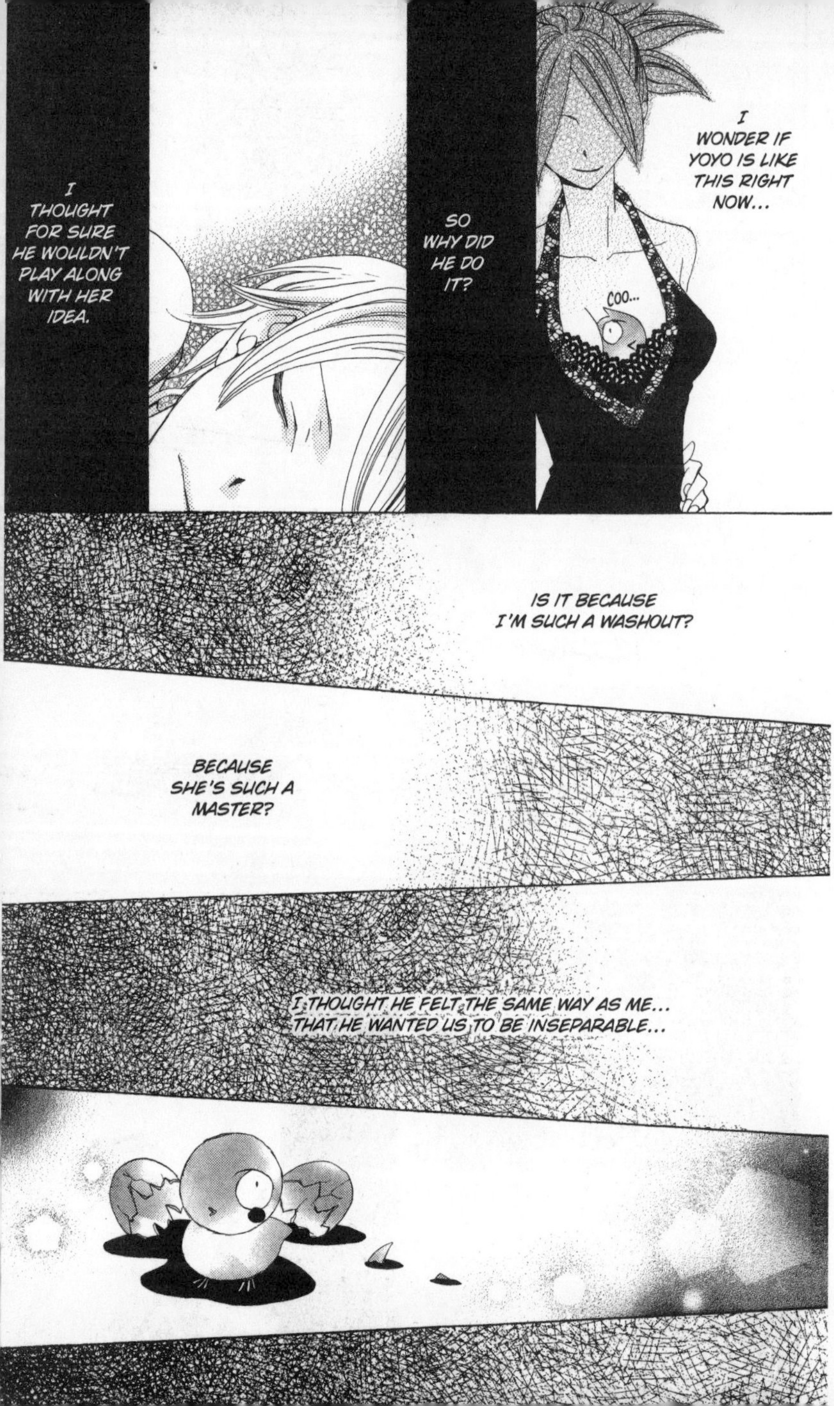
I WONDER IF YOYO IS LIKE THIS RIGHT NOW...
COO...
SO WHY DID HE DO IT?
I THOUGHT FOR SURE HE WOULDN'T PLAY ALONG WITH HER IDEA.
IS IT BECAUSE I'M SUCH A WASHOUT?
BECAUSE SHE'S SUCH A MASTER?
I THOUGHT HE FELT THE SAME WAY AS ME... THAT HE WANTED US TO BE INSEPARABLE...

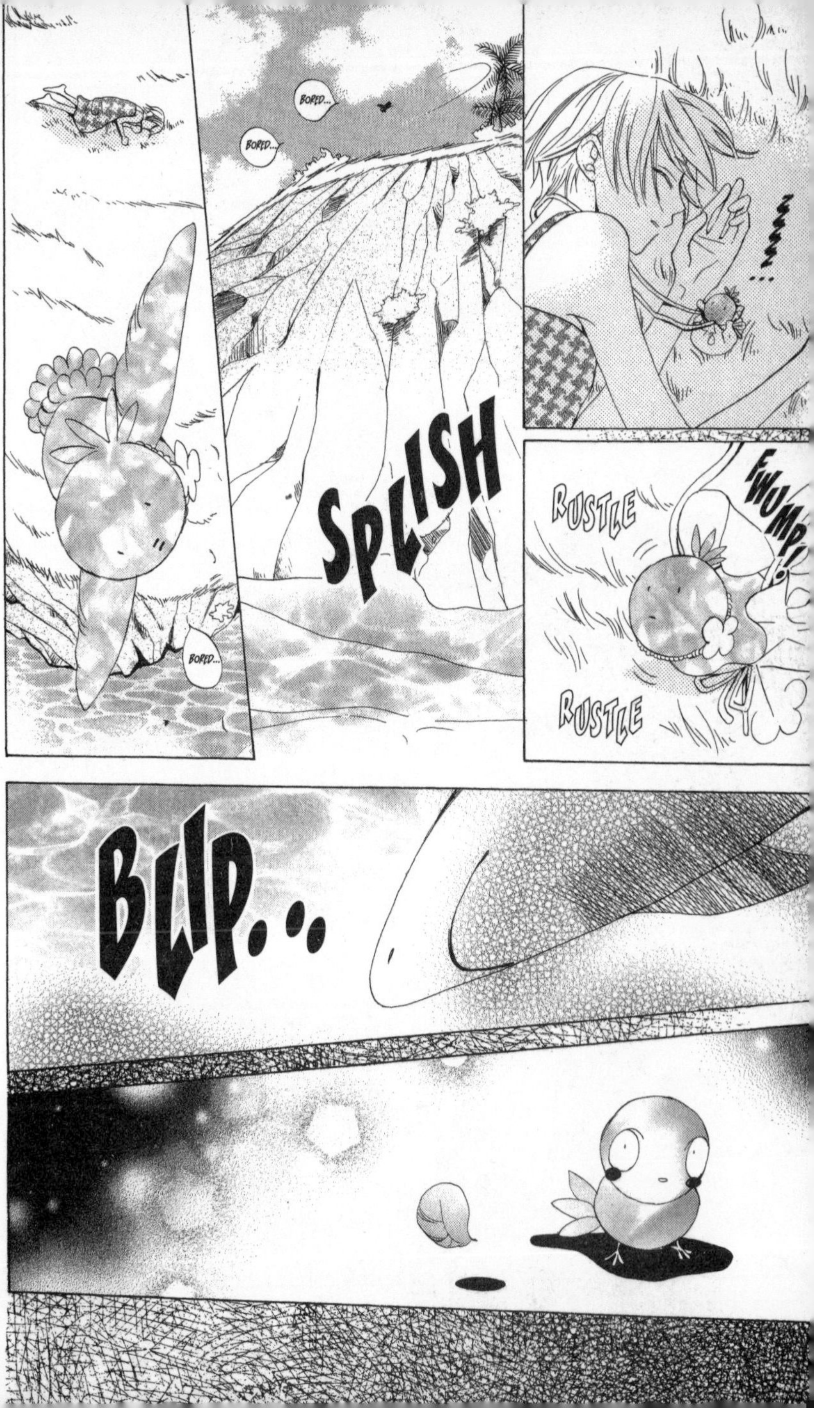
ZZZZ...
RUSTLE
FWUMP!
RUSTLE
BORED...
BORED...
SPLISH
BORED...
BLIP...

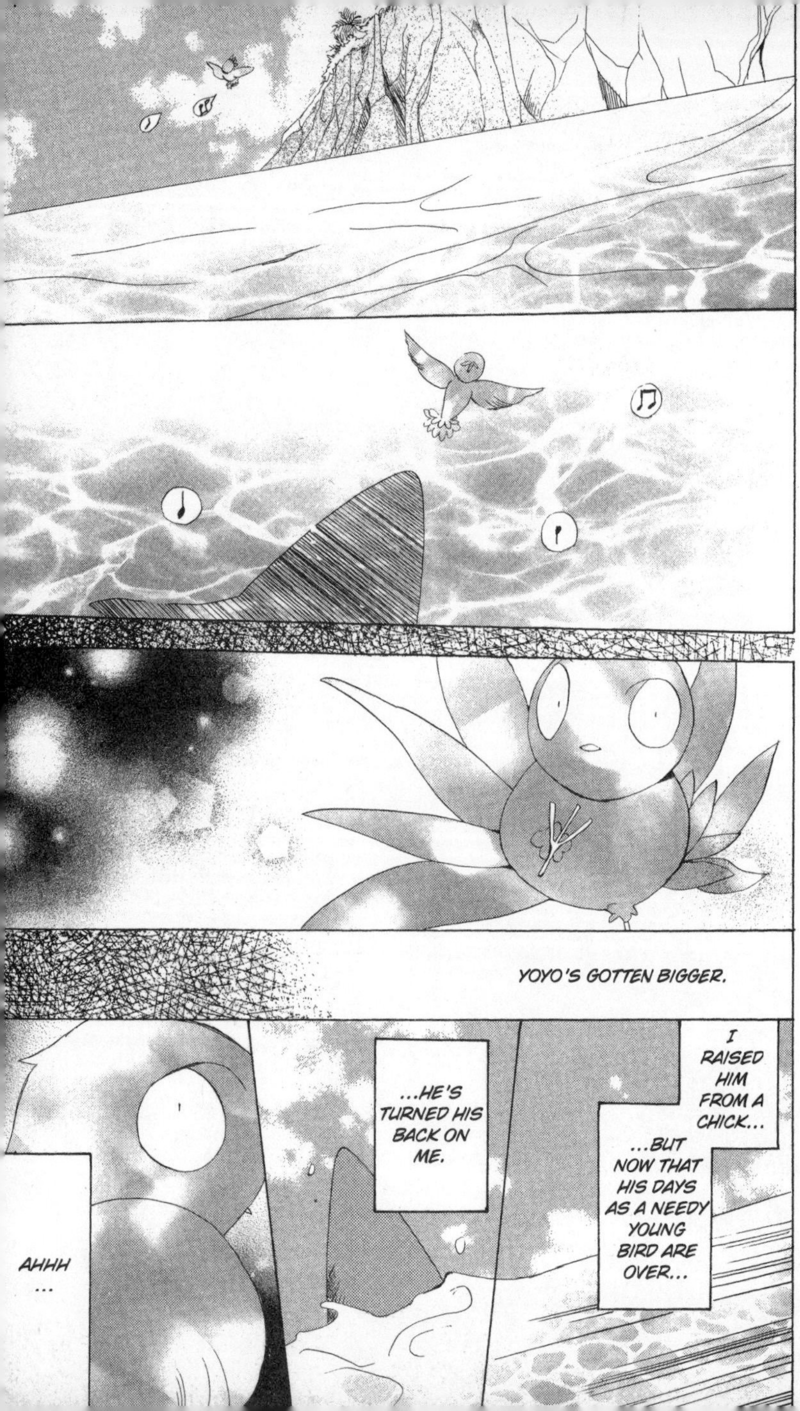
YOYO'S GOTTEN BIGGER.
I RAISED HIM FROM A CHICK...
...BUT NOW THAT HIS DAYS AS A NEEDY YOUNG BIRD ARE OVER...
...HE'S TURNED HIS BACK ON ME.
AHHH ...

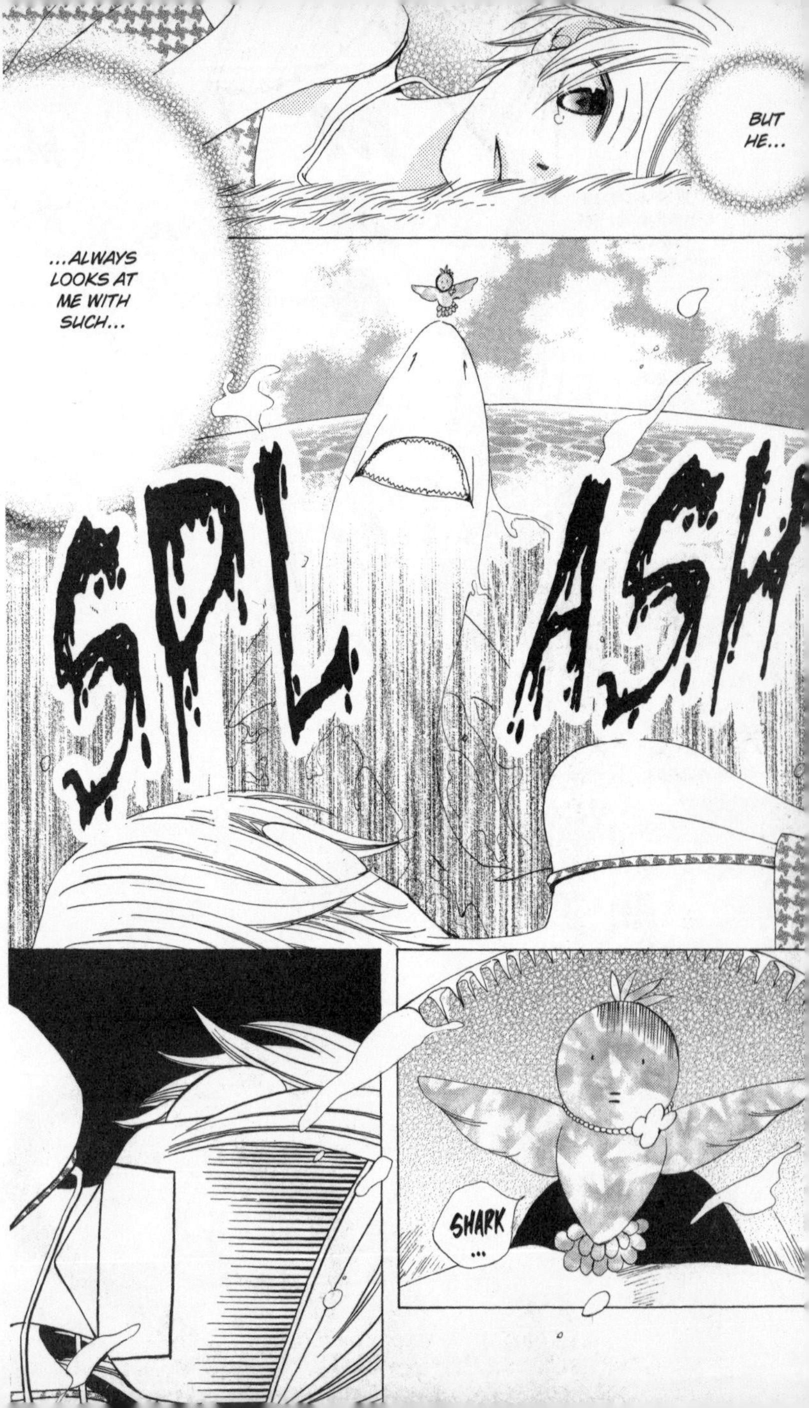
BUT HE...
...ALWAYS LOOKS AT ME WITH SUCH...
SPLASH
SHARK ...

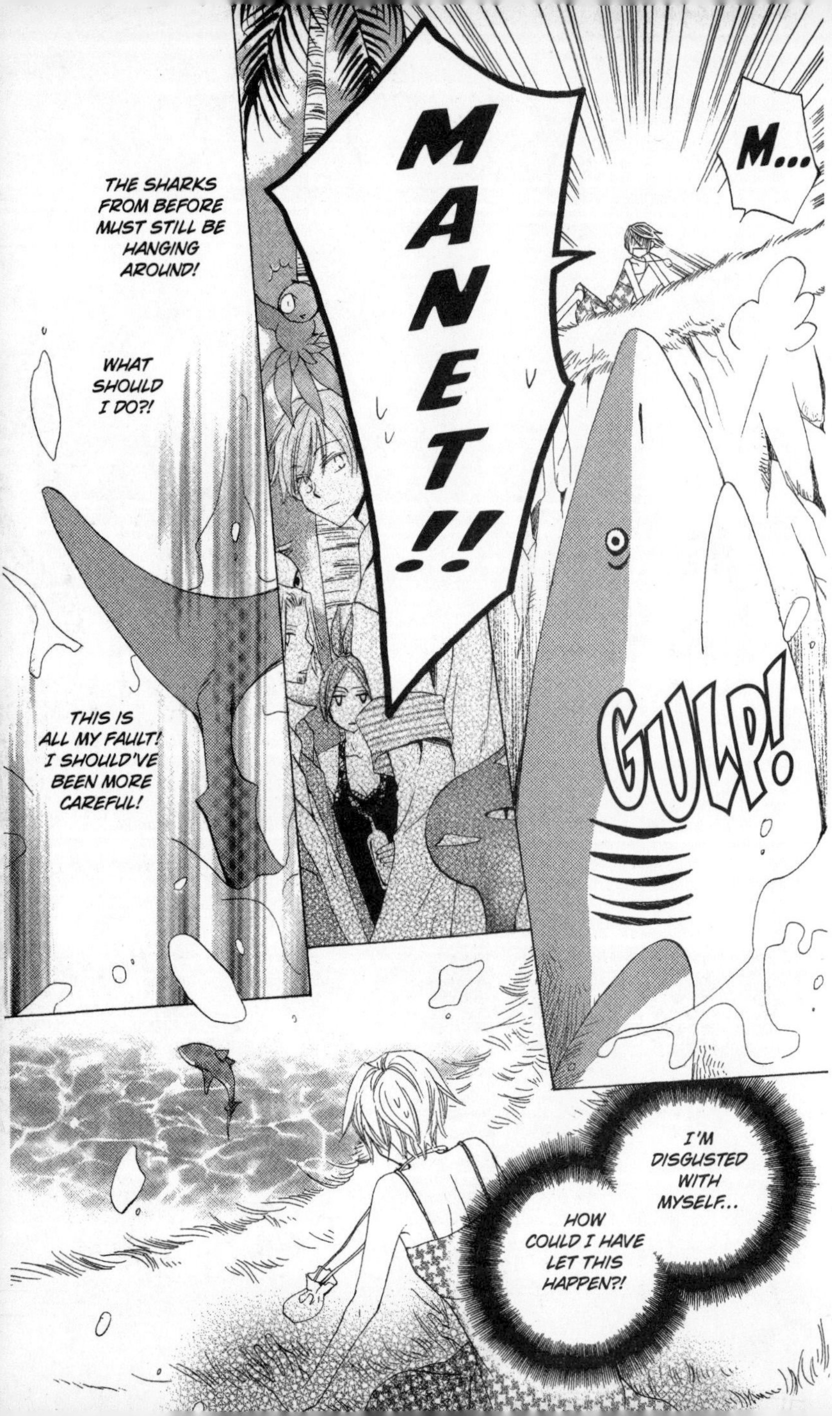
M...
MANET!!
GULP!
THE SHARKS FROM BEFORE MUST STILL BE HANGING AROUND!
WHAT SHOULD I DO?!
THIS IS ALL MY FAULT! I SHOULD'VE BEEN MORE CAREFUL!
I'M DISGUSTED WITH MYSELF...
HOW COULD I HAVE LET THIS HAPPEN?!

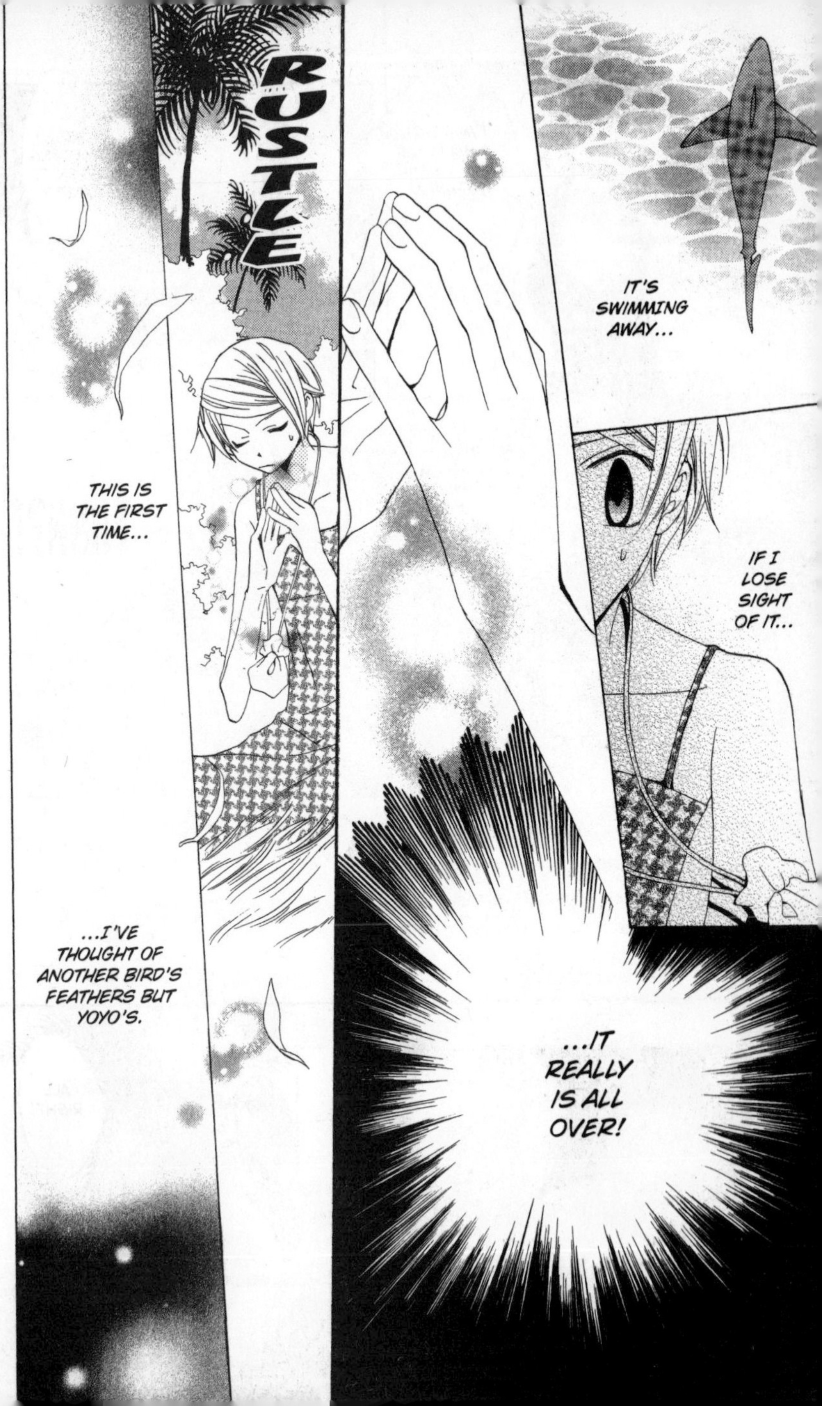
IT'S SWIMMING AWAY...
IF I LOSE SIGHT OF IT...
...IT REALLY IS ALL OVER!
RUSTLE
THIS IS THE FIRST TIME...
...I'VE THOUGHT OF ANOTHER BIRD'S FEATHERS BUT YOYO'S.

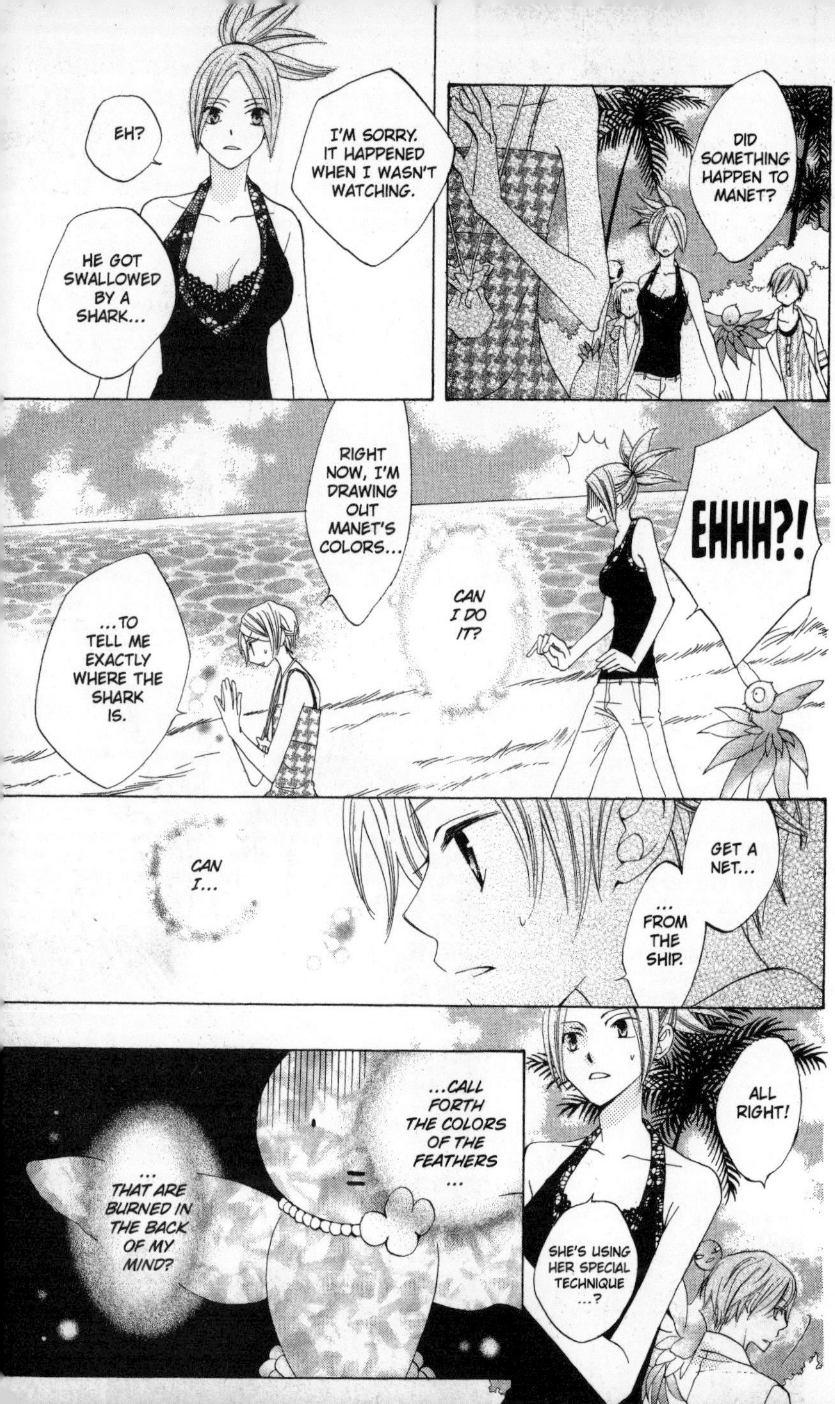
DID SOMETHING HAPPEN TO MANET?
I'M SORRY. IT HAPPENED WHEN I WASN'T WATCHING.
EH?
HE GOT SWALLOWED BY A SHARK...
EHHH?!
RIGHT NOW, I'M DRAWING OUT MANET'S COLORS...
CAN I DO IT?
...TO TELL ME EXACTLY WHERE THE SHARK IS.
GET A NET...
...FROM THE SHIP.
CAN I...
ALL RIGHT!
SHE'S USING HER SPECIAL TECHNIQUE...?
...CALL FORTH THE COLORS OF THE FEATHERS...
...THAT ARE BURNED IN THE BACK OF MY MIND?

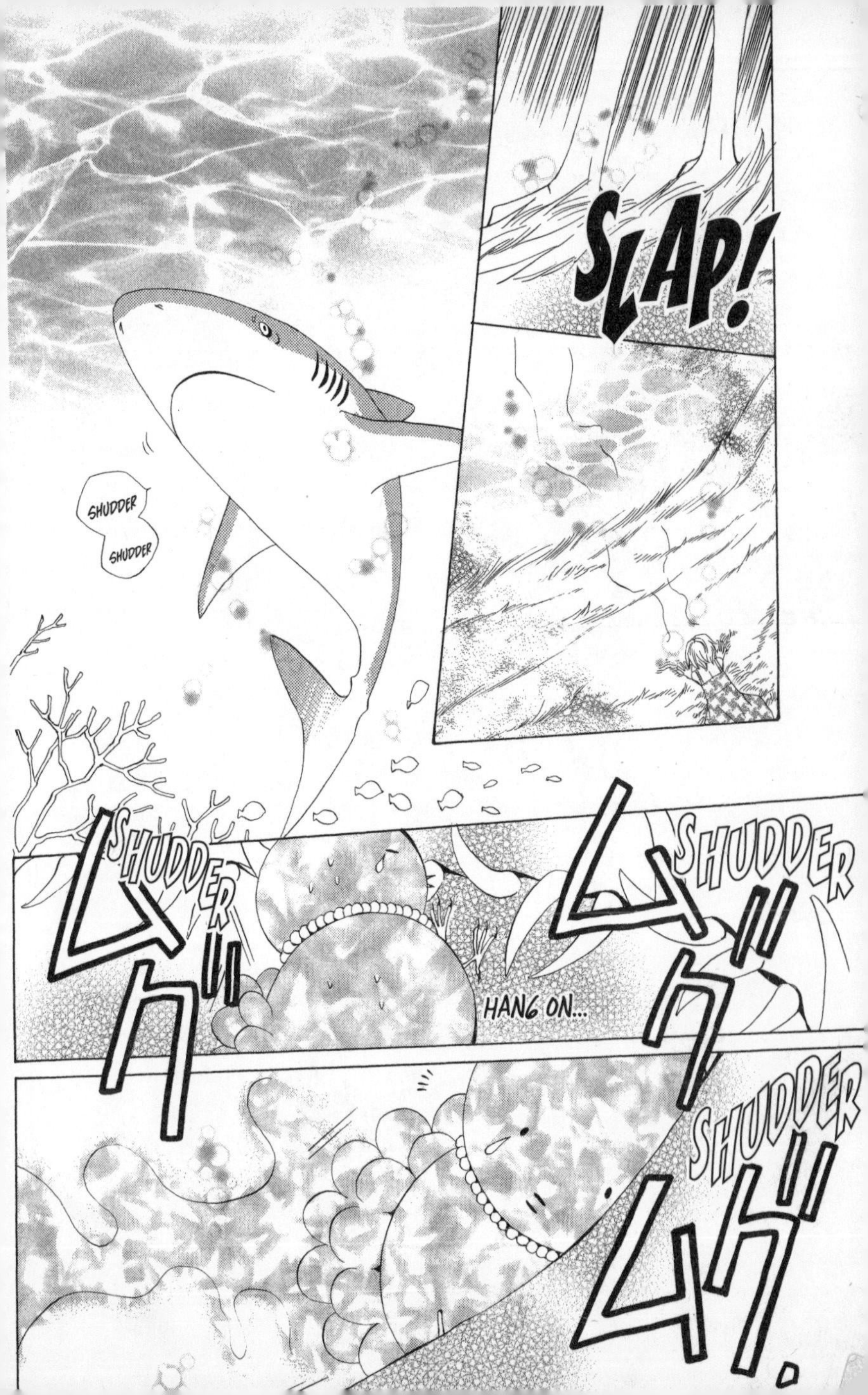
SLAP!
SHUDDER
SHUDDER
SHUDDER
ムガ
HANG ON...
SHUDDER
ムガ
SHUDDER
ムガ!

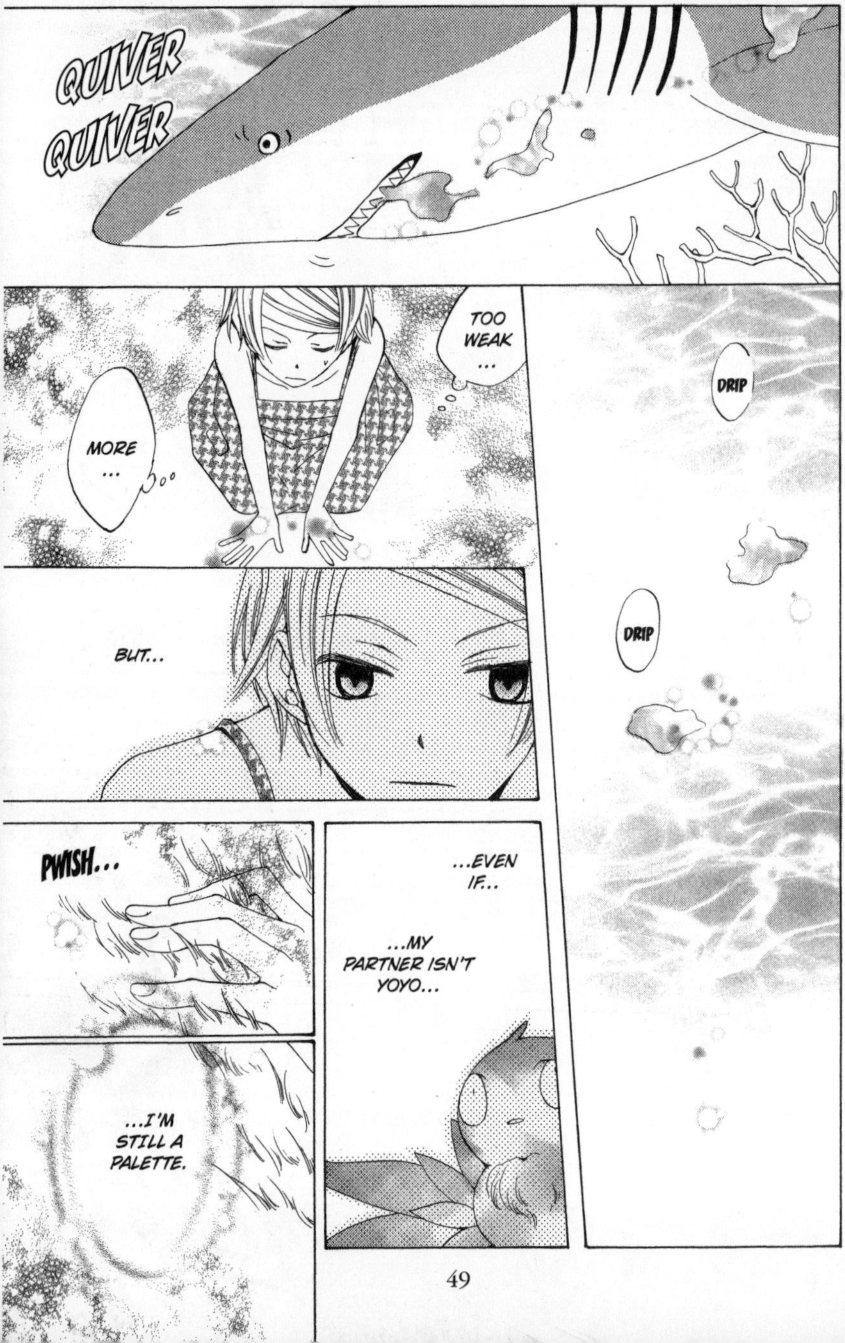
QUIVER QUIVER
DRIP
DRIP
TOO WEAK ...
MORE ...
BUT...
...EVEN IF...
...MY PARTNER ISN'T YOYO...
PWISH...
...I'M STILL A PALETTE.

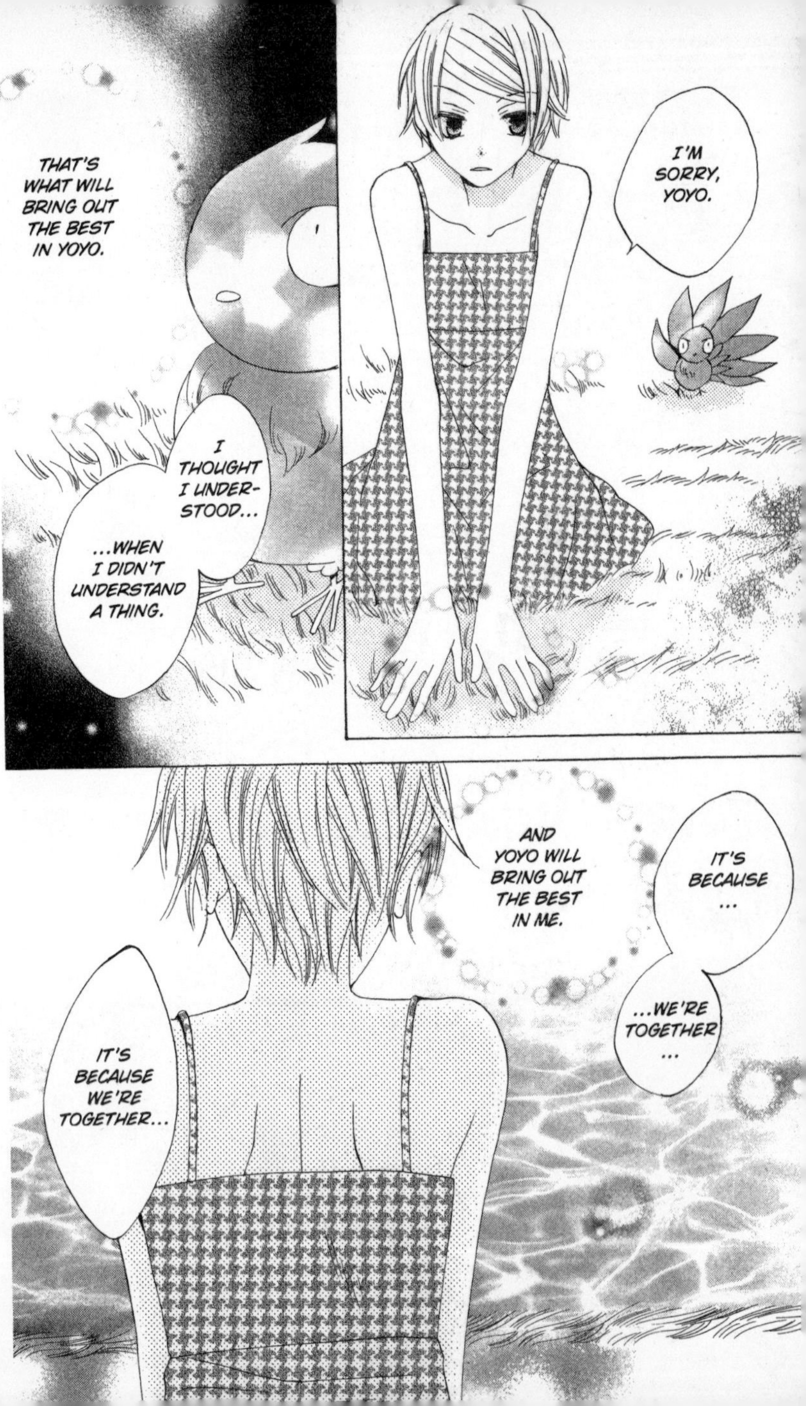
I'M SORRY, YOYO.
I THOUGHT I UNDER-STOOD...
...WHEN I DIDN'T UNDERSTAND A THING.
THAT'S WHAT WILL BRING OUT THE BEST IN YOYO.
IT'S BECAUSE...
...WE'RE TOGETHER...
AND YOYO WILL BRING OUT THE BEST IN ME.
IT'S BECAUSE WE'RE TOGETHER...

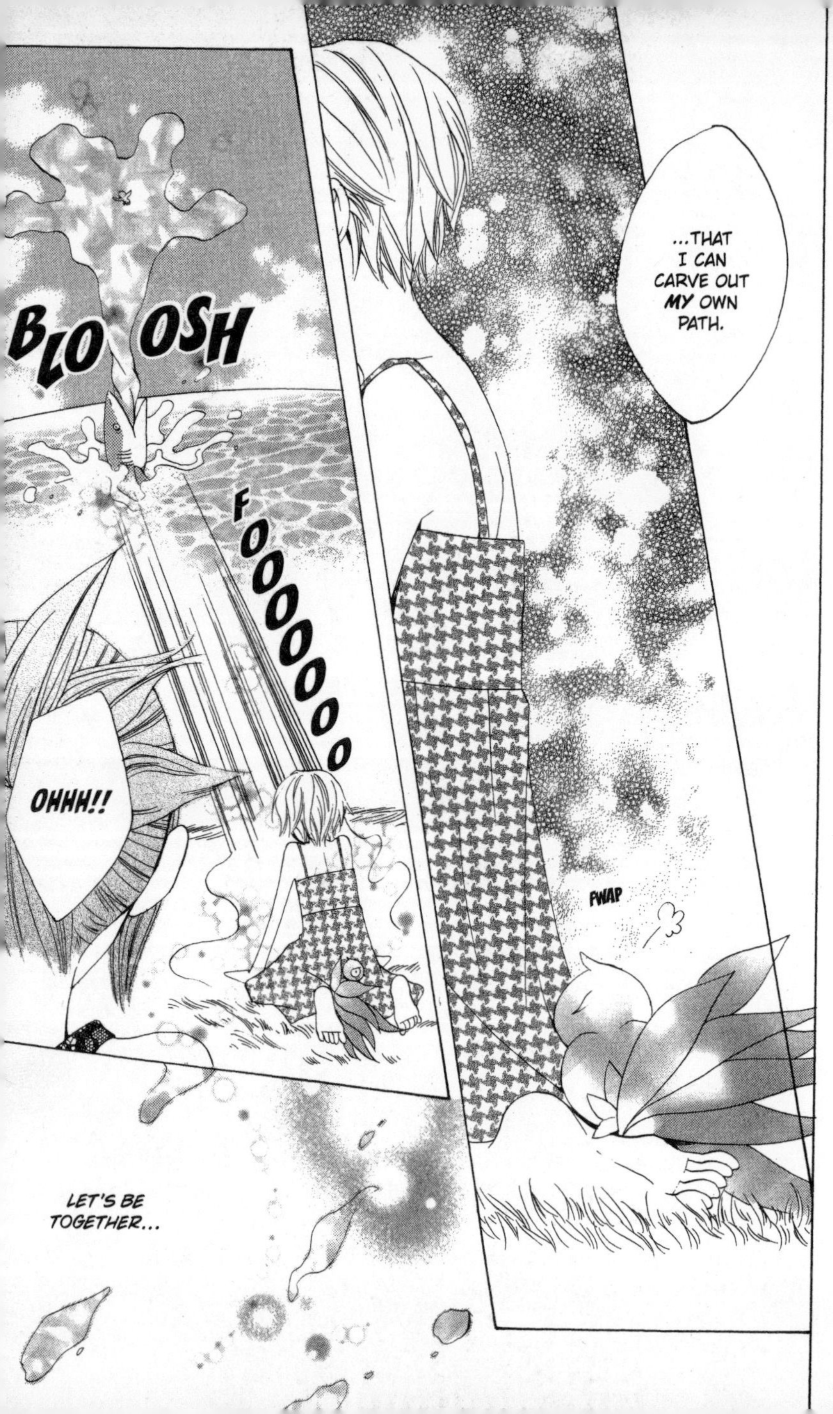
...THAT I CAN CARVE OUT MY OWN PATH.
PWAP
BLOOSH
FOOOOOOOO
OHHH!!
LET'S BE TOGETHER...

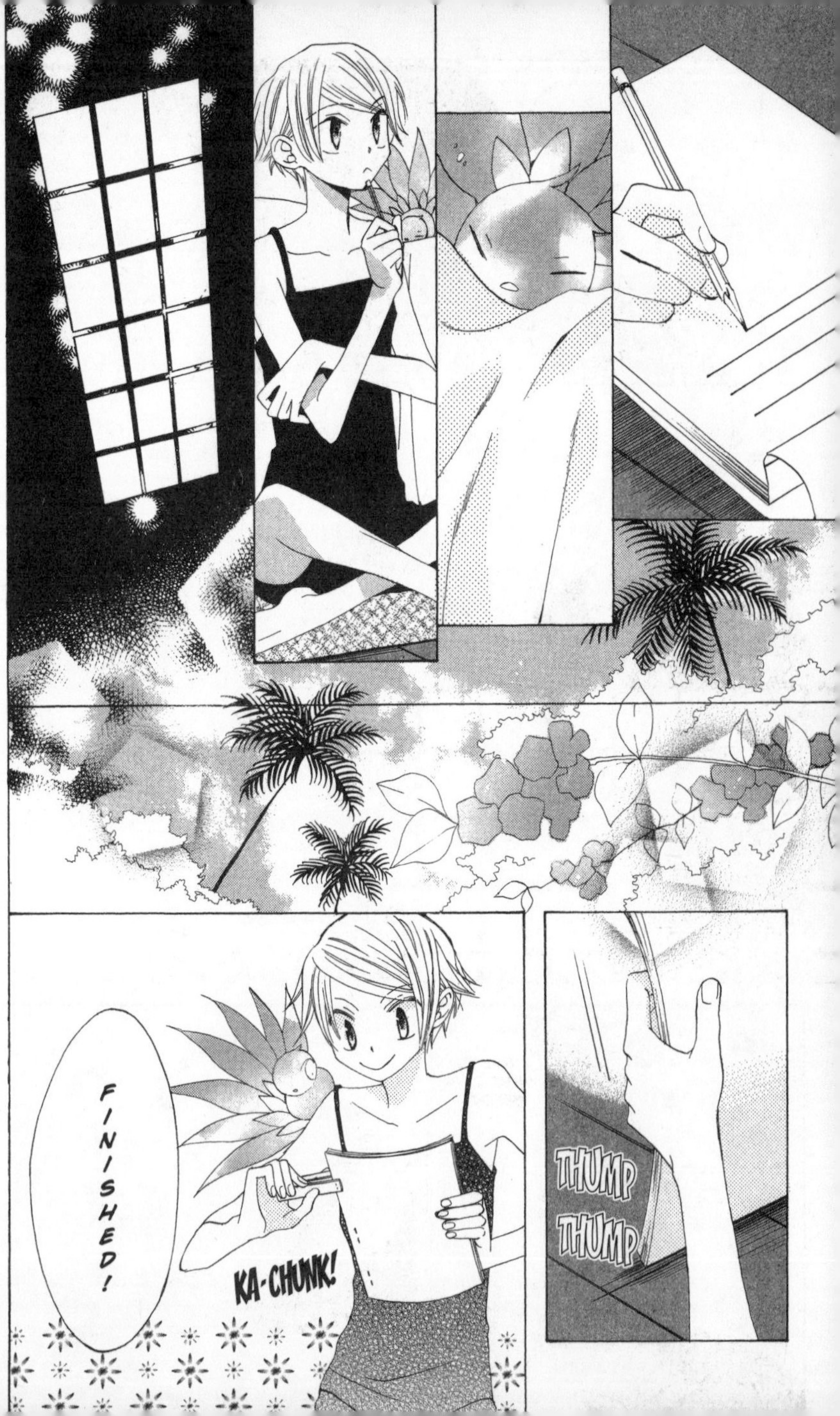
THUMP
THUMP
FINISHED!
KA-CHUNK!

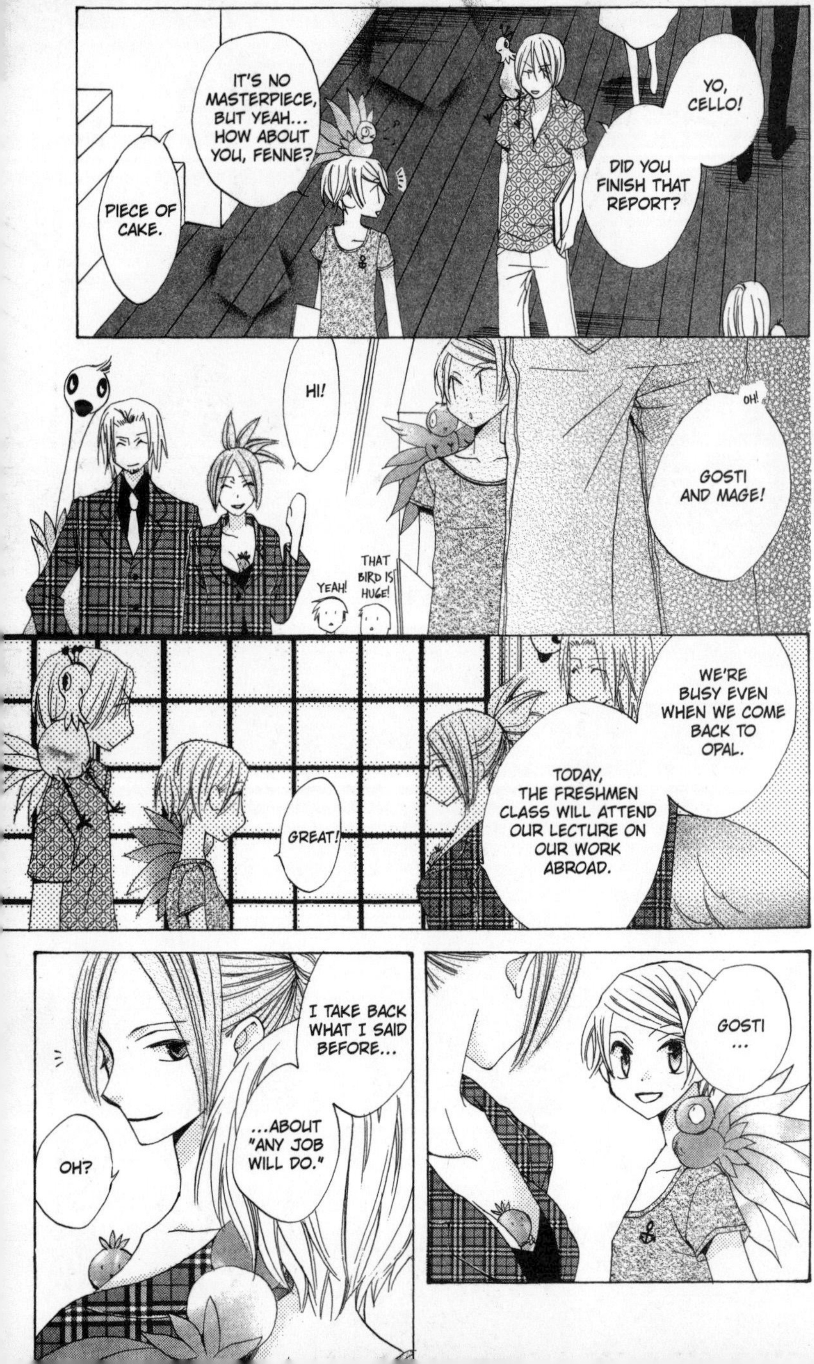
YO, CELLO!
DID YOU FINISH THAT REPORT?
IT'S NO MASTERPIECE, BUT YEAH... HOW ABOUT YOU, FENNE?
PIECE OF CAKE.
OH!
GOSTI AND MAGE!
HI!
THAT BIRD IS HUGE!
YEAH!
WE'RE BUSY EVEN WHEN WE COME BACK TO OPAL.
TODAY, THE FRESHMEN CLASS WILL ATTEND OUR LECTURE ON OUR WORK ABROAD.
GREAT!
GOSTI ...
I TAKE BACK WHAT I SAID BEFORE...
...ABOUT "ANY JOB WILL DO."
OH?

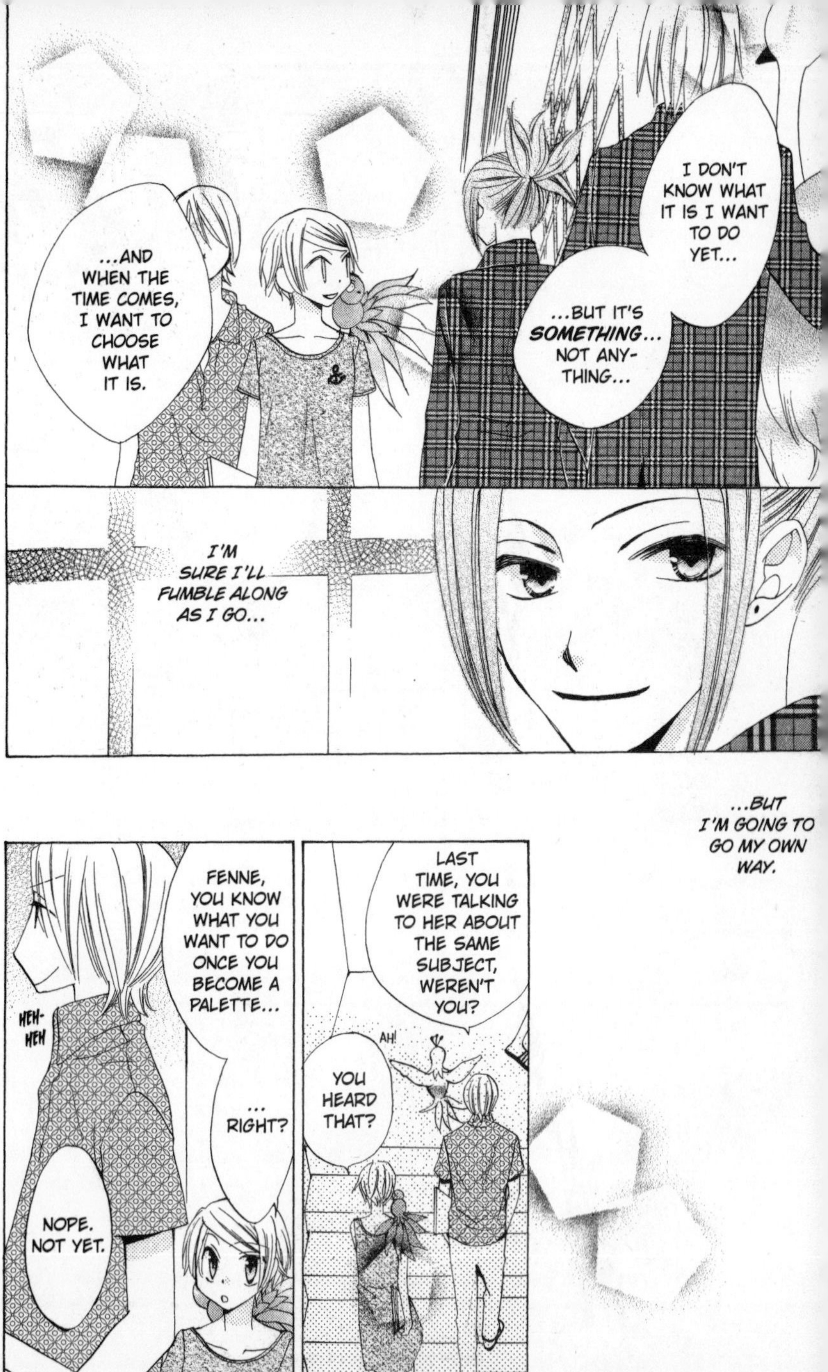
I DON'T KNOW WHAT IT IS I WANT TO DO YET...
...BUT IT'S **SOMETHING**... NOT ANYTHING...
...AND WHEN THE TIME COMES, I WANT TO CHOOSE WHAT IT IS.
I'M SURE I'LL FUMBLE ALONG AS I GO...
...BUT I'M GOING TO GO MY OWN WAY.
LAST TIME, YOU WERE TALKING TO HER ABOUT THE SAME SUBJECT, WEREN'T YOU?
AH!
YOU HEARD THAT?
FENNE, YOU KNOW WHAT YOU WANT TO DO ONCE YOU BECOME A PALETTE...
...RIGHT?
HEH-HEH
NOPE. NOT YET.

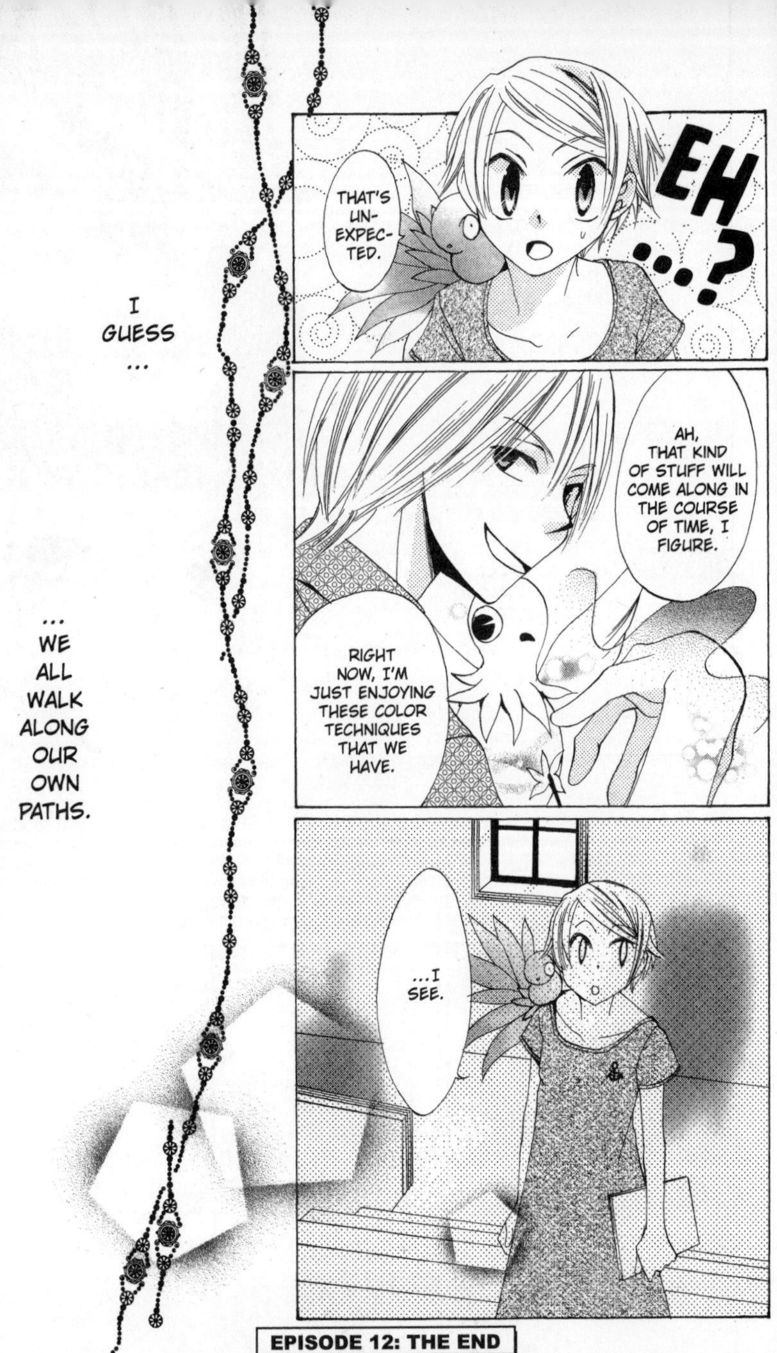
EH...?
THAT'S UN-EXPECTED.
AH, THAT KIND OF STUFF WILL COME ALONG IN THE COURSE OF TIME, I FIGURE.
RIGHT NOW, I'M JUST ENJOYING THESE COLOR TECHNIQUES THAT WE HAVE.
...I SEE.
I GUESS...
...WE ALL WALK ALONG OUR OWN PATHS.
EPISODE 12: THE END

Yoyo became even more hidden
here than I was aiming for.

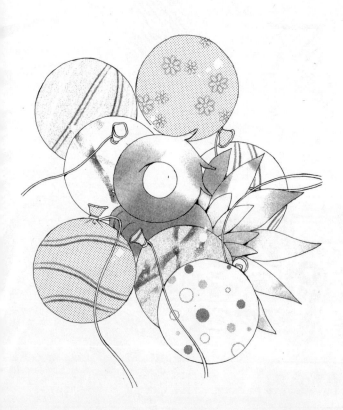

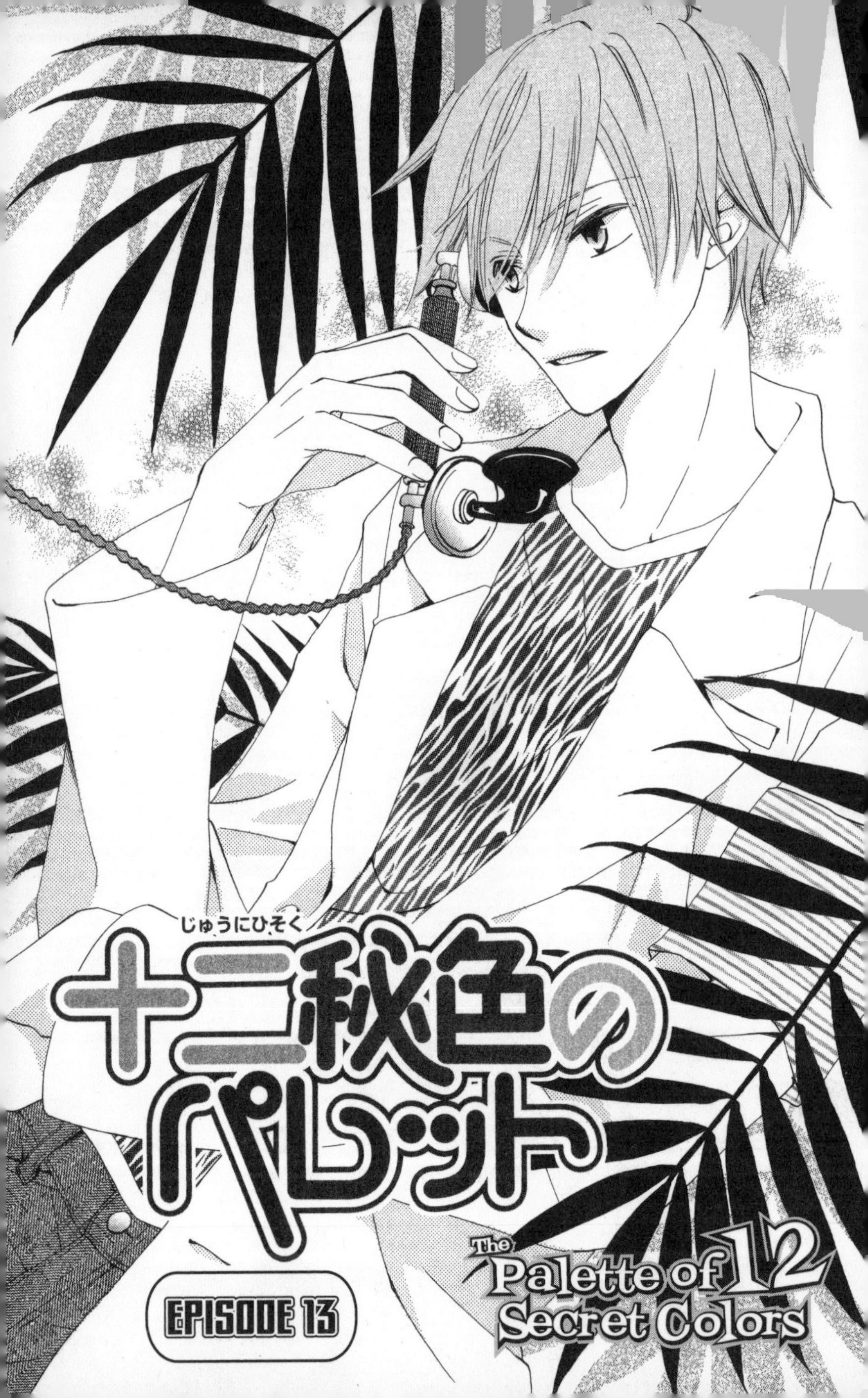
じゅうにひそく
十二秘色のパレット
The Palette of 12 Secret Colors
EPISODE 13

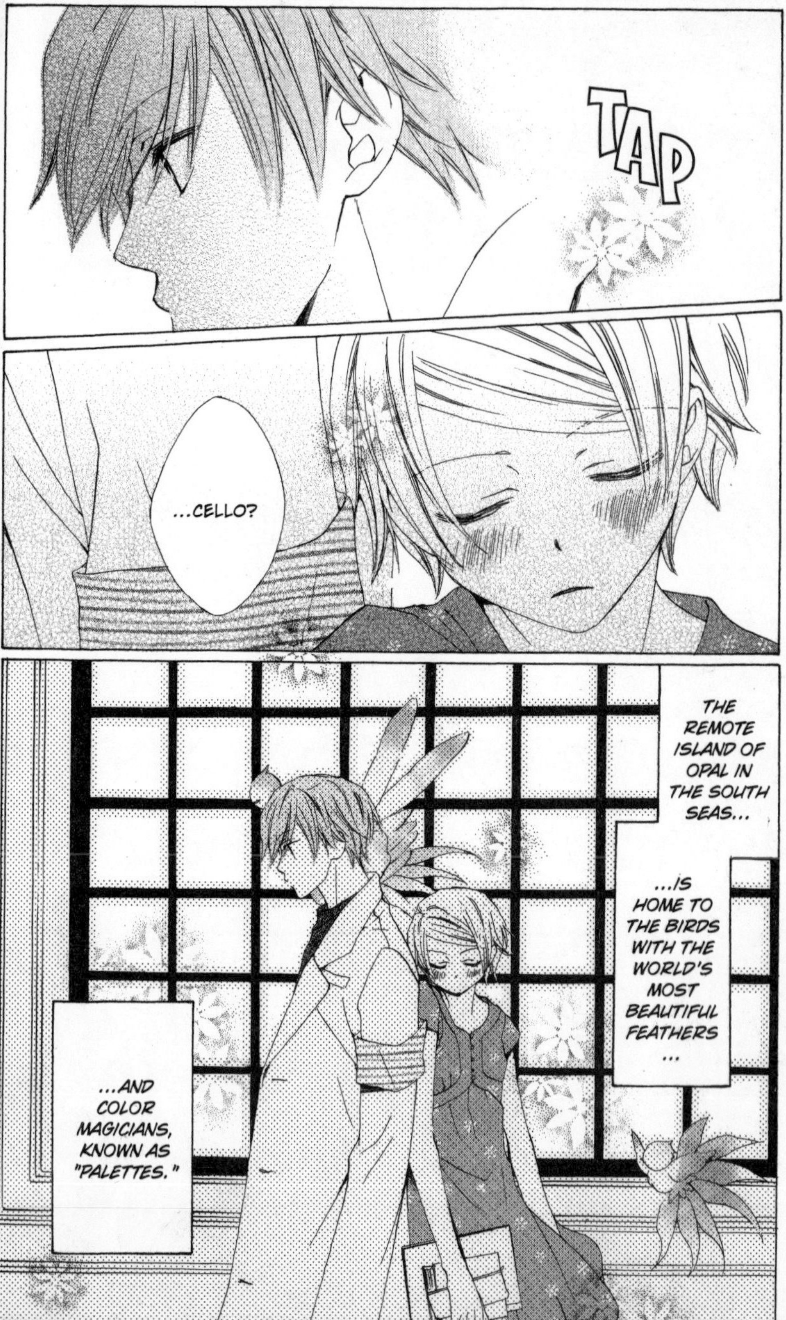
TAP
...CELLO?
THE REMOTE ISLAND OF OPAL IN THE SOUTH SEAS...
...IS HOME TO THE BIRDS WITH THE WORLD'S MOST BEAUTIFUL FEATHERS...
...AND COLOR MAGICIANS, KNOWN AS "PALETTES."

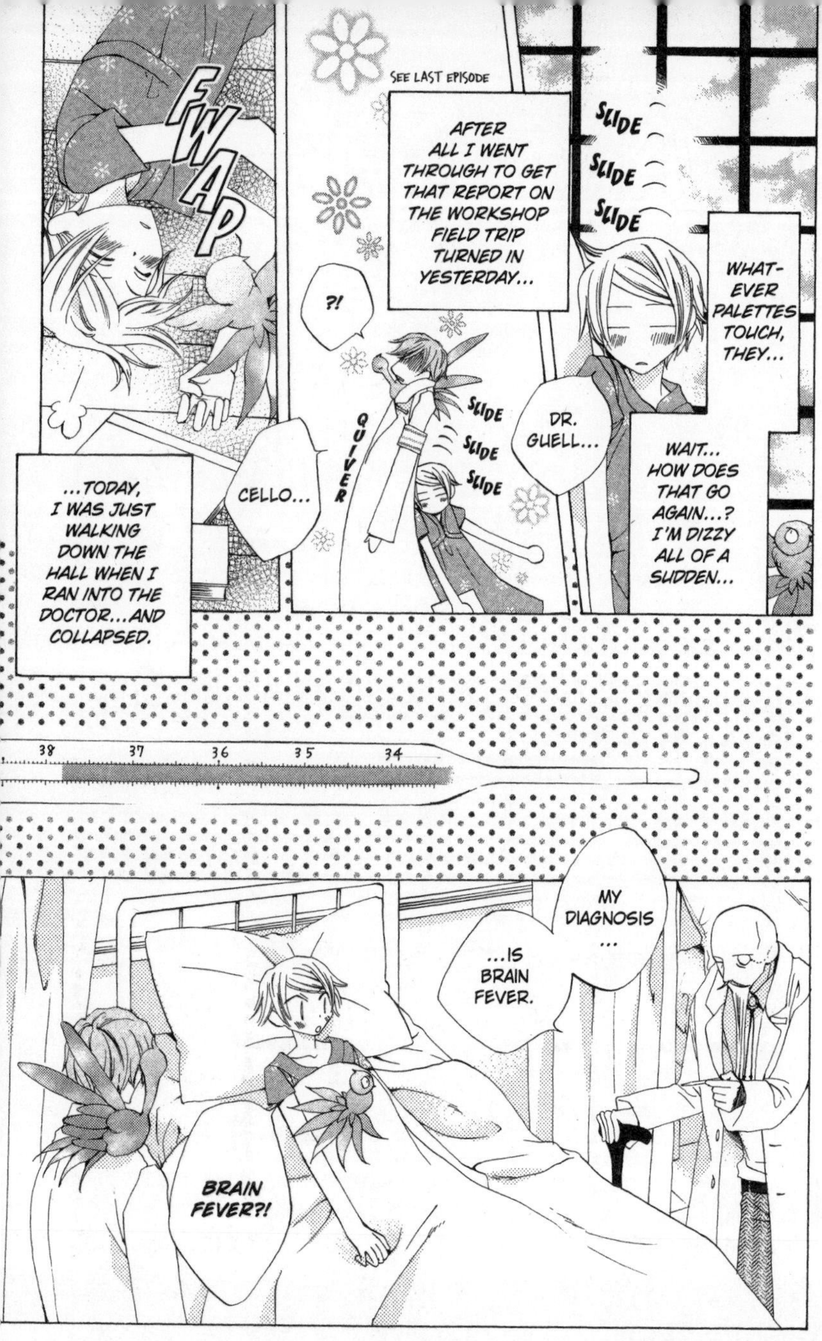
SLIDE
SLIDE
SLIDE
WHAT-EVER PALETTES TOUCH, THEY...
DR. GUELL...
WAIT... HOW DOES THAT GO AGAIN...? I'M DIZZY ALL OF A SUDDEN...
SEE LAST EPISODE
AFTER ALL I WENT THROUGH TO GET THAT REPORT ON THE WORKSHOP FIELD TRIP TURNED IN YESTERDAY...
?!
SLIDE
SLIDE
SLIDE
QUIVER
CELLO...
FWAP
...TODAY, I WAS JUST WALKING DOWN THE HALL WHEN I RAN INTO THE DOCTOR...AND COLLAPSED.
38 37 36 35 34
MY DIAGNOSIS ...
...IS BRAIN FEVER.
BRAIN FEVER?!

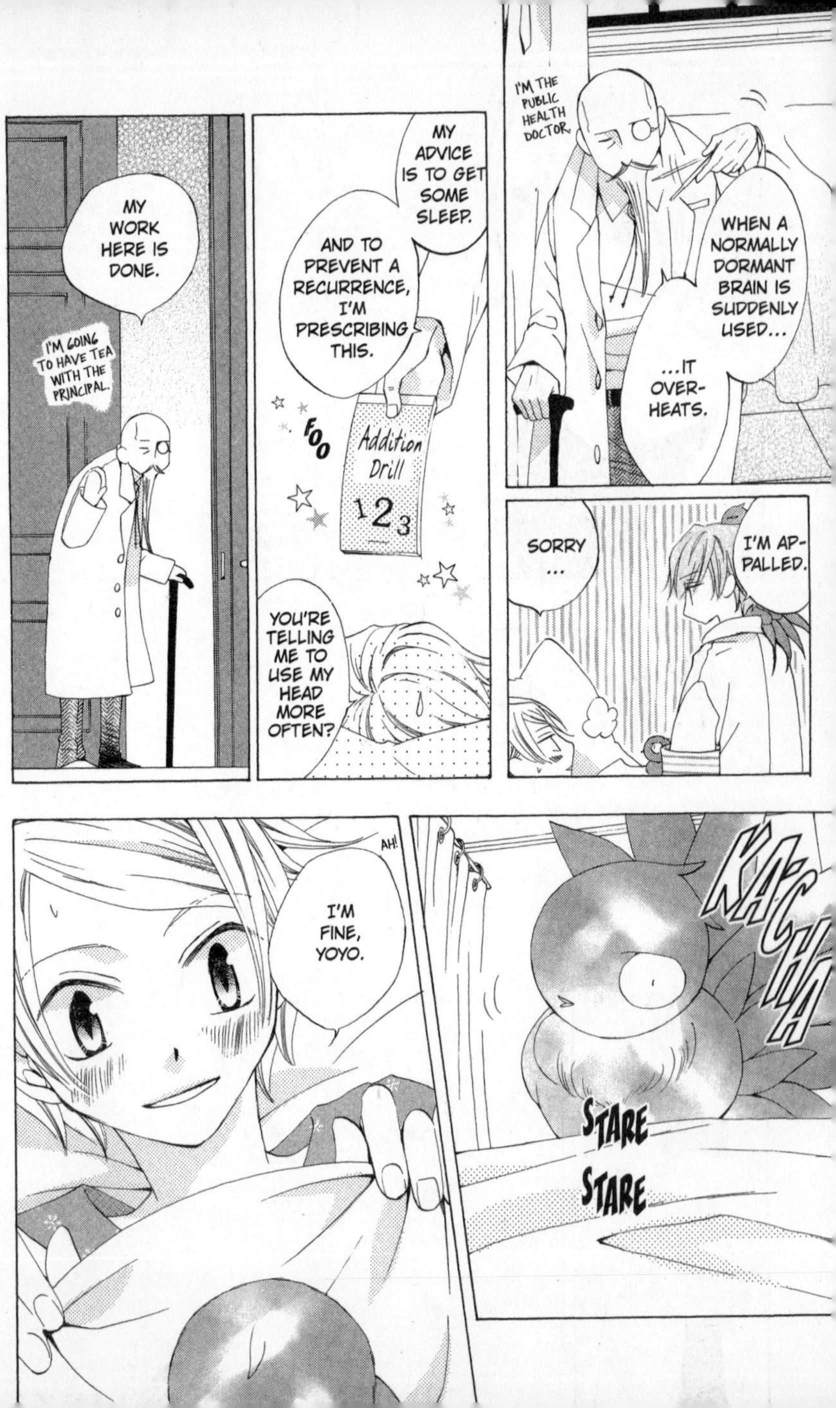
I'M THE PUBLIC HEALTH DOCTOR.
WHEN A NORMALLY DORMANT BRAIN IS SUDDENLY USED...
...IT OVER-HEATS.
I'M AP-PALLED.
SORRY...
MY ADVICE IS TO GET SOME SLEEP.
AND TO PREVENT A RECURRENCE, I'M PRESCRIBING THIS.
Addition Drill
1 2 3
FOO
YOU'RE TELLING ME TO USE MY HEAD MORE OFTEN?
MY WORK HERE IS DONE.
I'M GOING TO HAVE TEA WITH THE PRINCIPAL.
KACHA
STARE
STARE
AH!
I'M FINE, YOYO.

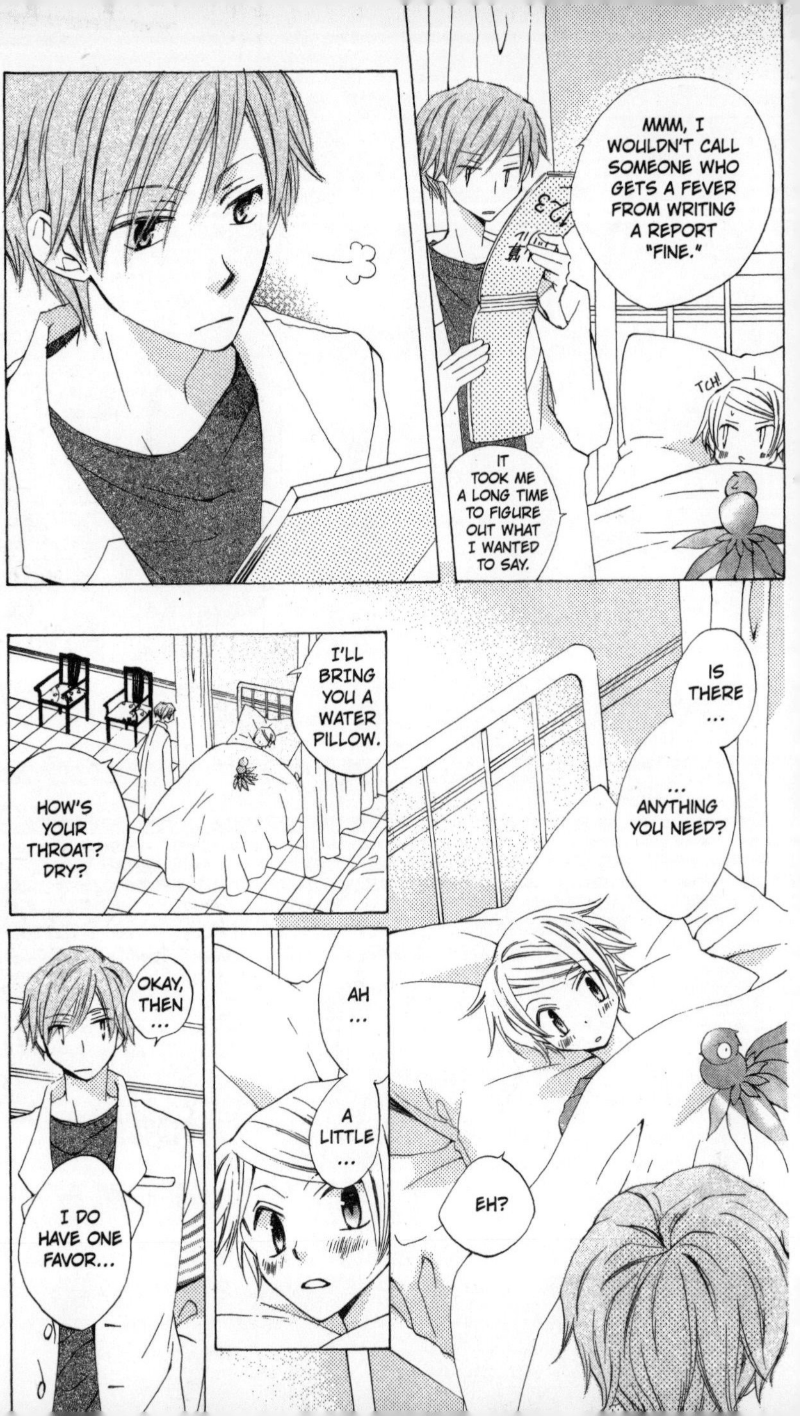
MMM, I WOULDN'T CALL SOMEONE WHO GETS A FEVER FROM WRITING A REPORT "FINE."
TCH!
IT TOOK ME A LONG TIME TO FIGURE OUT WHAT I WANTED TO SAY.
IS THERE ...
... ANYTHING YOU NEED?
I'LL BRING YOU A WATER PILLOW.
HOW'S YOUR THROAT? DRY?
EH?
AH ...
A LITTLE ...
OKAY, THEN ...
I DO HAVE ONE FAVOR...

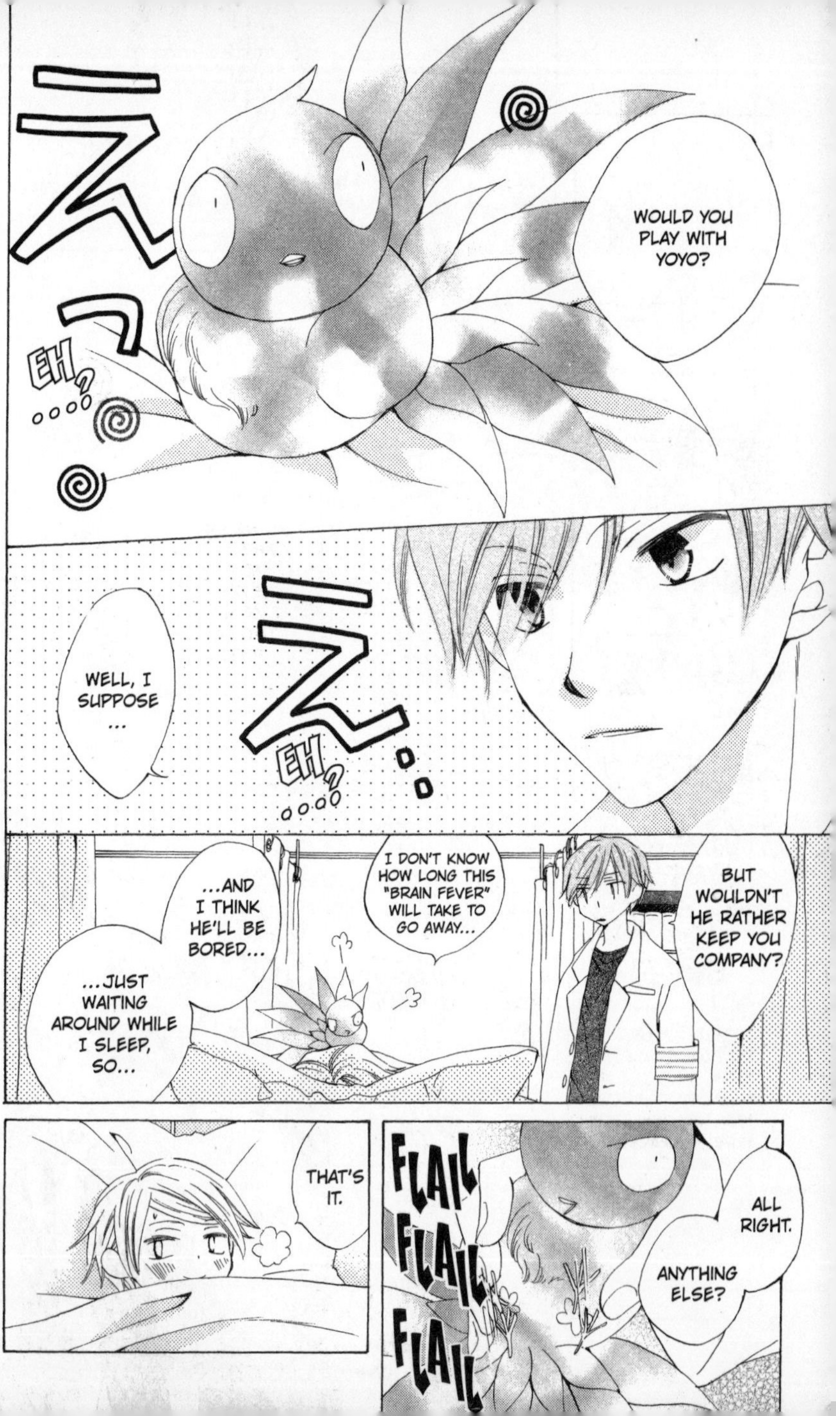
WOULD YOU PLAY WITH YOYO?
EH?....
EH?....
WELL, I SUPPOSE ...
BUT WOULDN'T HE RATHER KEEP YOU COMPANY?
I DON'T KNOW HOW LONG THIS "BRAIN FEVER" WILL TAKE TO GO AWAY...
...AND I THINK HE'LL BE BORED...
...JUST WAITING AROUND WHILE I SLEEP, SO...
ALL RIGHT.
ANYTHING ELSE?
FLAIL FLAIL FLAIL
THAT'S IT.

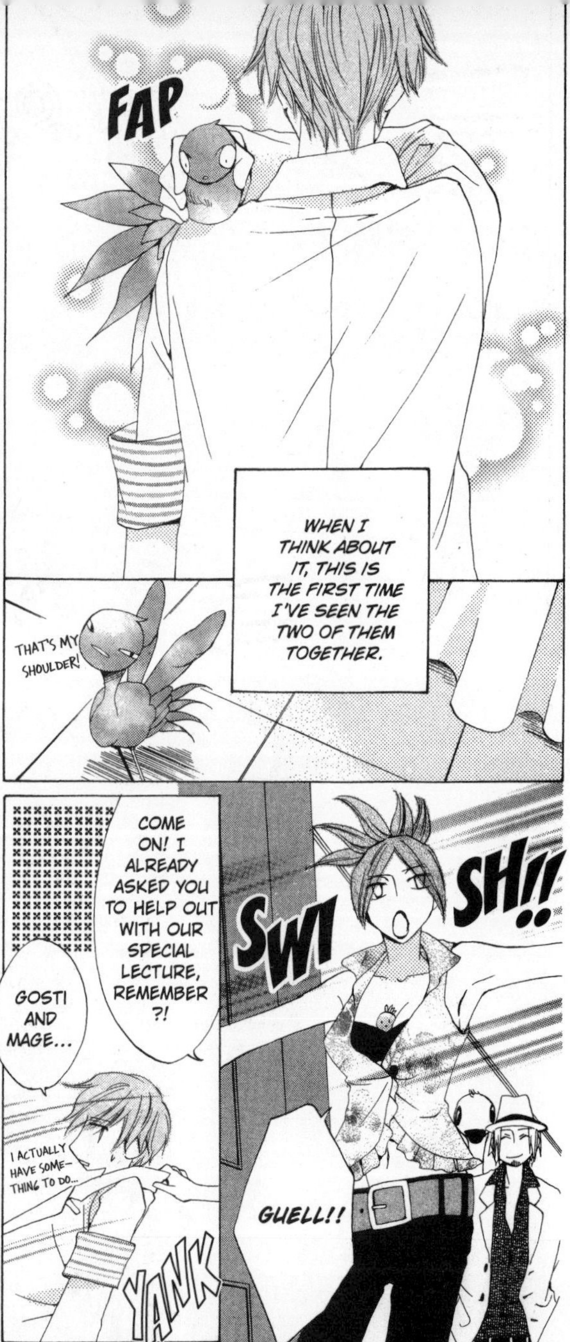
FAP
WHEN I THINK ABOUT IT, THIS IS THE FIRST TIME I'VE SEEN THE TWO OF THEM TOGETHER.
THAT'S MY SHOULDER!
SWISH!!
COME ON! I ALREADY ASKED YOU TO HELP OUT WITH OUR SPECIAL LECTURE, REMEMBER ?!
GOSTI AND MAGE...
I ACTUALLY HAVE SOME-THING TO DO...
YANK
GUELL!!

4

OTHER COUNTRIES (2)

THIS IS THE CHINESE VERSION.

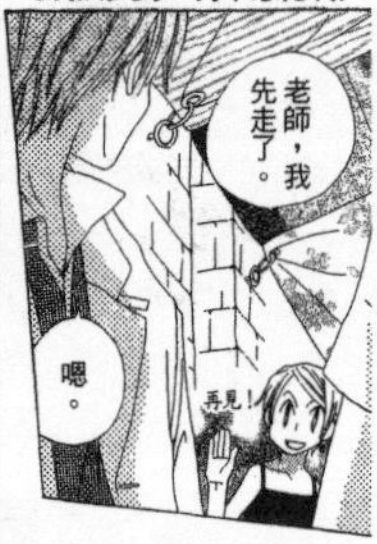
老師，我先走了。
嗯。
再見！

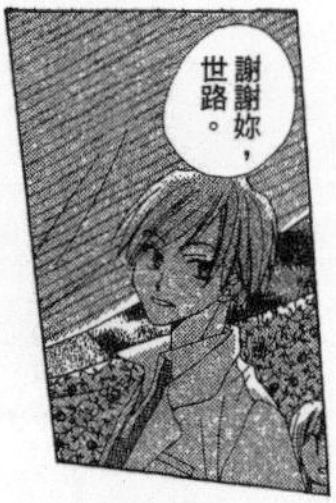
謝謝妳，世路。

IN THE CHINESE, NO HONORIFICS LIKE "SAN" OR "KUN" ARE USED. BY THE WAY, EVEN MY SMALL TALK HERE IS TRANSLATED. I APOLOGIZE FOR ALWAYS WRITING ABOUT TRIVIAL MATTERS.

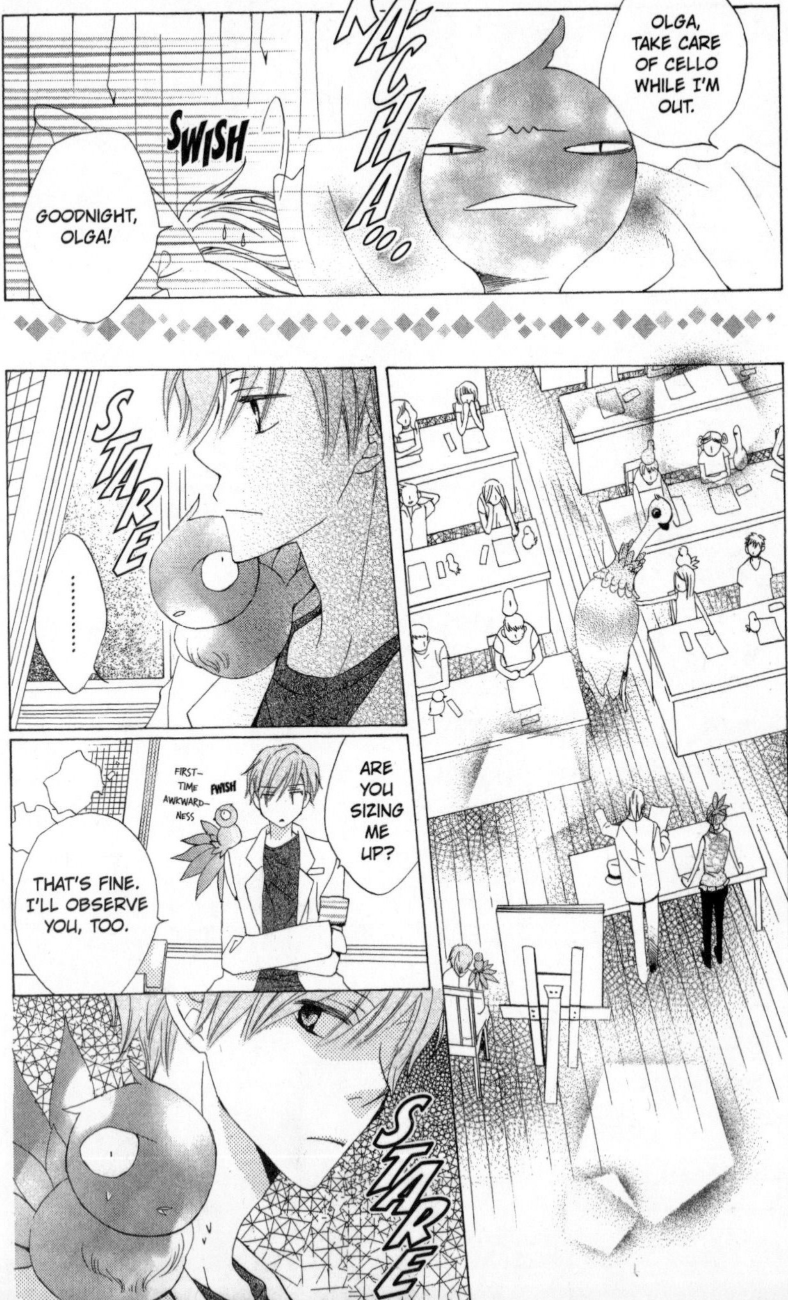

OLGA, TAKE CARE OF CELLO WHILE I'M OUT.
KA-CHA...
SWISH
GOODNIGHT, OLGA!
STARE
......
ARE YOU SIZING ME UP?
FIRST-TIME AWKWARDNESS
FWISH
THAT'S FINE. I'LL OBSERVE YOU, TOO.
STARE

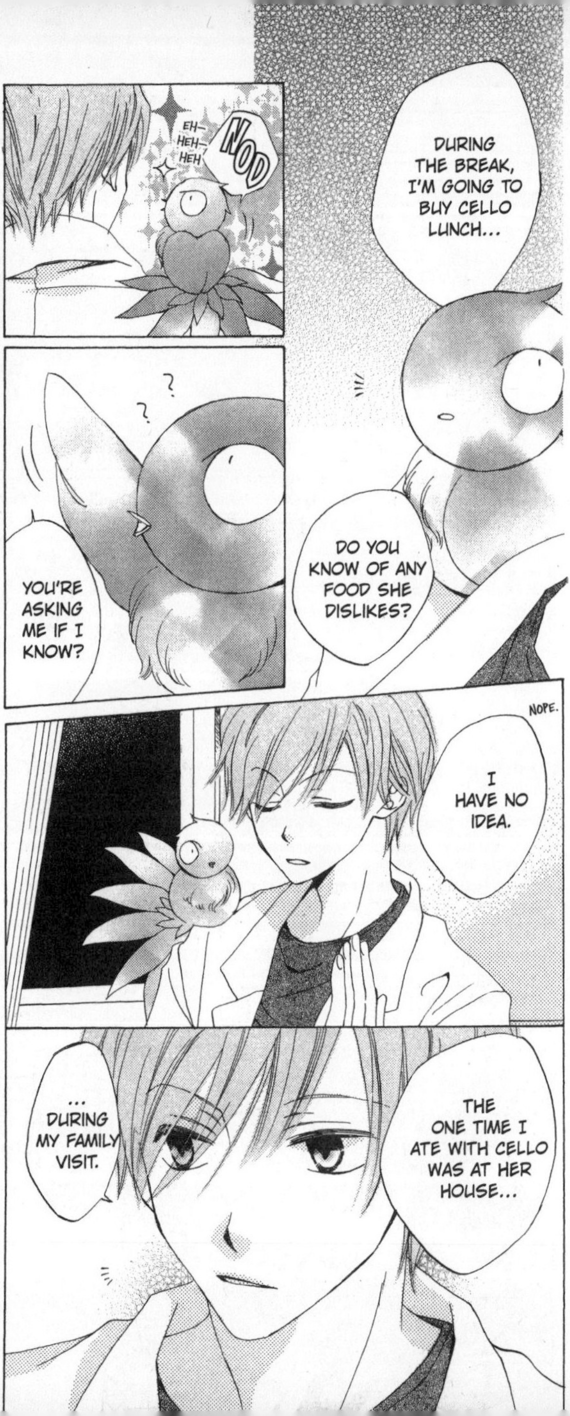
DURING THE BREAK, I'M GOING TO BUY CELLO LUNCH...
DO YOU KNOW OF ANY FOOD SHE DISLIKES?
EH-HEH-HEH
NOD
YOU'RE ASKING ME IF I KNOW?
NOPE.
I HAVE NO IDEA.
THE ONE TIME I ATE WITH CELLO WAS AT HER HOUSE...
...DURING MY FAMILY VISIT.

5

LIKES AND DISLIKES:

I DON'T LIKE EGGS IN GENERAL, BUT DEPENDING ON THE METHOD OF COOKING, MY LEVEL OF DISLIKE DIFFERS. THERE'S NO WAY I'LL EAT FRIED EGGS, BOILED EGGS (SOFT OR HARD-BOILED) OR EGG ON RICE. HOWEVER, I CAN EAT *TAMAGOYAKI* (A SWEETENED, SOY-FLAVORED OMELET) AND OTHER KINDS OF OMELETS. WITH SUKIYAKI, I'LL USE A RAW EGG, BUT I'VE NEVER ORDERED *TSUKIMI SOBA* (NOODLES WITH AN EGG ON TOP). FOR ME THE KEY POINT IS WHETHER THE EGG'S FLAVOR TAKES PRECEDENCE IN THE DISH OR WHETHER THE OTHER FLAVORS ARE STRONG ENOUGH SO THAT I DON'T MIND THE EGG.

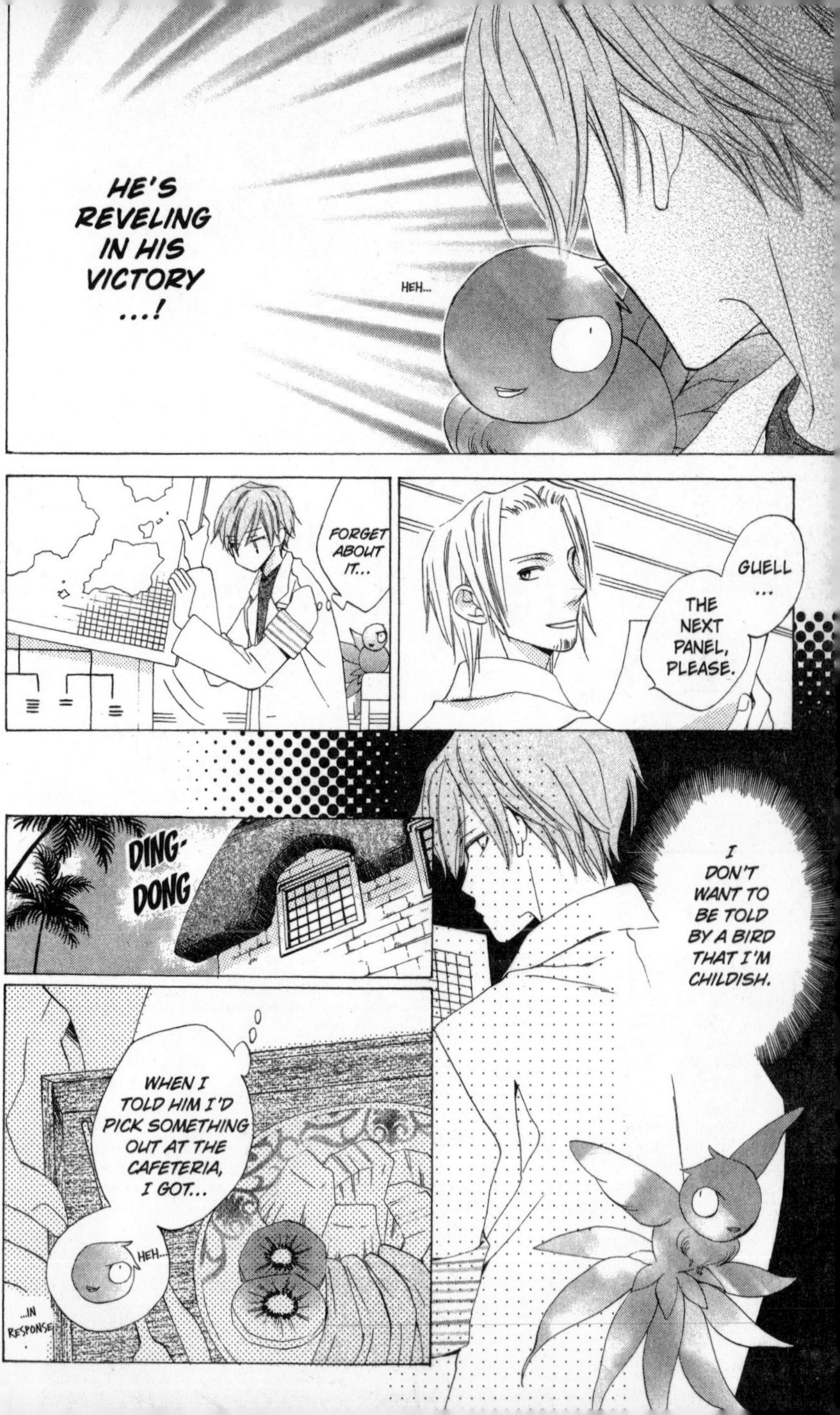
HEH...
HE'S REVELING IN HIS VICTORY ...!
GUELL ... THE NEXT PANEL, PLEASE.
FORGET ABOUT IT...
I DON'T WANT TO BE TOLD BY A BIRD THAT I'M CHILDISH.
DING-DONG
WHEN I TOLD HIM I'D PICK SOMETHING OUT AT THE CAFETERIA, I GOT...
HEH...
...IN RESPONSE.

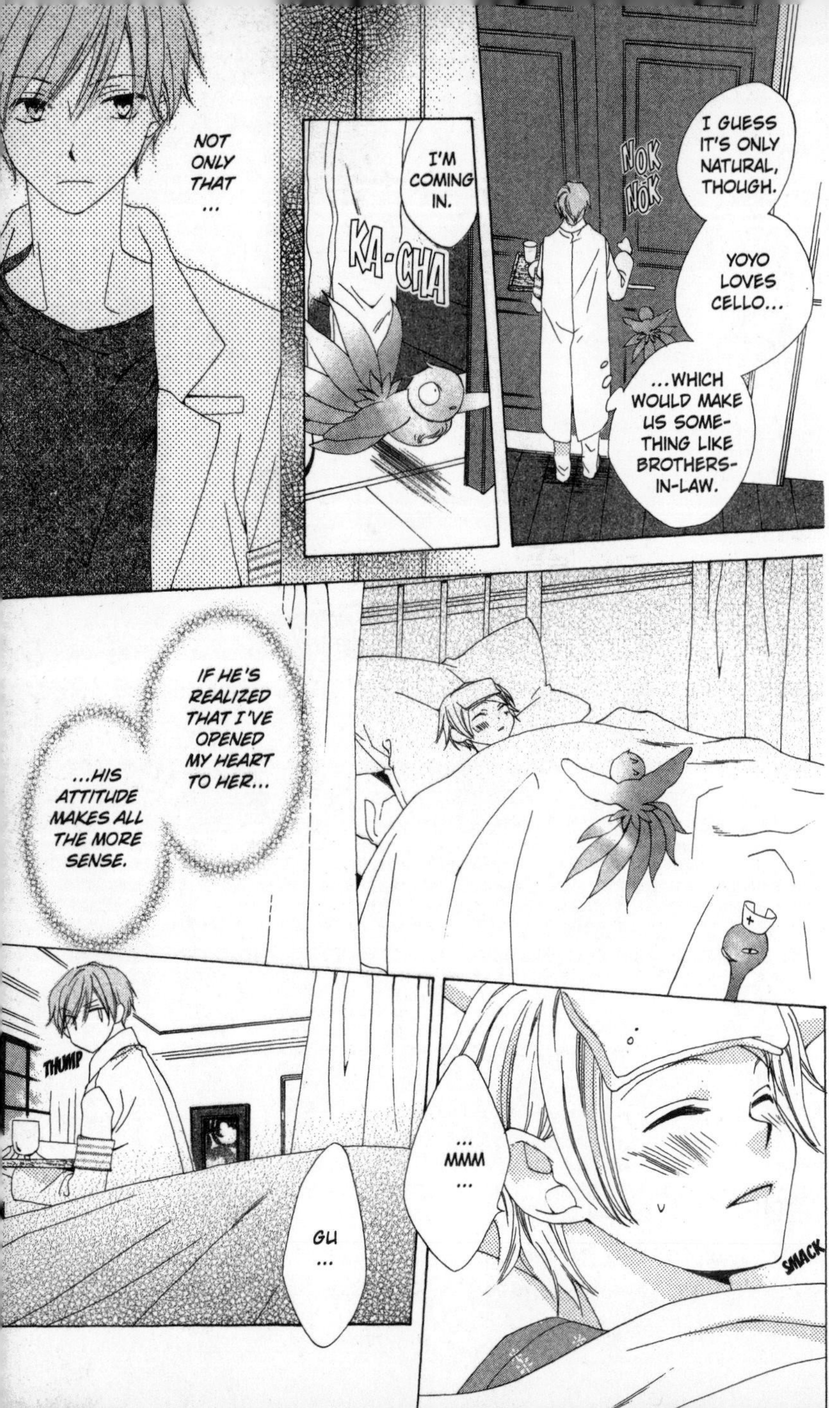
I GUESS IT'S ONLY NATURAL, THOUGH.
NOK NOK
YOYO LOVES CELLO...
...WHICH WOULD MAKE US SOME-THING LIKE BROTHERS-IN-LAW.
I'M COMING IN.
KA-CHA
NOT ONLY THAT ...
IF HE'S REALIZED THAT I'VE OPENED MY HEART TO HER...
...HIS ATTITUDE MAKES ALL THE MORE SENSE.
SMACK
... MMM ...
GU ...
THUMP

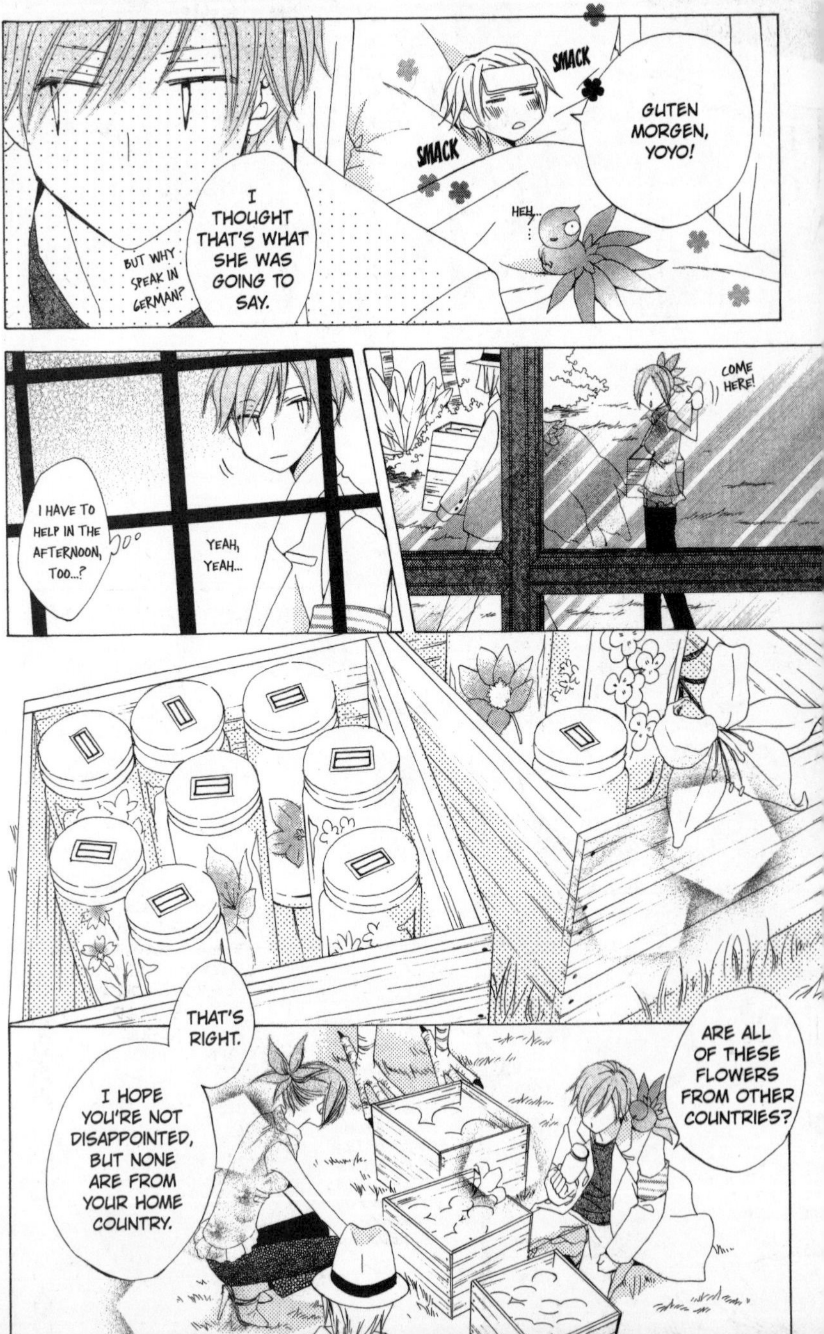
SMACK
GUTEN MORGEN, YOYO!
SMACK
HEH...
I THOUGHT THAT'S WHAT SHE WAS GOING TO SAY.
BUT WHY SPEAK IN GERMAN?
COME HERE!
YEAH, YEAH...
I HAVE TO HELP IN THE AFTERNOON, TOO...?
ARE ALL OF THESE FLOWERS FROM OTHER COUNTRIES?
THAT'S RIGHT.
I HOPE YOU'RE NOT DISAPPOINTED, BUT NONE ARE FROM YOUR HOME COUNTRY.

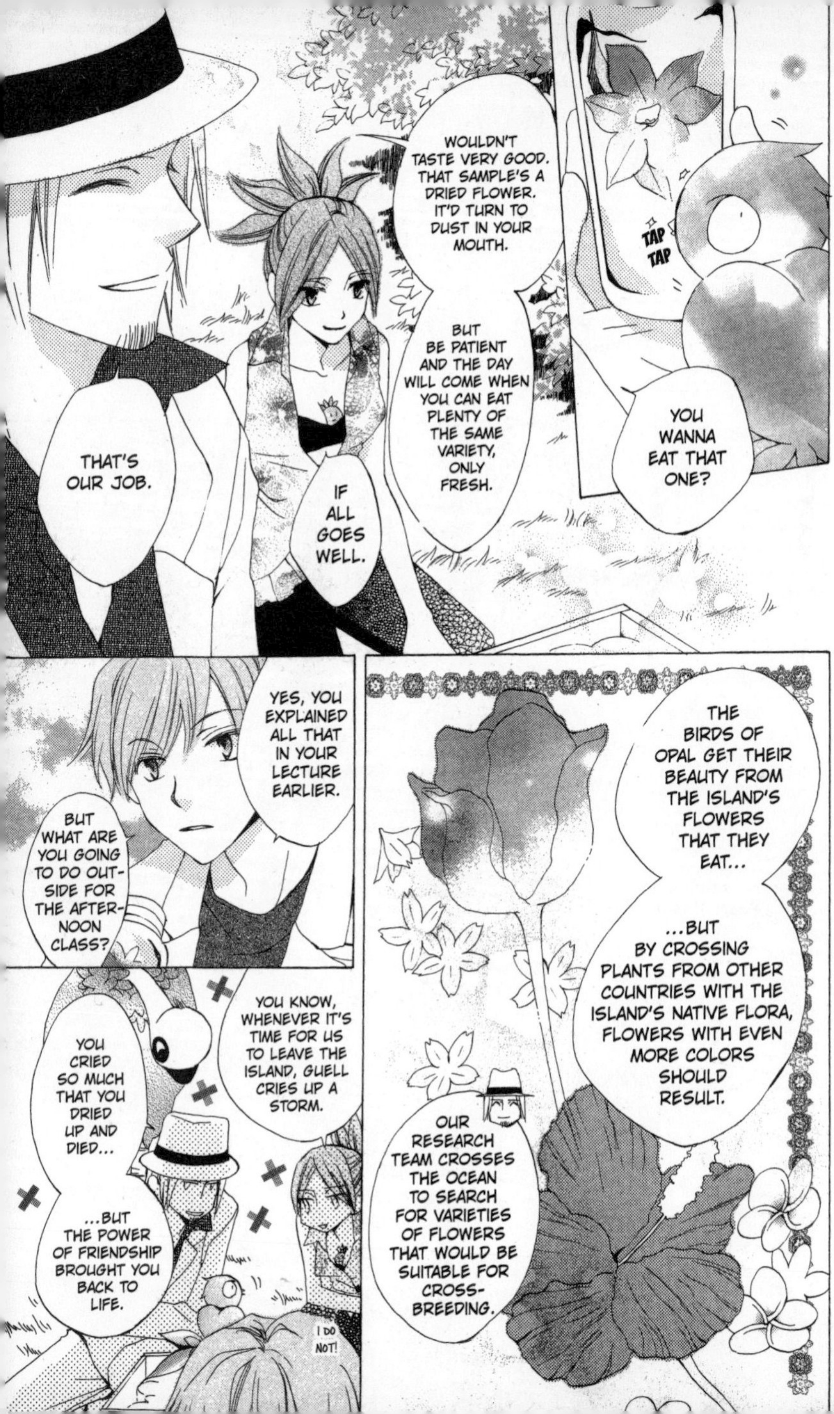
TAP TAP
YOU WANNA EAT THAT ONE?
WOULDN'T TASTE VERY GOOD. THAT SAMPLE'S A DRIED FLOWER. IT'D TURN TO DUST IN YOUR MOUTH.
BUT BE PATIENT AND THE DAY WILL COME WHEN YOU CAN EAT PLENTY OF THE SAME VARIETY, ONLY FRESH.
IF ALL GOES WELL.
THAT'S OUR JOB.
THE BIRDS OF OPAL GET THEIR BEAUTY FROM THE ISLAND'S FLOWERS THAT THEY EAT...
...BUT BY CROSSING PLANTS FROM OTHER COUNTRIES WITH THE ISLAND'S NATIVE FLORA, FLOWERS WITH EVEN MORE COLORS SHOULD RESULT.
OUR RESEARCH TEAM CROSSES THE OCEAN TO SEARCH FOR VARIETIES OF FLOWERS THAT WOULD BE SUITABLE FOR CROSS-BREEDING.
YES, YOU EXPLAINED ALL THAT IN YOUR LECTURE EARLIER.
BUT WHAT ARE YOU GOING TO DO OUTSIDE FOR THE AFTERNOON CLASS?
YOU KNOW, WHENEVER IT'S TIME FOR US TO LEAVE THE ISLAND, GUELL CRIES UP A STORM.
YOU CRIED SO MUCH THAT YOU DRIED UP AND DIED...
...BUT THE POWER OF FRIENDSHIP BROUGHT YOU BACK TO LIFE.
I DO NOT!

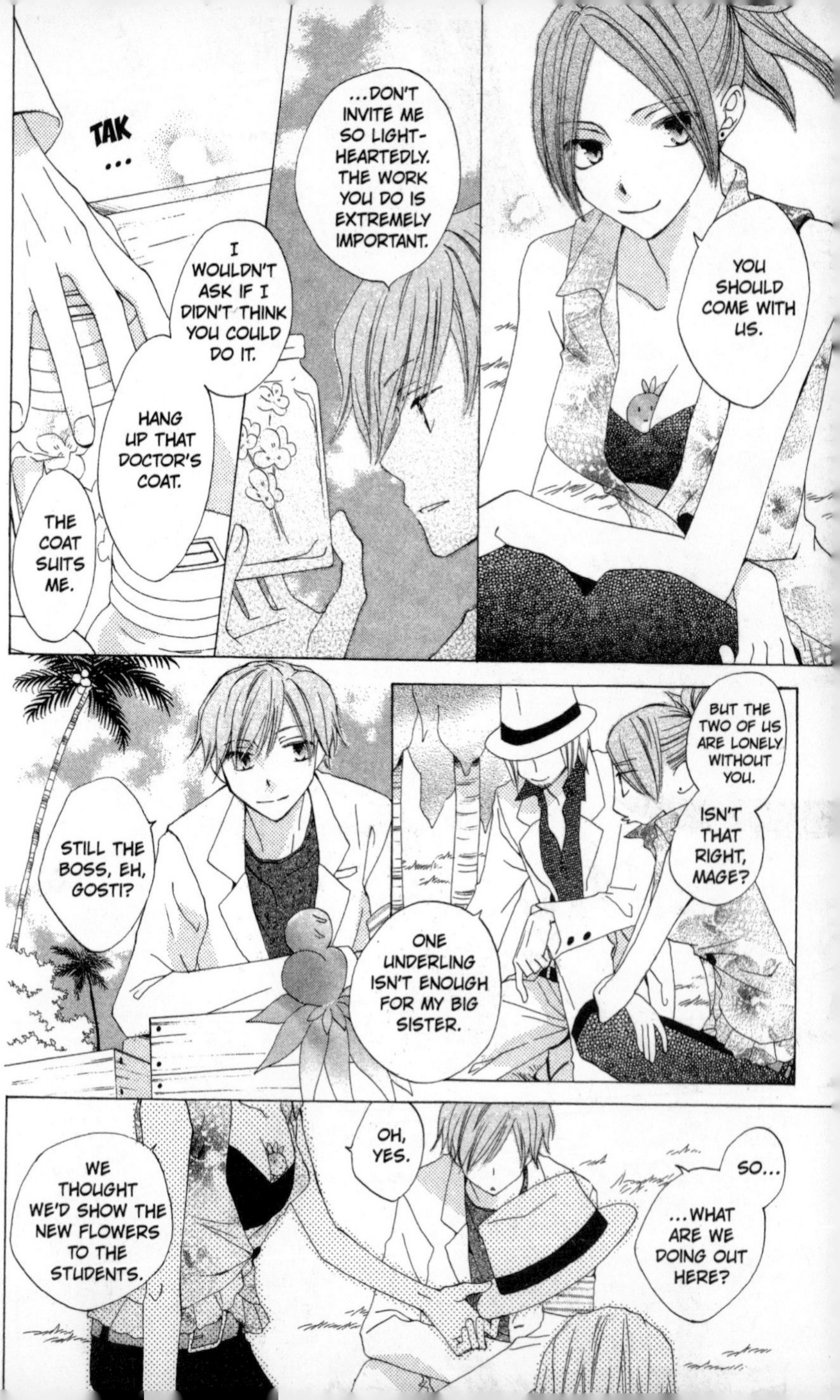
YOU SHOULD COME WITH US.
...DON'T INVITE ME SO LIGHT-HEARTEDLY. THE WORK YOU DO IS EXTREMELY IMPORTANT.
I WOULDN'T ASK IF I DIDN'T THINK YOU COULD DO IT.
HANG UP THAT DOCTOR'S COAT.
TAK
...
THE COAT SUITS ME.
BUT THE TWO OF US ARE LONELY WITHOUT YOU.
ISN'T THAT RIGHT, MAGE?
ONE UNDERLING ISN'T ENOUGH FOR MY BIG SISTER.
STILL THE BOSS, EH, GOSTI?
SO...
...WHAT ARE WE DOING OUT HERE?
OH, YES.
WE THOUGHT WE'D SHOW THE NEW FLOWERS TO THE STUDENTS.

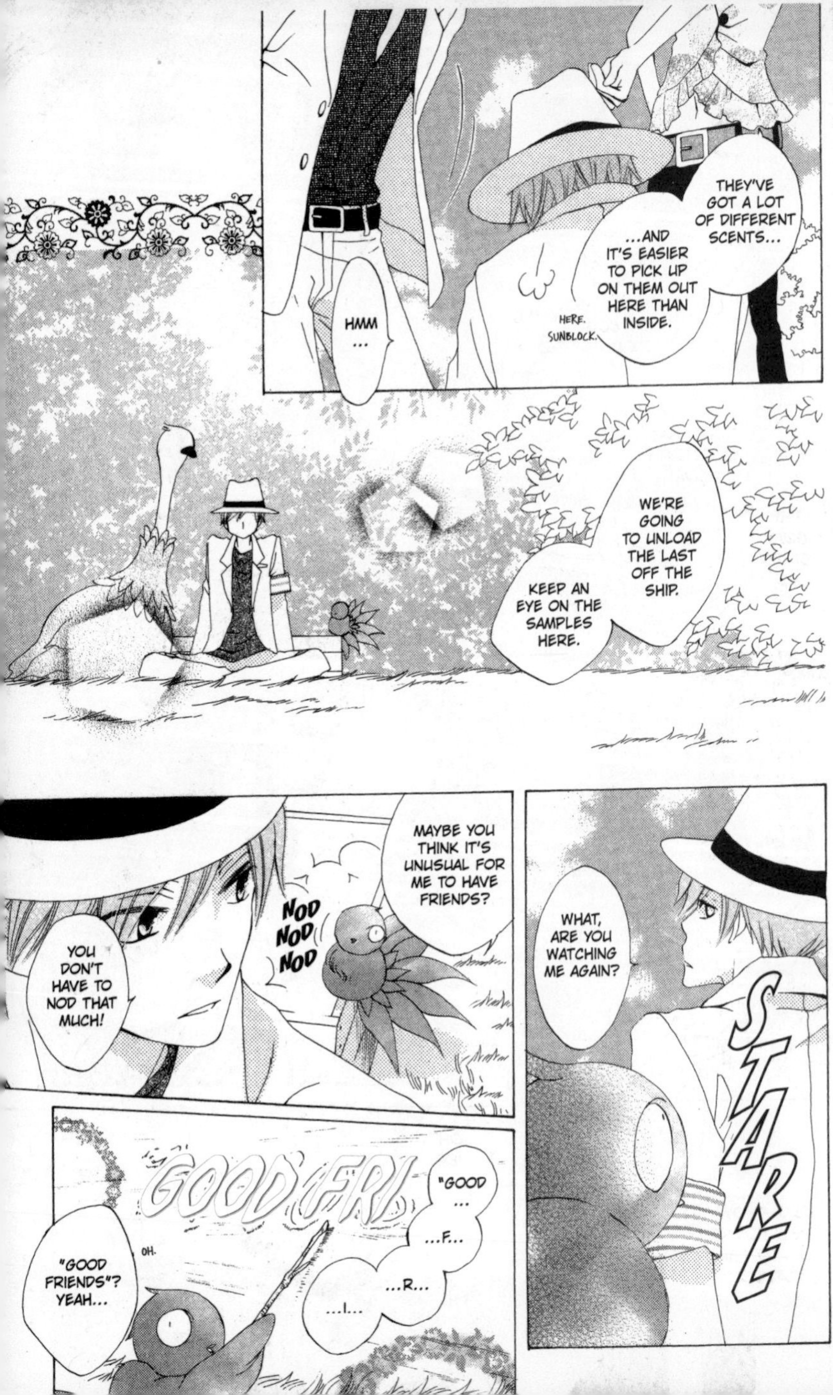
THEY'VE GOT A LOT OF DIFFERENT SCENTS...
...AND IT'S EASIER TO PICK UP ON THEM OUT HERE THAN INSIDE.
HERE. SUNBLOCK.
HMM...
WE'RE GOING TO UNLOAD THE LAST OFF THE SHIP.
KEEP AN EYE ON THE SAMPLES HERE.
WHAT, ARE YOU WATCHING ME AGAIN?
STARE
MAYBE YOU THINK IT'S UNUSUAL FOR ME TO HAVE FRIENDS?
NOD NOD NOD
YOU DON'T HAVE TO NOD THAT MUCH!
GOOD FRI
"GOOD ...
...F...
...R...
...I...
OH.
"GOOD FRIENDS"? YEAH...

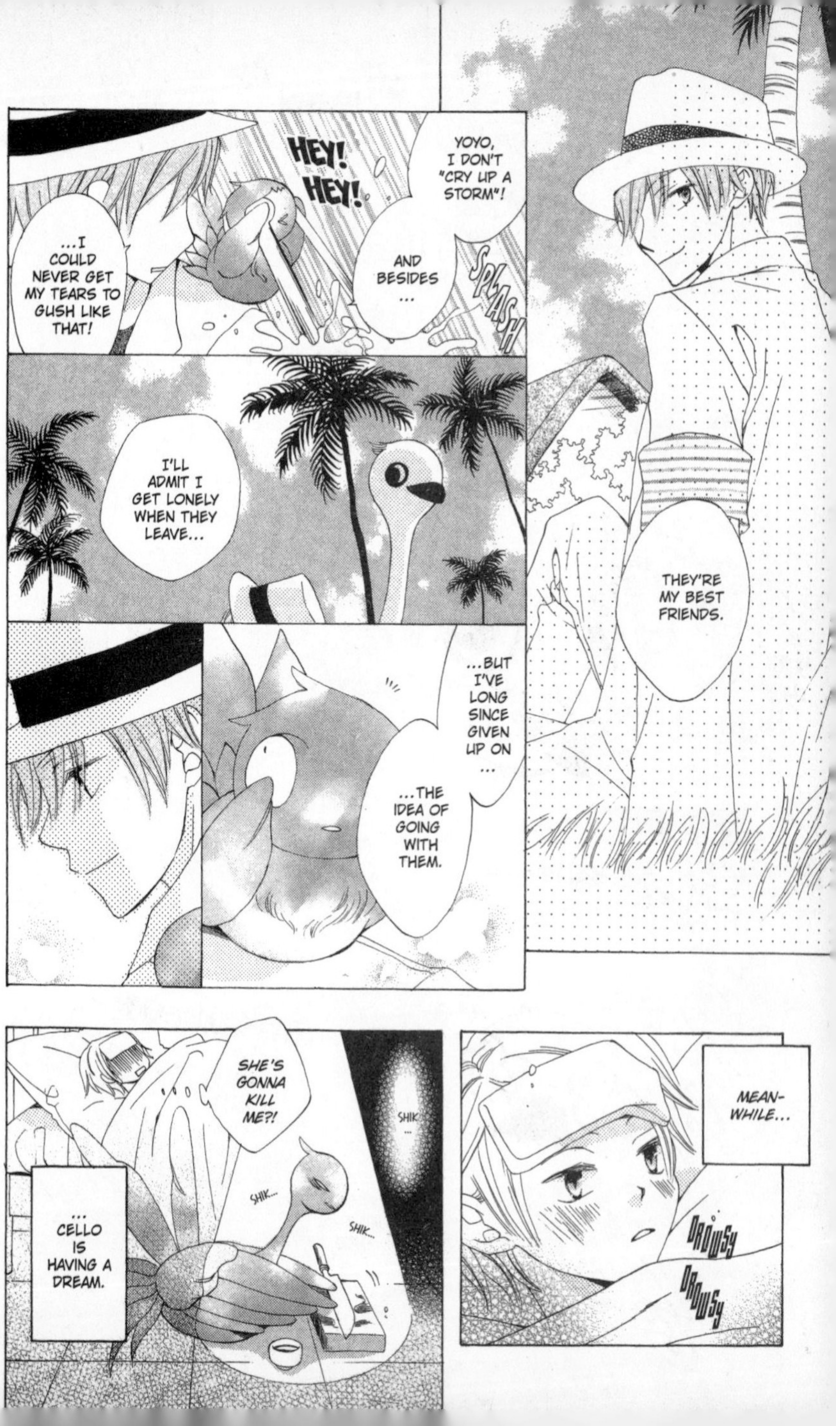
THEY'RE MY BEST FRIENDS.
YOYO, I DON'T "CRY UP A STORM"!
HEY! HEY!
AND BESIDES ...
SPLASH
...I COULD NEVER GET MY TEARS TO GUSH LIKE THAT!
I'LL ADMIT I GET LONELY WHEN THEY LEAVE...
...BUT I'VE LONG SINCE GIVEN UP ON ...
...THE IDEA OF GOING WITH THEM.
MEAN-WHILE...
DROWSY
DROWSY
SHE'S GONNA KILL ME?!
SHIK ...
SHIK...
SHIK...
... CELLO IS HAVING A DREAM.

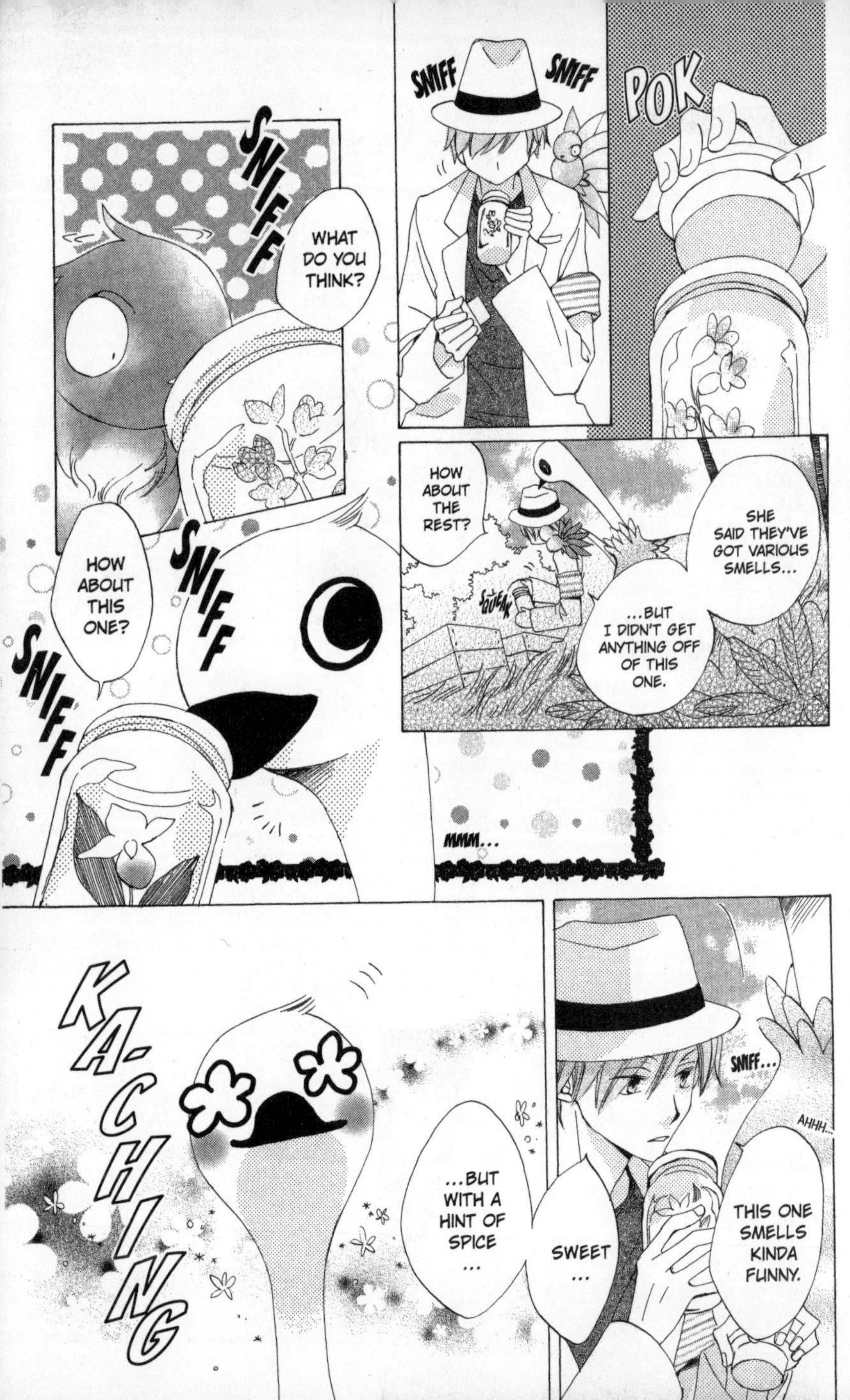
POK
SNIFF
SNIFF
SNIFF
WHAT DO YOU THINK?
HOW ABOUT THE REST?
SQUEAK
SHE SAID THEY'VE GOT VARIOUS SMELLS...
...BUT I DIDN'T GET ANYTHING OFF OF THIS ONE.
SNIFF
HOW ABOUT THIS ONE?
SNIFF
MMM...
SNIFF...
AHHH...
THIS ONE SMELLS KINDA FUNNY.
SWEET...
...BUT WITH A HINT OF SPICE...
KA-CHING

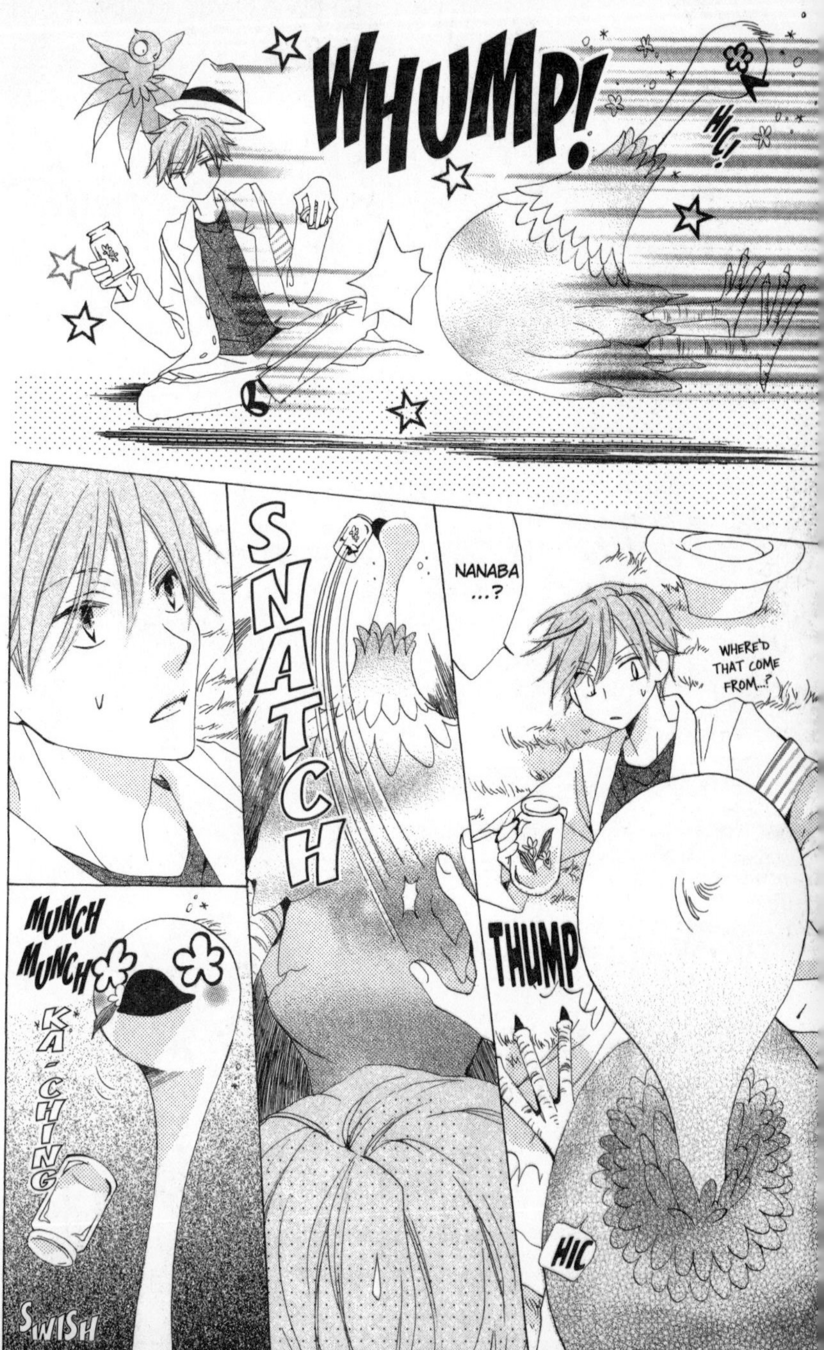
HIC!
WHUMP!
WHERE'D THAT COME FROM...?
NANABA ...?
THUMP
HIC
SNATCH
MUNCH MUNCH
KA-CHING
SWISH

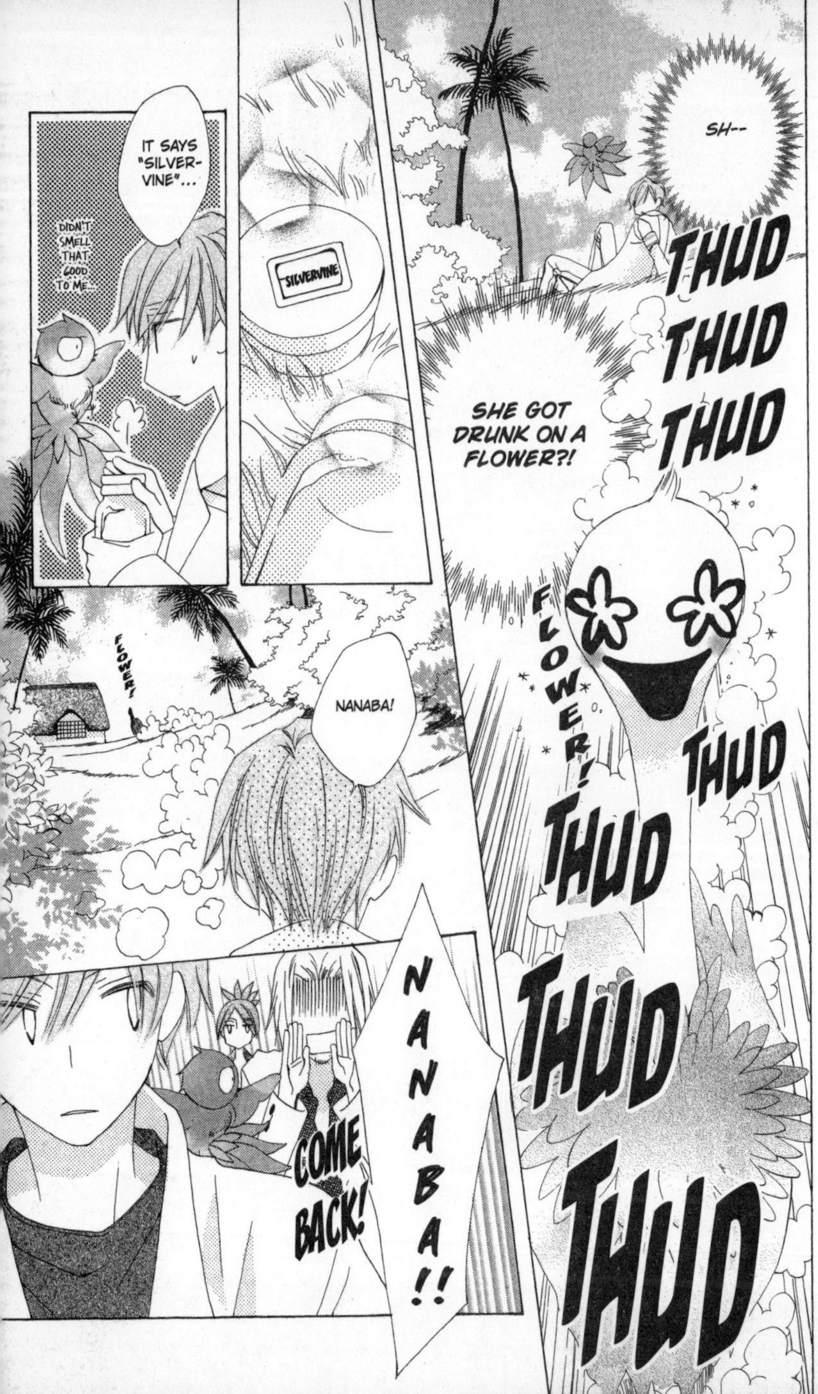

SH--
THUD THUD THUD
SHE GOT DRUNK ON A FLOWER?!
FLOWER!
THUD THUD
THUD
THUD
THUD
SILVERVINE
IT SAYS "SILVER-VINE"...
DIDN'T SMELL THAT GOOD TO ME...
NANABA!
FLOWER!
NANABA!!
COME BACK!

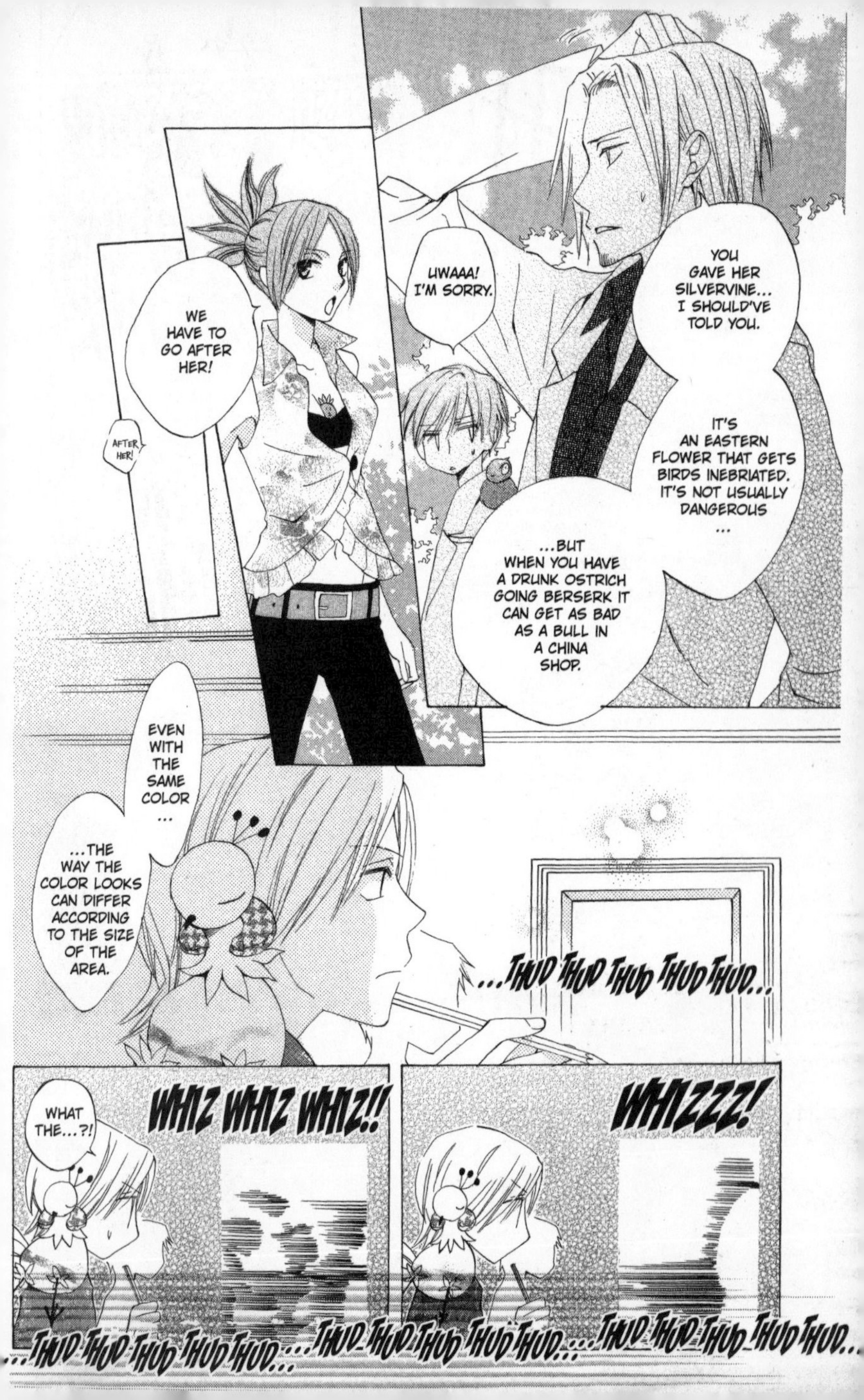
YOU GAVE HER SILVERVINE... I SHOULD'VE TOLD YOU.
IT'S AN EASTERN FLOWER THAT GETS BIRDS INEBRIATED. IT'S NOT USUALLY DANGEROUS...
...BUT WHEN YOU HAVE A DRUNK OSTRICH GOING BERSERK IT CAN GET AS BAD AS A BULL IN A CHINA SHOP.
UWAAA! I'M SORRY.
WE HAVE TO GO AFTER HER!
AFTER HER!
EVEN WITH THE SAME COLOR...
...THE WAY THE COLOR LOOKS CAN DIFFER ACCORDING TO THE SIZE OF THE AREA.
...THUD THUD THUD THUD THUD...
WHIZZZ!
WHAT THE...?!
WHIZ WHIZ WHIZ!!
...THUD THUD THUD THUD THUD... ...THUD THUD THUD THUD THUD... ...THUD THUD THUD THUD THUD...

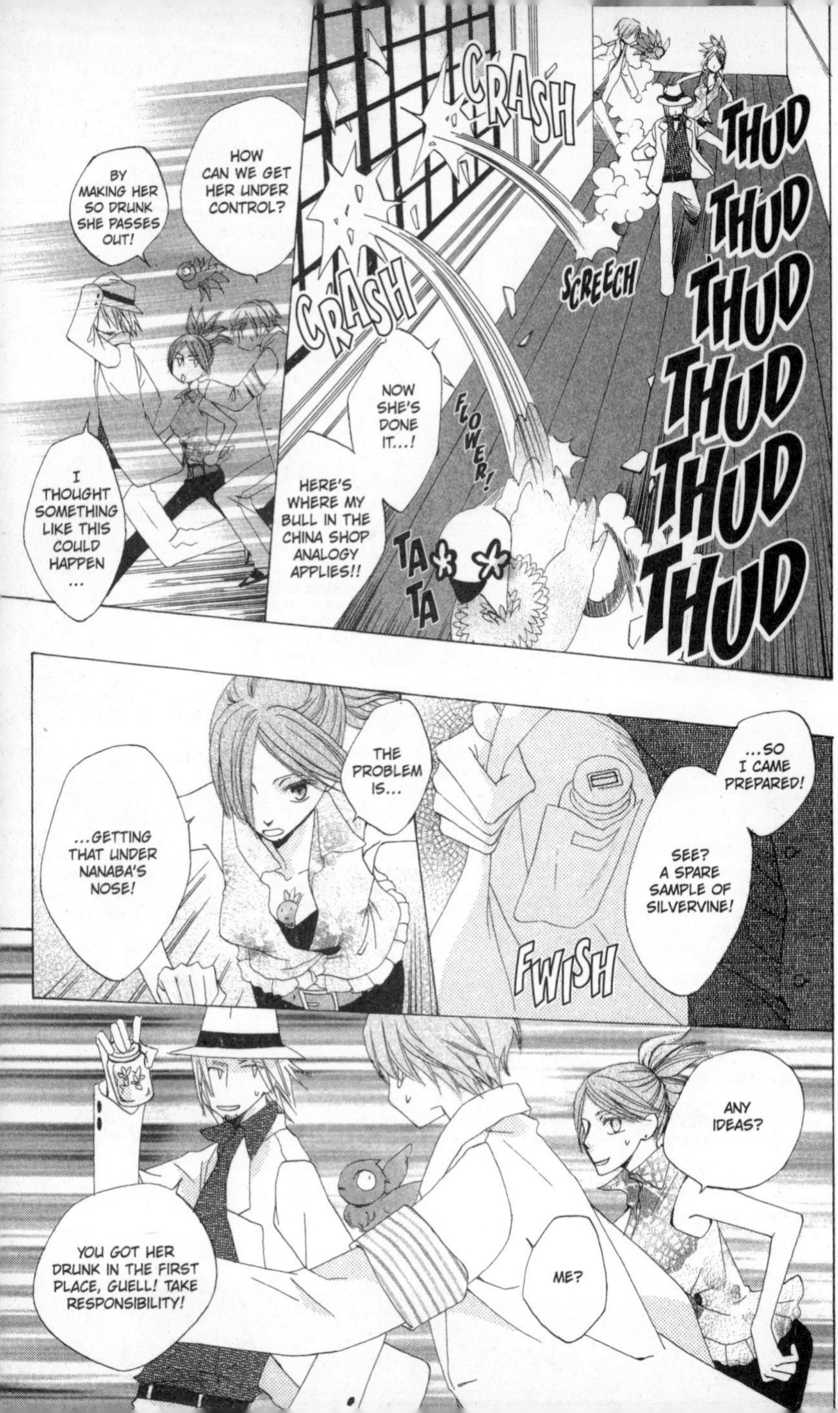
CRASH
THUD THUD THUD THUD THUD THUD
SCREECH
CRASH
FLOWER!
NOW SHE'S DONE IT...!
HERE'S WHERE MY BULL IN THE CHINA SHOP ANALOGY APPLIES!!
TA TA
HOW CAN WE GET HER UNDER CONTROL?
BY MAKING HER SO DRUNK SHE PASSES OUT!
I THOUGHT SOMETHING LIKE THIS COULD HAPPEN...
...SO I CAME PREPARED!
SEE? A SPARE SAMPLE OF SILVERVINE!
FWISH
THE PROBLEM IS...
...GETTING THAT UNDER NANABA'S NOSE!
ANY IDEAS?
ME?
YOU GOT HER DRUNK IN THE FIRST PLACE, GUELL! TAKE RESPONSIBILITY!

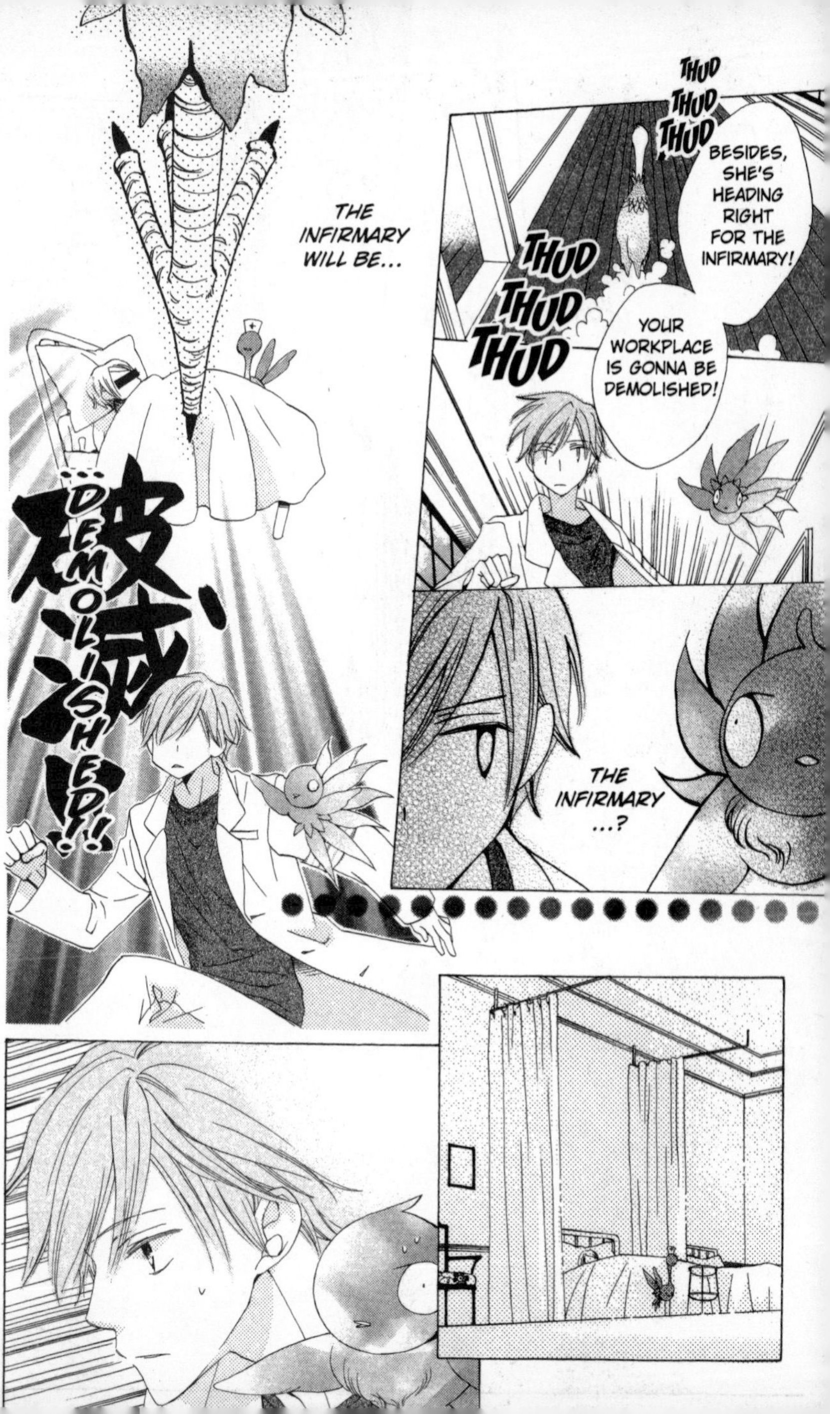
THUD THUD THUD
THUD THUD THUD
BESIDES, SHE'S HEADING RIGHT FOR THE INFIRMARY!
YOUR WORKPLACE IS GONNA BE DEMOLISHED!
THE INFIRMARY ...?
THE INFIRMARY WILL BE...
...DEMOLISHED!!

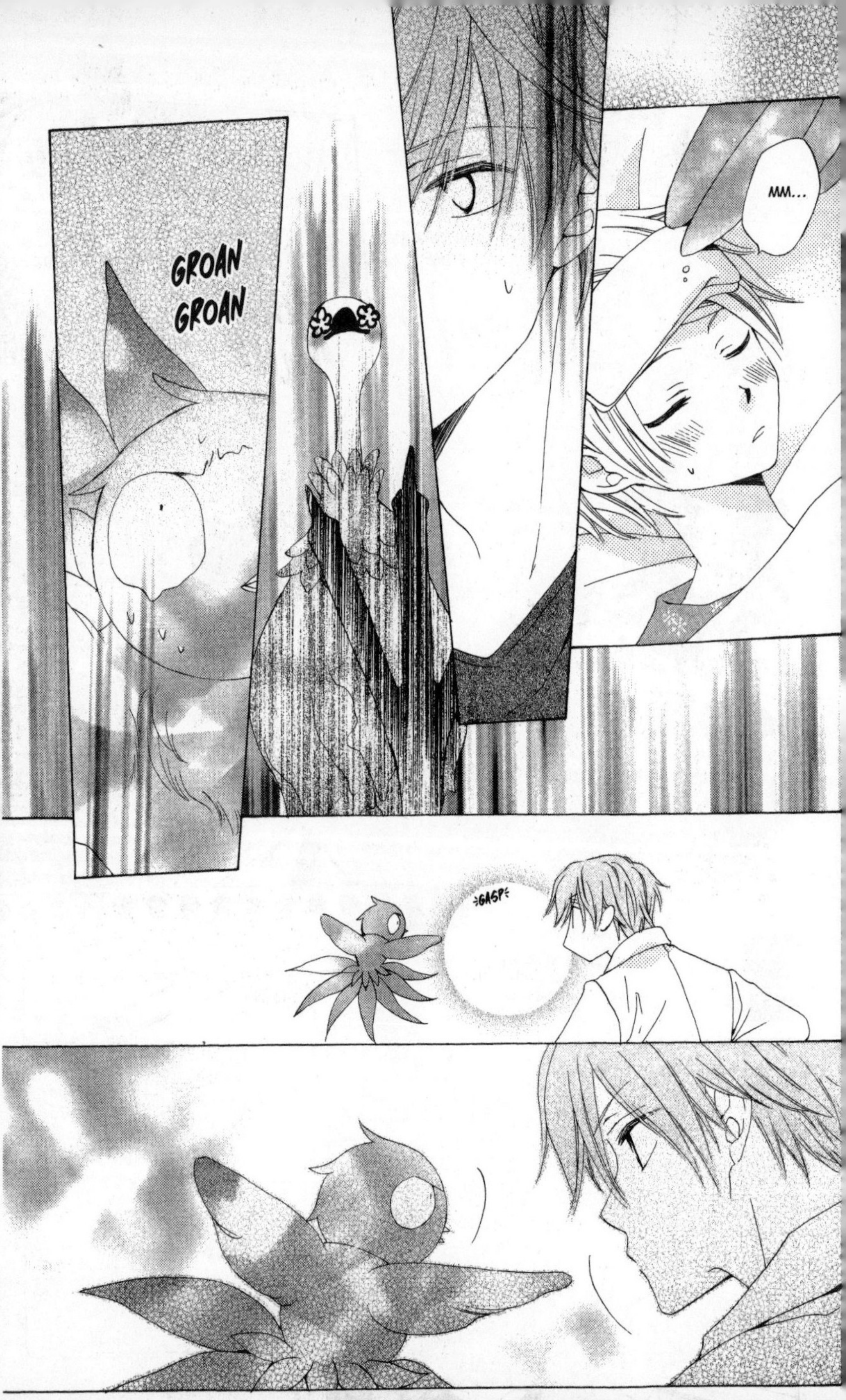
MM...
GROAN
GROAN
GASP

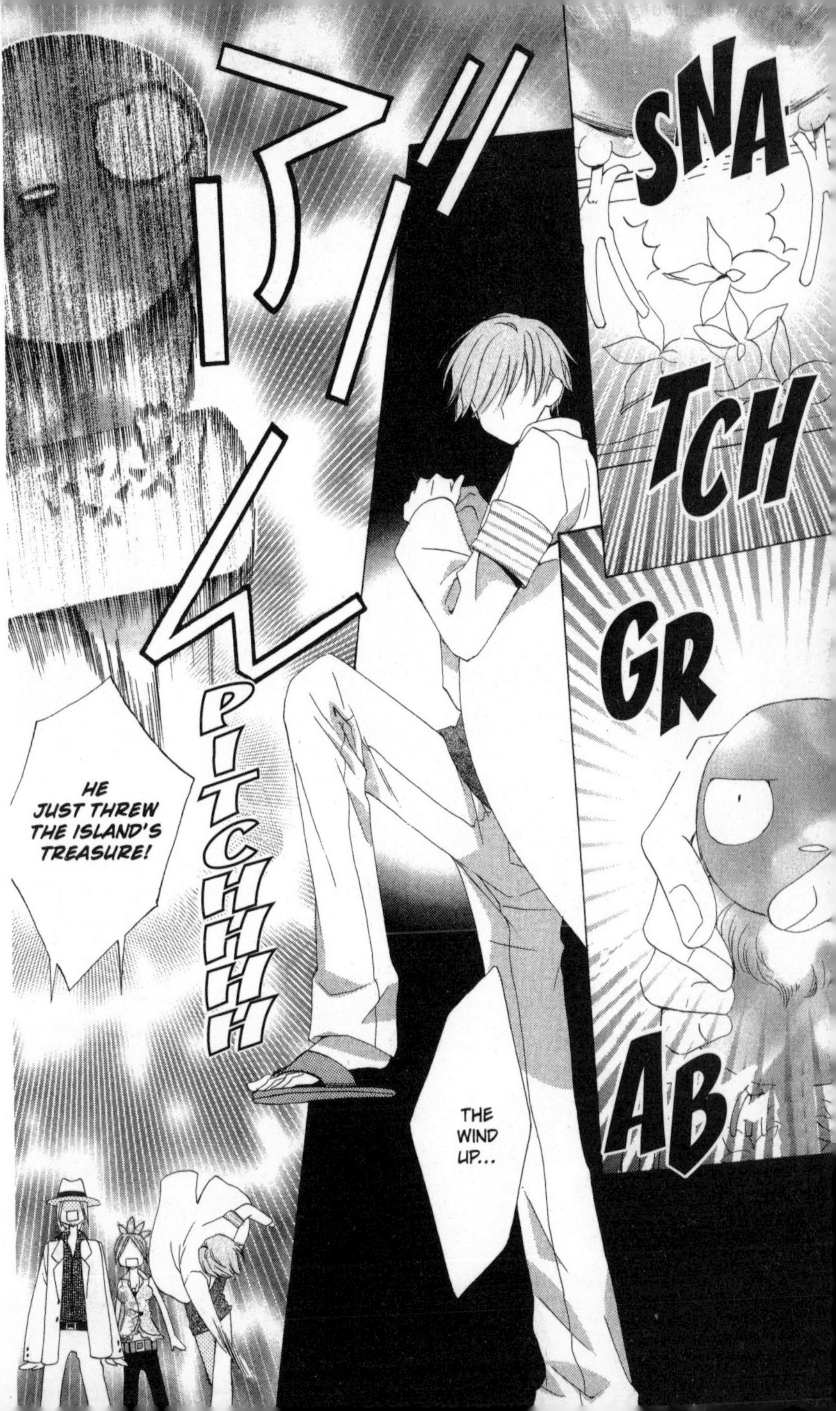
SNATCH
GRAB
THE WIND UP...
PITCHHHH
HE JUST THREW THE ISLAND'S TREASURE!

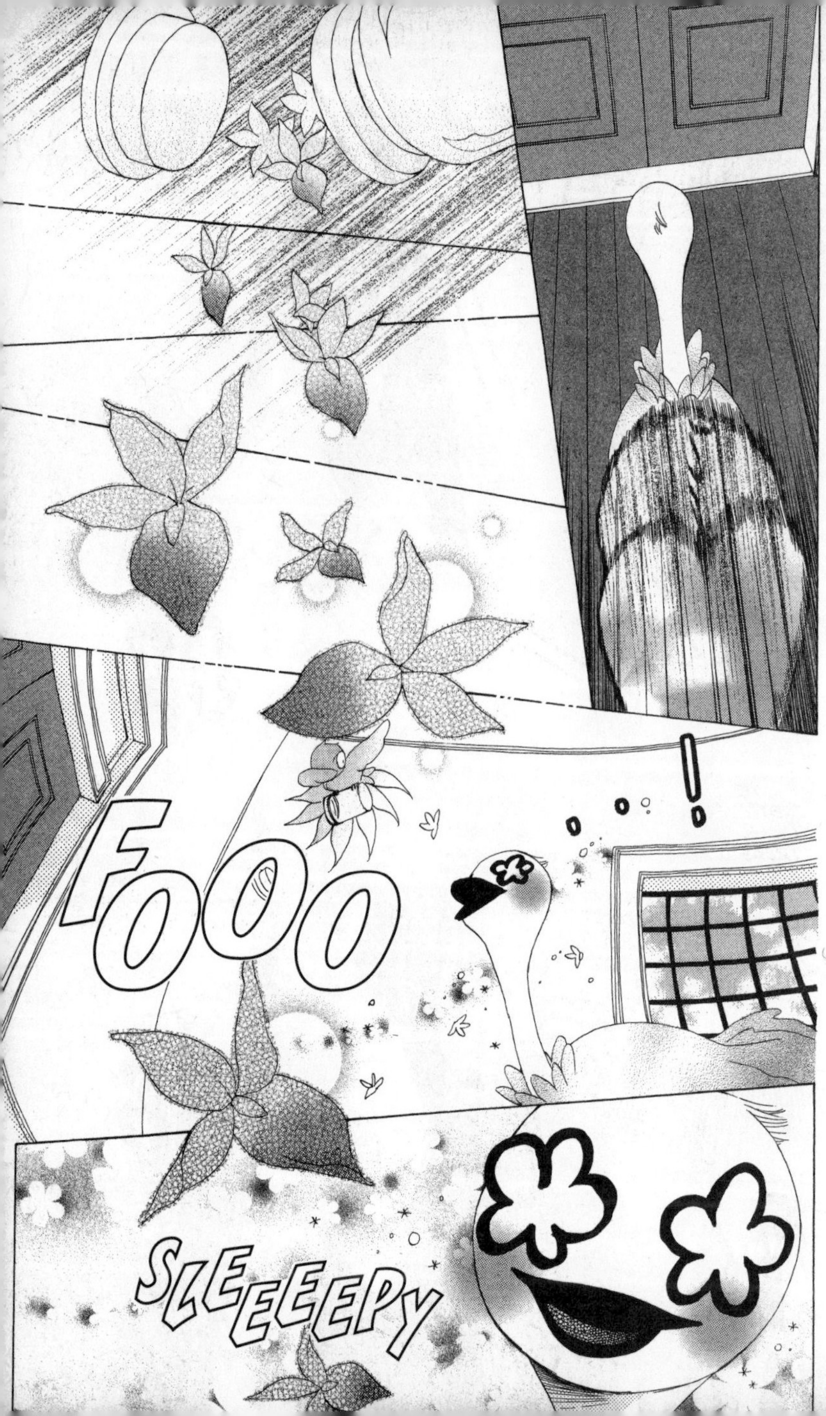

!
FOOO
SLEEEEPY

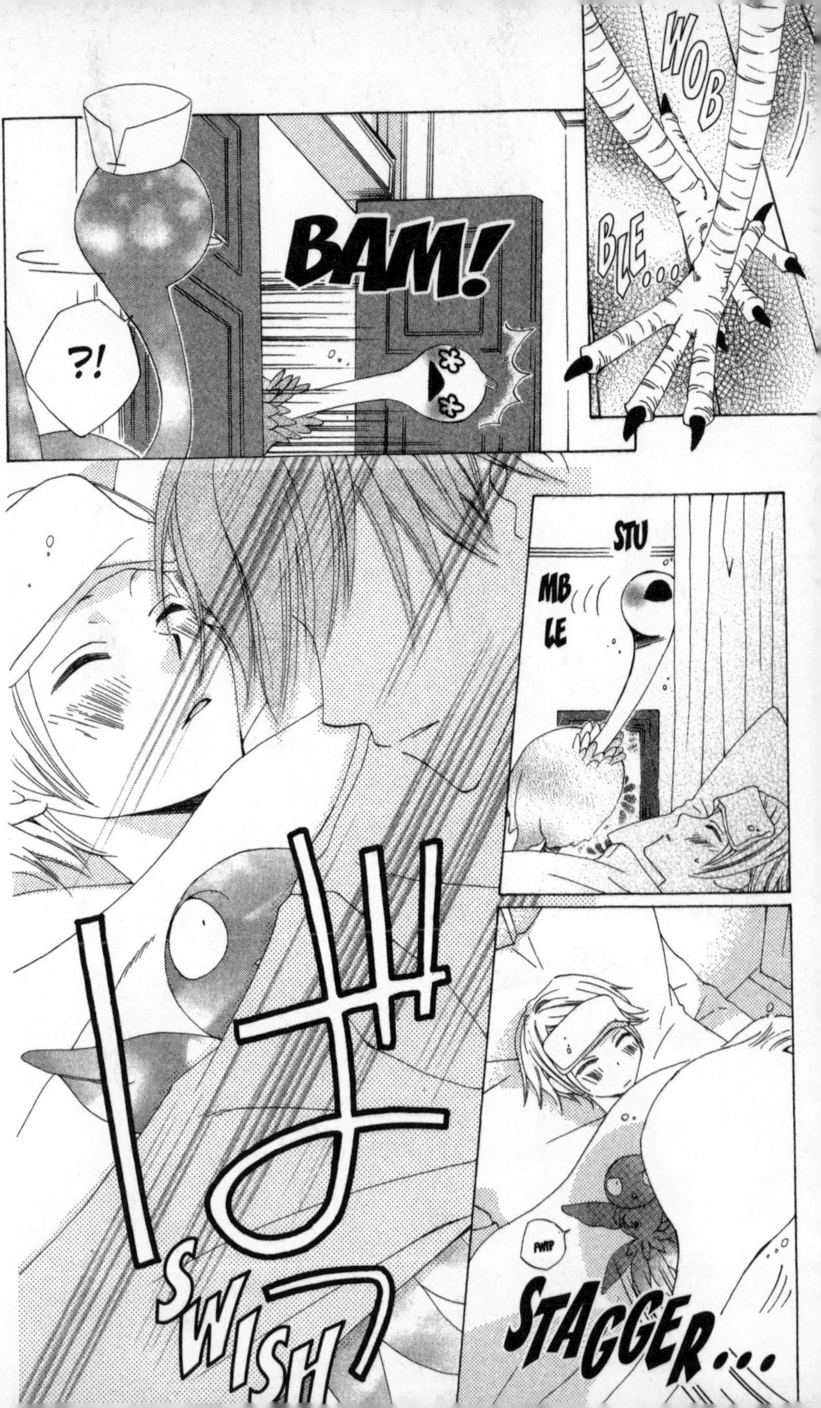
WOBBLE...
BAM!
?!
STUMBLE
PWIP
STAGGER...
SWISH

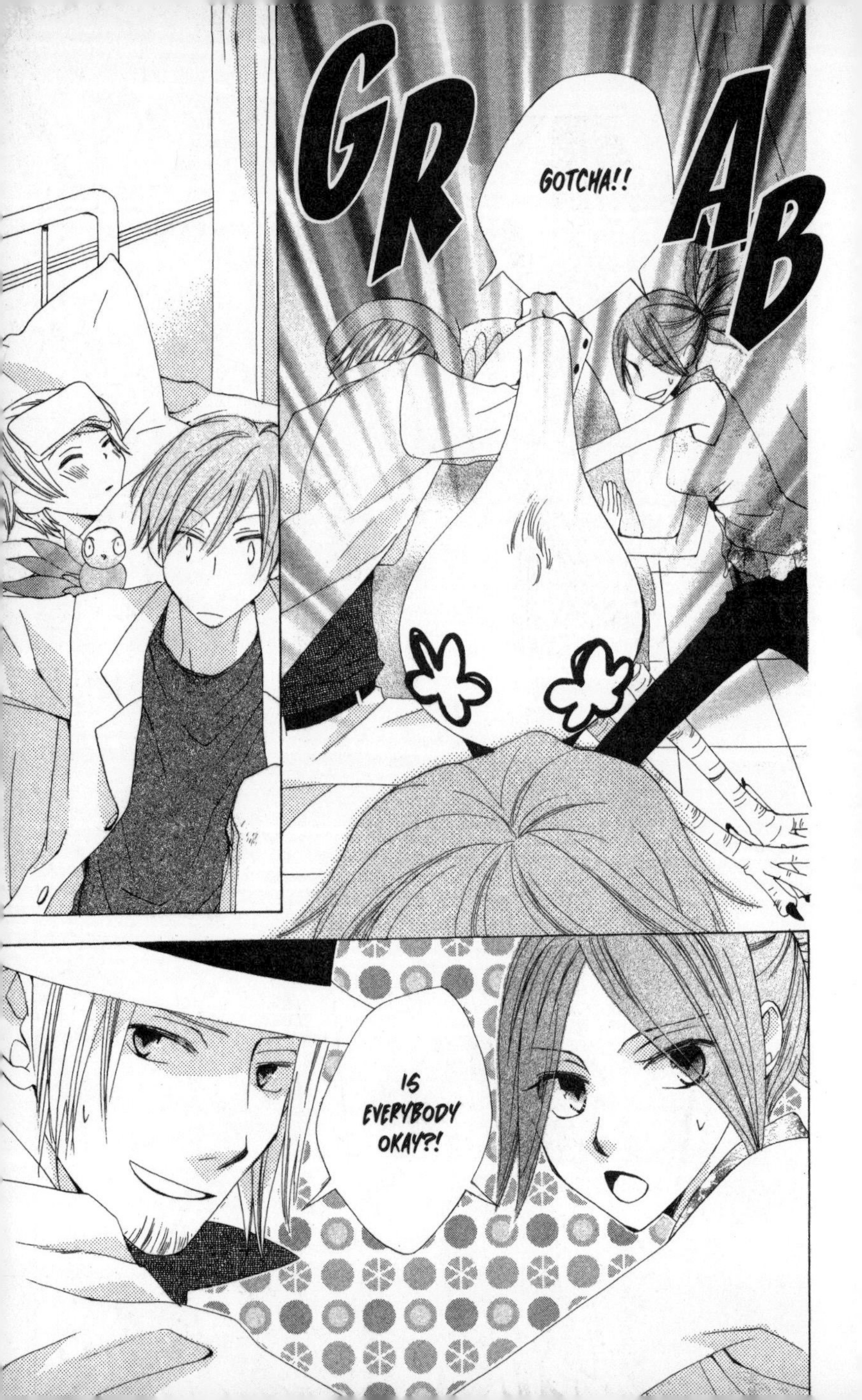
GRAB
GOTCHA!!
IS EVERYBODY OKAY?!

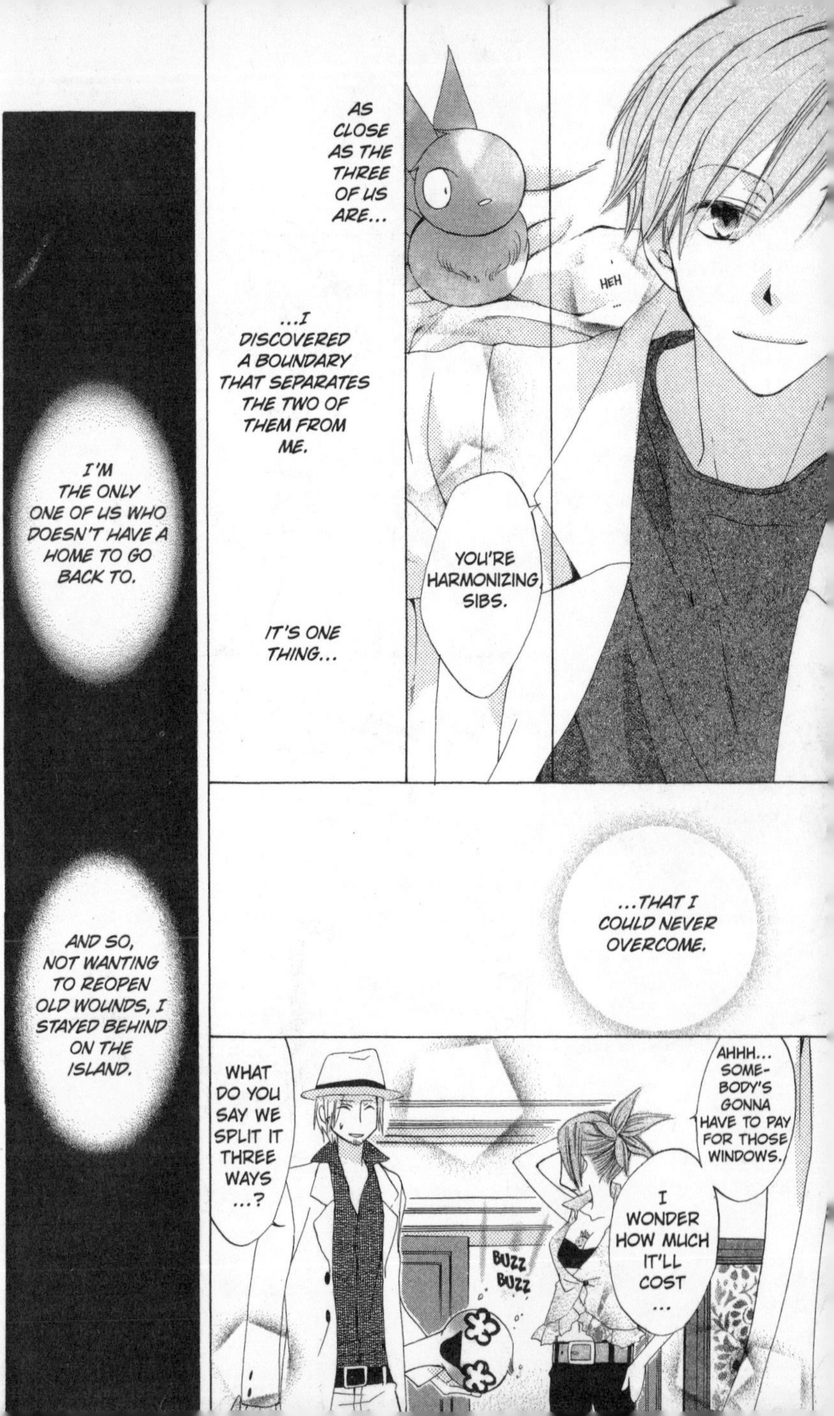
HEH...
YOU'RE HARMONIZING SIBS.
AS CLOSE AS THE THREE OF US ARE...
...I DISCOVERED A BOUNDARY THAT SEPARATES THE TWO OF THEM FROM ME.
IT'S ONE THING...
...THAT I COULD NEVER OVERCOME.
AHHH... SOMEBODY'S GONNA HAVE TO PAY FOR THOSE WINDOWS.
I WONDER HOW MUCH IT'LL COST...
BUZZ BUZZ
WHAT DO YOU SAY WE SPLIT IT THREE WAYS...?
I'M THE ONLY ONE OF US WHO DOESN'T HAVE A HOME TO GO BACK TO.
AND SO, NOT WANTING TO REOPEN OLD WOUNDS, I STAYED BEHIND ON THE ISLAND.

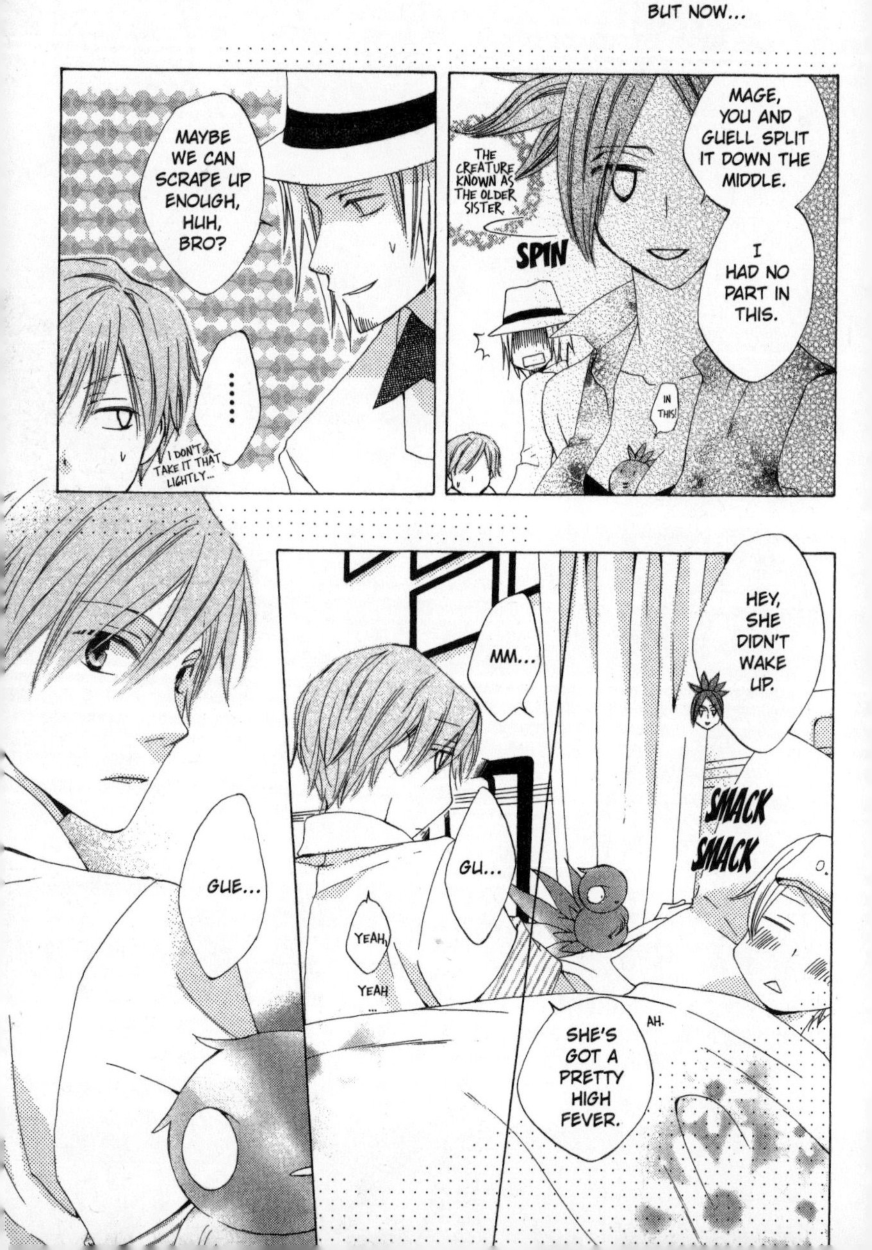
BUT NOW...
MAGE, YOU AND GUELL SPLIT IT DOWN THE MIDDLE.
I HAD NO PART IN THIS.
THE CREATURE KNOWN AS THE OLDER SISTER
SPIN
IN THIS!
MAYBE WE CAN SCRAPE UP ENOUGH, HUH, BRO?
......
I DON'T TAKE IT THAT LIGHTLY...
HEY, SHE DIDN'T WAKE UP.
SMACK
SMACK
MM...
GU...
YEAH, YEAH...
AH.
SHE'S GOT A PRETTY HIGH FEVER.
GUE...

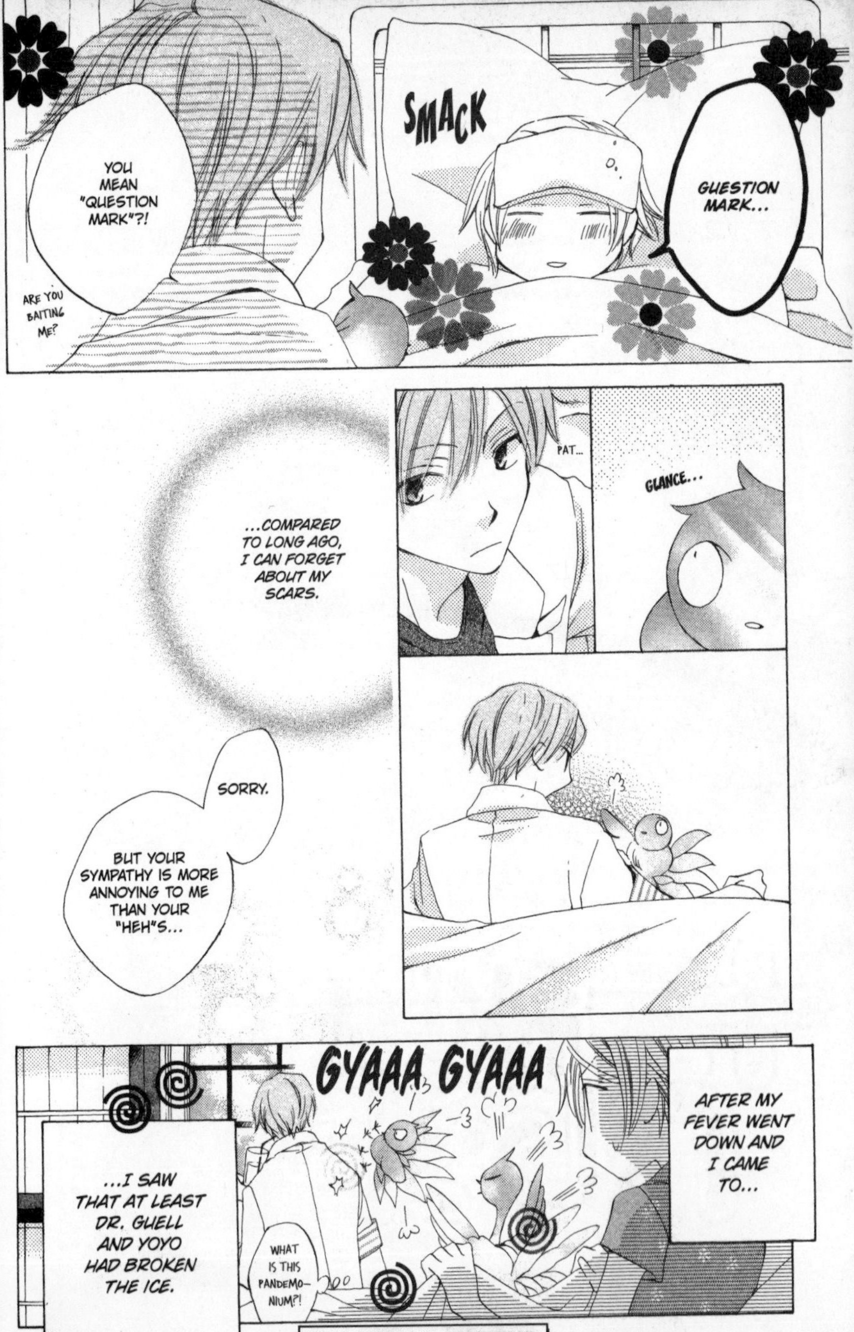
GUESTION MARK...
SMACK
YOU MEAN "QUESTION MARK"?!
ARE YOU BAITING ME?
GLANCE...
PAT...
...COMPARED TO LONG AGO, I CAN FORGET ABOUT MY SCARS.
SORRY.
BUT YOUR SYMPATHY IS MORE ANNOYING TO ME THAN YOUR "HEH"S...
AFTER MY FEVER WENT DOWN AND I CAME TO...
GYAAA GYAAA
WHAT IS THIS PANDEMONIUM?!
...I SAW THAT AT LEAST DR. GUELL AND YOYO HAD BROKEN THE ICE.

EPISODE 13: THE END

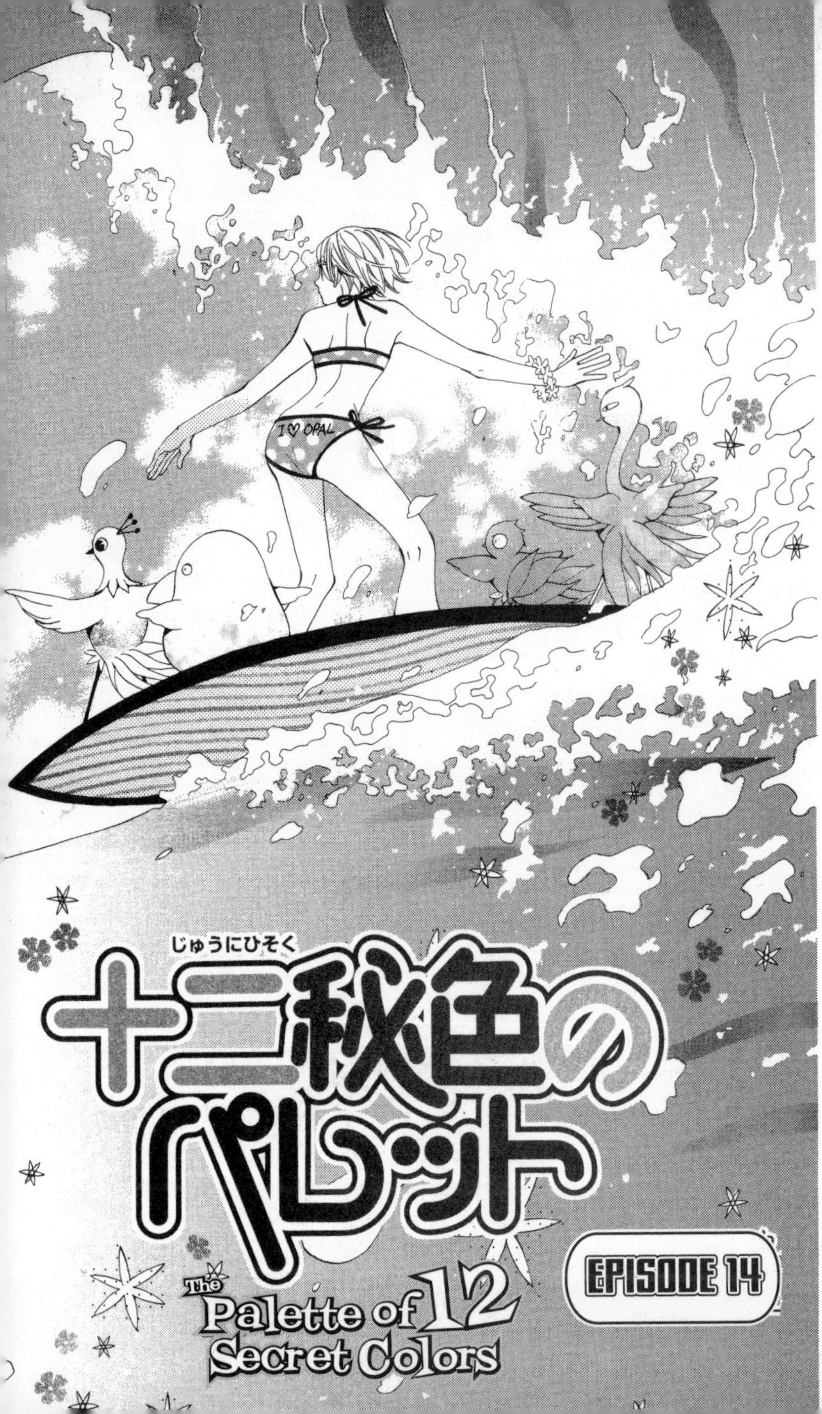
I ♡ OPAL
じゅうにひそく
十二秘色のパレット
The Palette of 12 Secret Colors
EPISODE 14

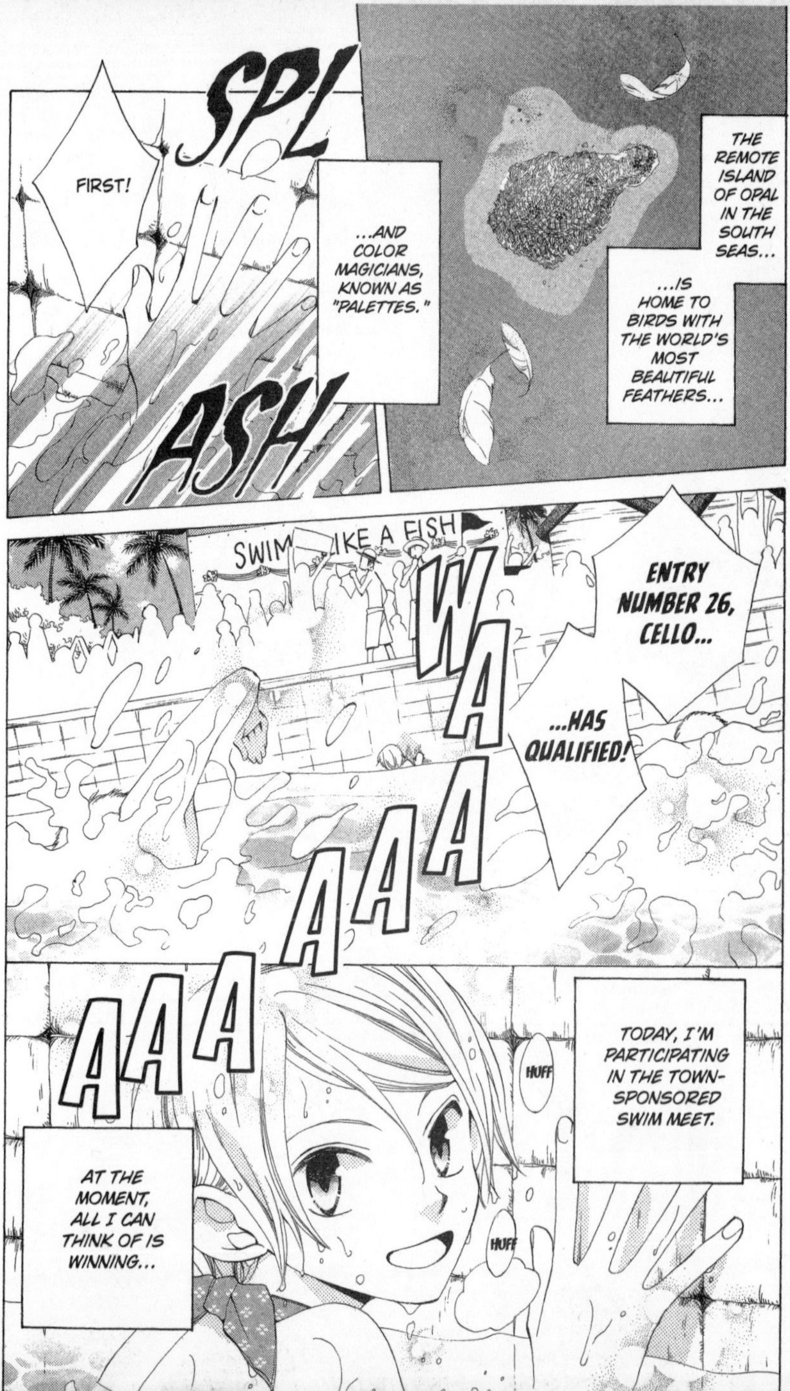
THE REMOTE ISLAND OF OPAL IN THE SOUTH SEAS...
...IS HOME TO BIRDS WITH THE WORLD'S MOST BEAUTIFUL FEATHERS...
...AND COLOR MAGICIANS, KNOWN AS "PALETTES."
SPLASH
FIRST!
SWIM IKE A FISH
ENTRY NUMBER 26, CELLO...
...HAS QUALIFIED!
WAAAAAAAAA
TODAY, I'M PARTICIPATING IN THE TOWN-SPONSORED SWIM MEET.
HUFF
HUFF
AT THE MOMENT, ALL I CAN THINK OF IS WINNING...

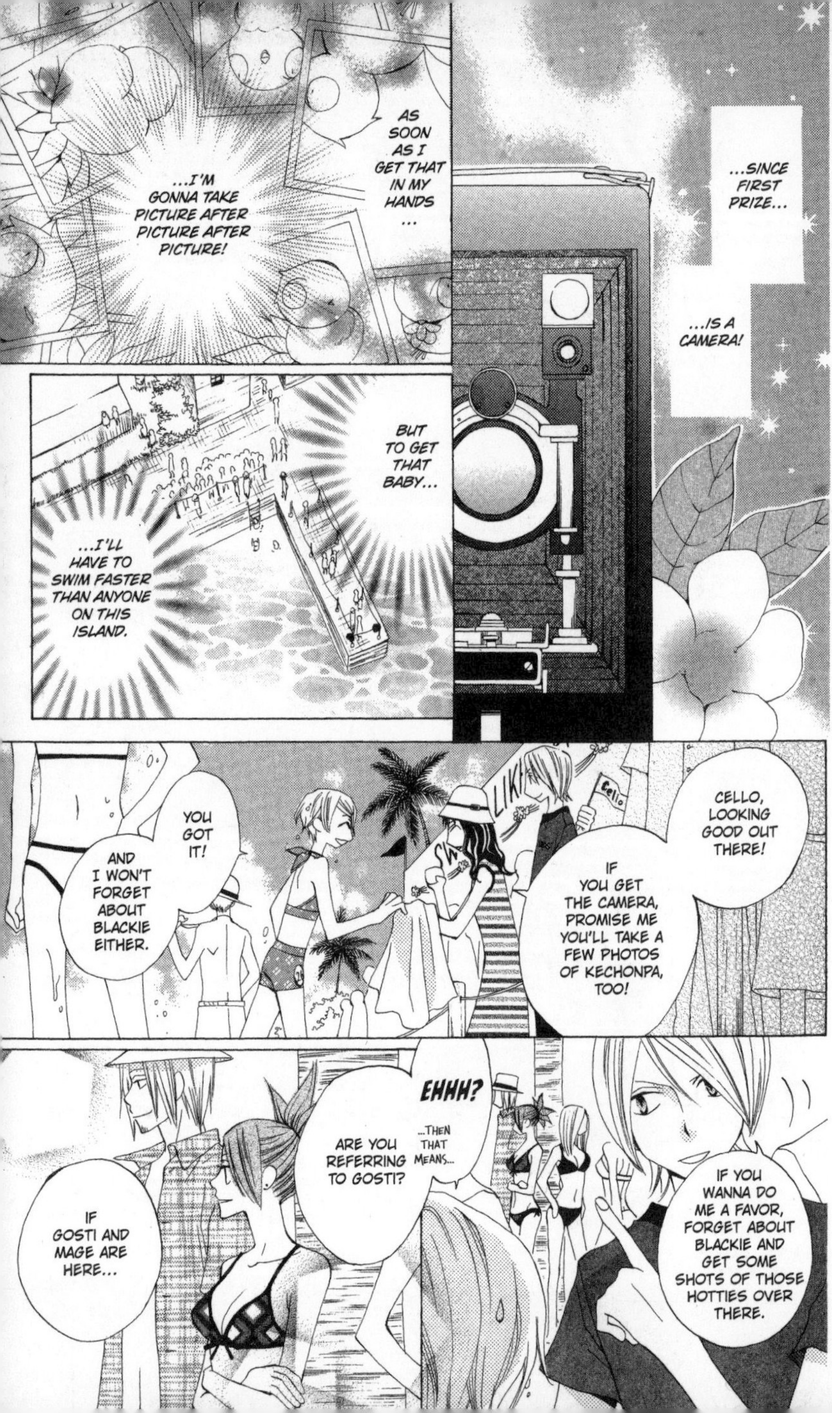
...SINCE FIRST PRIZE...
...IS A CAMERA!
AS SOON AS I GET THAT IN MY HANDS...
...I'M GONNA TAKE PICTURE AFTER PICTURE AFTER PICTURE!
BUT TO GET THAT BABY...
...I'LL HAVE TO SWIM FASTER THAN ANYONE ON THIS ISLAND.
Cello
CELLO, LOOKING GOOD OUT THERE!
IF YOU GET THE CAMERA, PROMISE ME YOU'LL TAKE A FEW PHOTOS OF KECHONPA, TOO!
YOU GOT IT!
AND I WON'T FORGET ABOUT BLACKIE EITHER.
IF YOU WANNA DO ME A FAVOR, FORGET ABOUT BLACKIE AND GET SOME SHOTS OF THOSE HOTTIES OVER THERE.
EHHH?
...THEN THAT MEANS...
ARE YOU REFERRING TO GOSTI?
IF GOSTI AND MAGE ARE HERE...

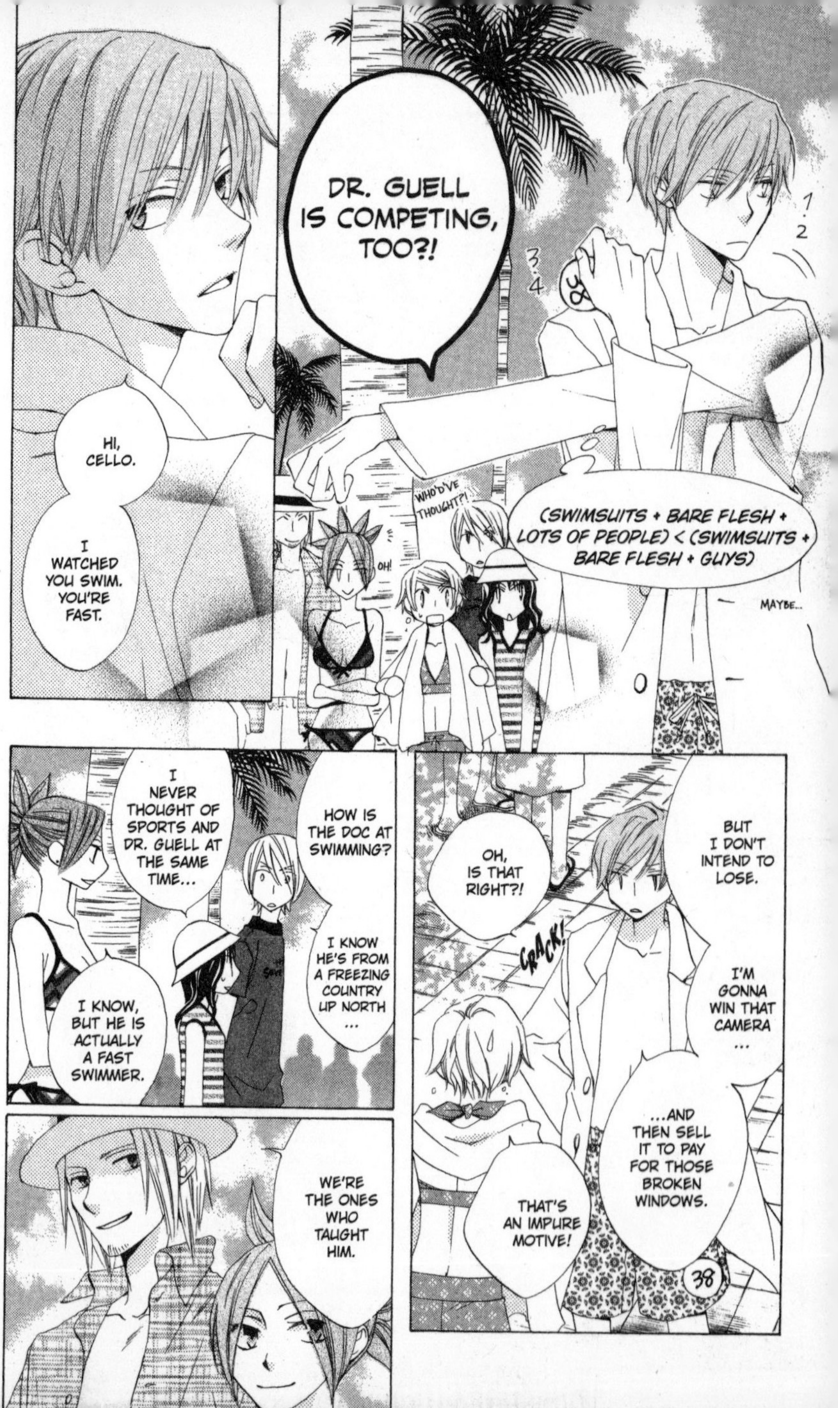
DR. GUELL IS COMPETING, TOO?!
1. 2
3. 4
WHO'D'VE THOUGHT?!
OH!
(SWIMSUITS + BARE FLESH + LOTS OF PEOPLE) < (SWIMSUITS + BARE FLESH + GUYS)
MAYBE...
HI, CELLO.
I WATCHED YOU SWIM. YOU'RE FAST.
BUT I DON'T INTEND TO LOSE.
OH, IS THAT RIGHT?!
CRACK!
I'M GONNA WIN THAT CAMERA...
...AND THEN SELL IT TO PAY FOR THOSE BROKEN WINDOWS.
THAT'S AN IMPURE MOTIVE!
HOW IS THE DOC AT SWIMMING?
I KNOW HE'S FROM A FREEZING COUNTRY UP NORTH...
I NEVER THOUGHT OF SPORTS AND DR. GUELL AT THE SAME TIME...
I KNOW, BUT HE IS ACTUALLY A FAST SWIMMER.
WE'RE THE ONES WHO TAUGHT HIM.

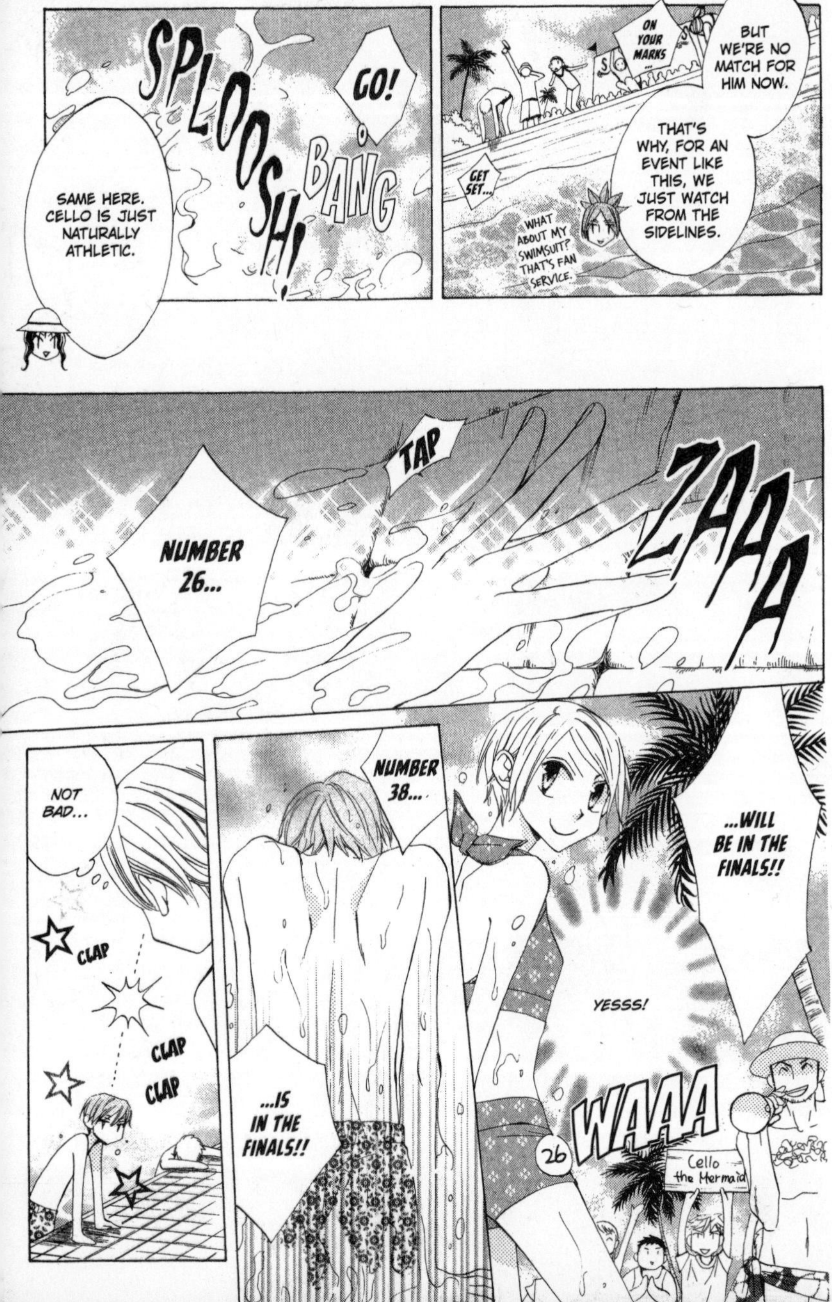

ON YOUR MARKS...
BUT WE'RE NO MATCH FOR HIM NOW.
THAT'S WHY, FOR AN EVENT LIKE THIS, WE JUST WATCH FROM THE SIDELINES.
GET SET...
WHAT ABOUT MY SWIMSUIT? THAT'S FAN SERVICE.
GO!
BANG
SPLOOSH!
SAME HERE. CELLO IS JUST NATURALLY ATHLETIC.
ZAAA
TAP
NUMBER 26...
...WILL BE IN THE FINALS!!
YESSS!
WAAA
26
Cello the Mermaid
NUMBER 38...
...IS IN THE FINALS!!
NOT BAD...
CLAP
CLAP
CLAP

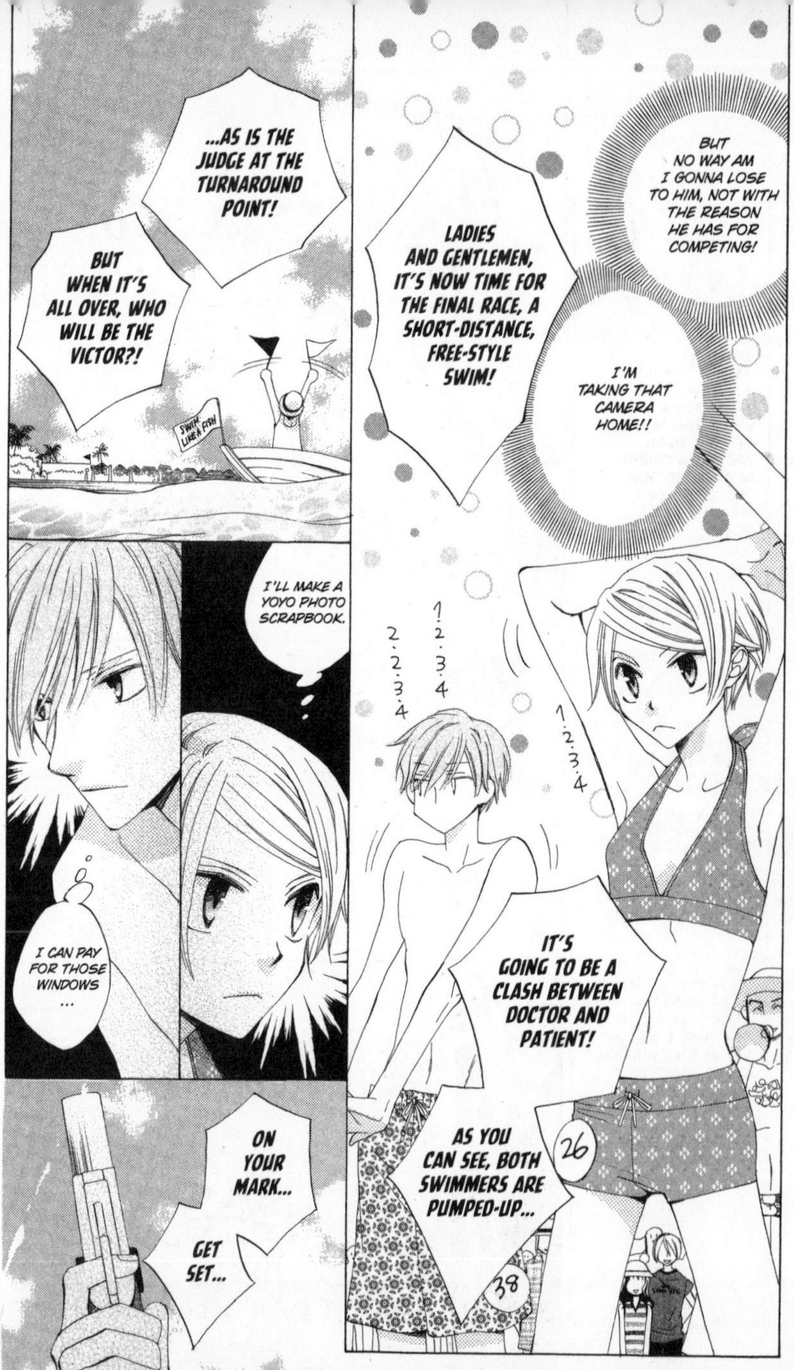
BUT NO WAY AM I GONNA LOSE TO HIM, NOT WITH THE REASON HE HAS FOR COMPETING!
I'M TAKING THAT CAMERA HOME!!
LADIES AND GENTLEMEN, IT'S NOW TIME FOR THE FINAL RACE, A SHORT-DISTANCE, FREE-STYLE SWIM!
1.2.3.4
1.2.3.4
2.2.3.4
IT'S GOING TO BE A CLASH BETWEEN DOCTOR AND PATIENT!
26
AS YOU CAN SEE, BOTH SWIMMERS ARE PUMPED-UP...
38
...AS IS THE JUDGE AT THE TURNAROUND POINT!
BUT WHEN IT'S ALL OVER, WHO WILL BE THE VICTOR?!
SWIM LIKE A FISH
I'LL MAKE A YOYO PHOTO SCRAPBOOK.
I CAN PAY FOR THOSE WINDOWS ...
ON YOUR MARK...
GET SET...

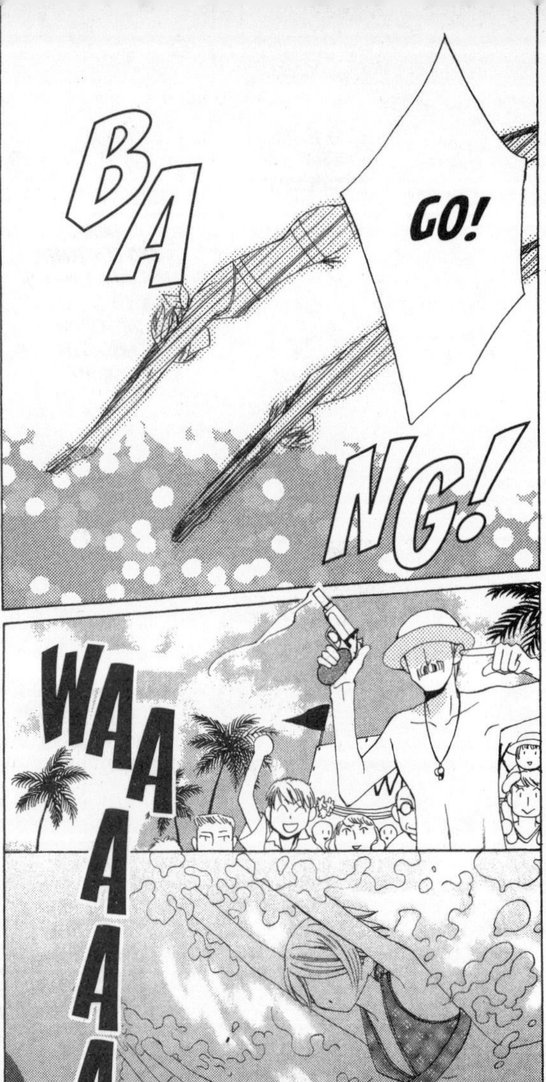
GO!
BANG!
WAAAAAAAAAAAA

6

SWIMMING
A LONG TIME AGO, A FRIEND OF MINE WHO WAS ON THE SWIM TEAM TAUGHT ME THAT WHEN YOU GET A CRAMP IN YOUR LEG, YOU SHOULD GO LIKE THIS TO GET RID OF IT:

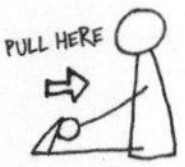
PULL HERE

ONCE, WHILE TAKING A NAP ON THE JOB, I SUDDENLY GOT A CRAMP IN MY CALF, SO I TRIED THE METHOD SHE PRESCRIBED, BUT IT DIDN'T WORK! IN FACT, IT FELT LIKE MY LEG WAS SURPRISED AT THE MOVEMENT AND CRANKED UP THE PAIN A NOTCH HIGHER. I'M NOT SO SURE MY FRIEND WAS RIGHT... I'VE FOUND THAT THE ONLY THING TO DO WHEN YOU GET A LEG CRAMP IS STICK IT OUT. THIS ONE TIME, I WAS IN BED WHEN I SUDDENLY GOT A CRAMP IN BOTH LEGS AT THE SAME TIME. I THOUGHT TO MYSELF, "SO THIS IS WHAT 'WRITHING IN AGONY' IS...".

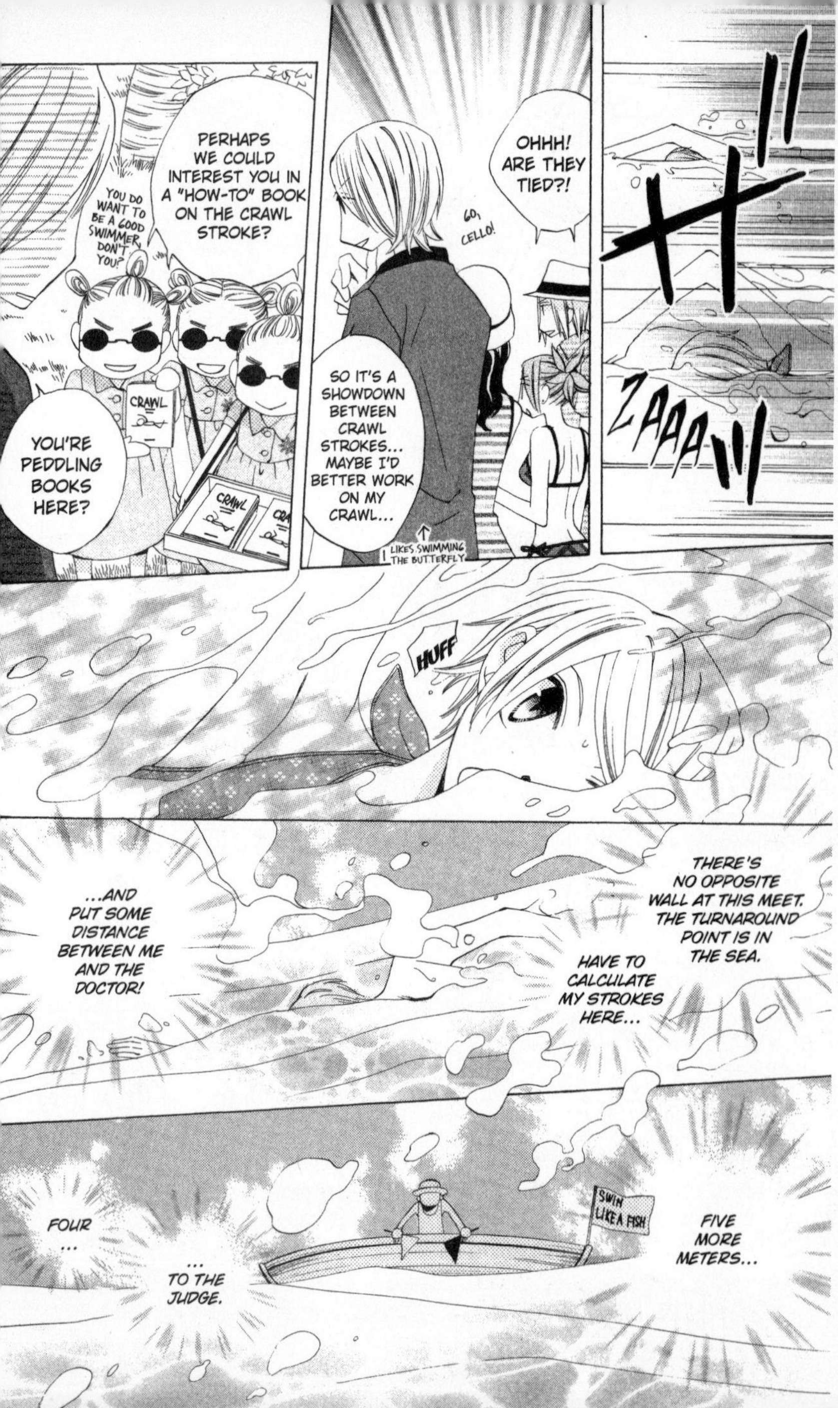
ZAAA
OHHH! ARE THEY TIED?!
GO, CELLO!
SO IT'S A SHOWDOWN BETWEEN CRAWL STROKES... MAYBE I'D BETTER WORK ON MY CRAWL...
LIKES SWIMMING THE BUTTERFLY
PERHAPS WE COULD INTEREST YOU IN A "HOW-TO" BOOK ON THE CRAWL STROKE?
YOU DO WANT TO BE A GOOD SWIMMER, DON'T YOU?
CRAWL
YOU'RE PEDDLING BOOKS HERE?
CRAWL
HUFF
THERE'S NO OPPOSITE WALL AT THIS MEET. THE TURNAROUND POINT IS IN THE SEA.
HAVE TO CALCULATE MY STROKES HERE...
...AND PUT SOME DISTANCE BETWEEN ME AND THE DOCTOR!
FIVE MORE METERS...
SWIM LIKE A FISH
... TO THE JUDGE.
FOUR ...

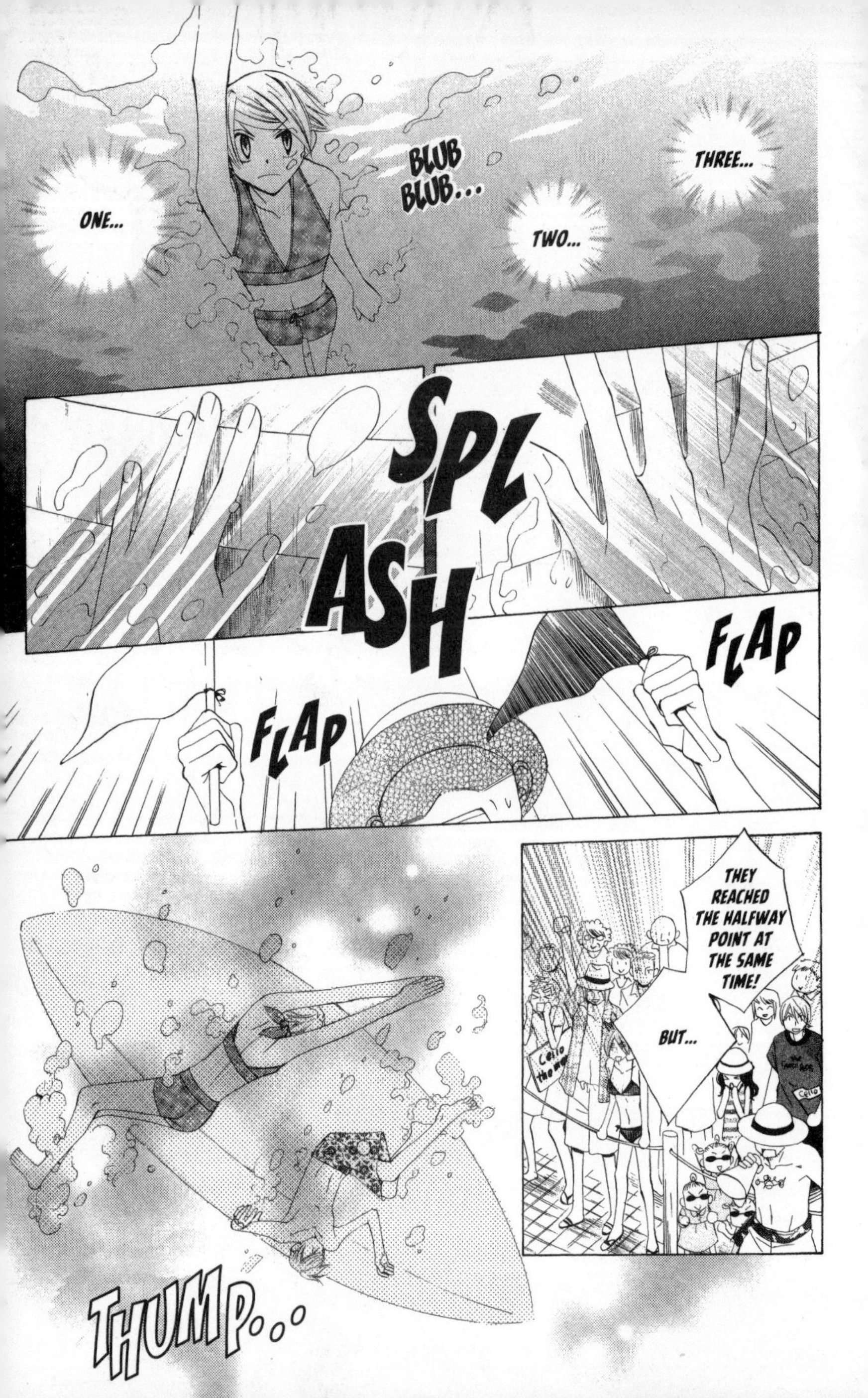
ONE...
BLUB BLUB...
TWO...
THREE...
SPLASH
FLAP
FLAP
THEY REACHED THE HALFWAY POINT AT THE SAME TIME!
BUT...
Cello
THUMP...

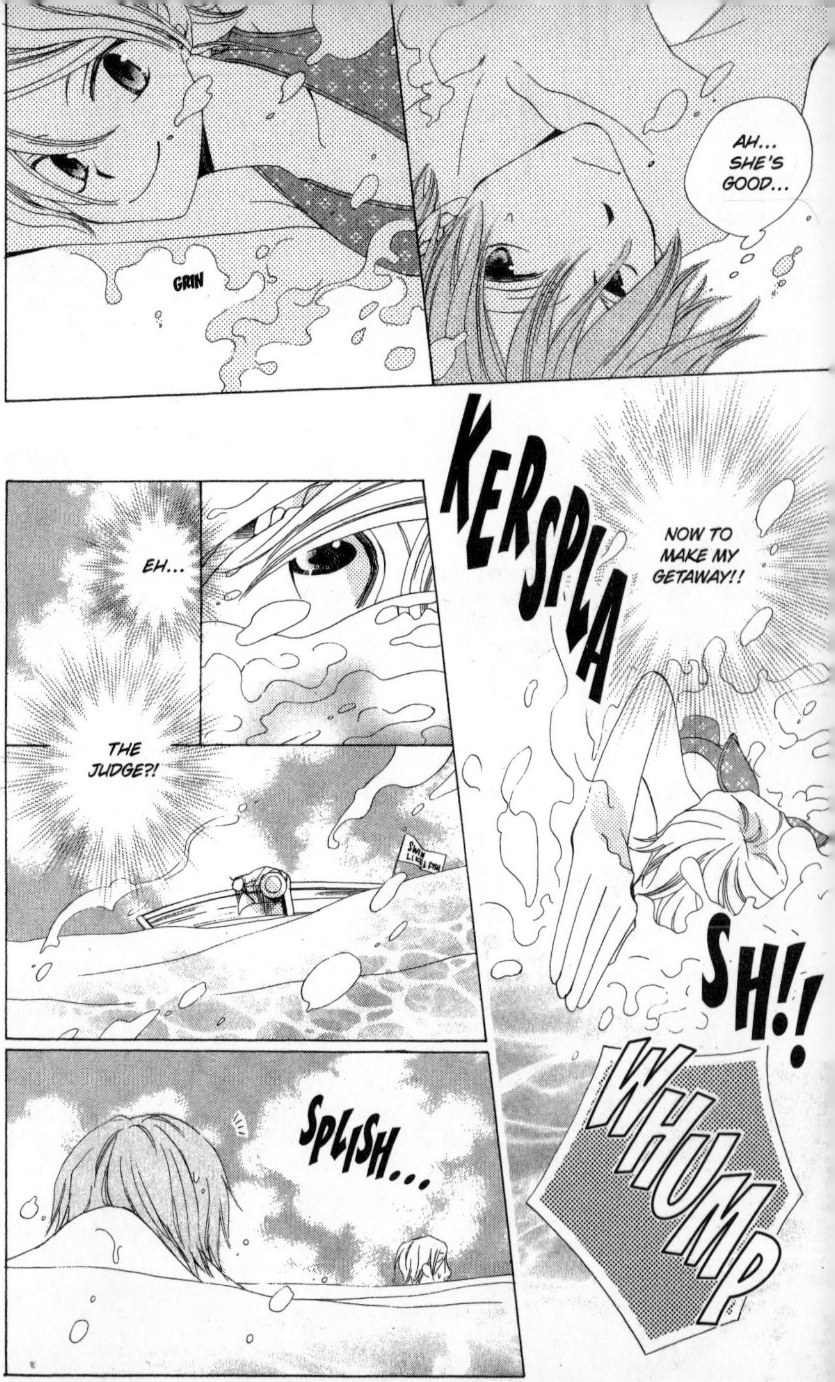

AH... SHE'S GOOD...
GRIN
KERSPLA
NOW TO MAKE MY GETAWAY!!
SH!!
WHUMP
EH...
THE JUDGE?!
SPLISH...

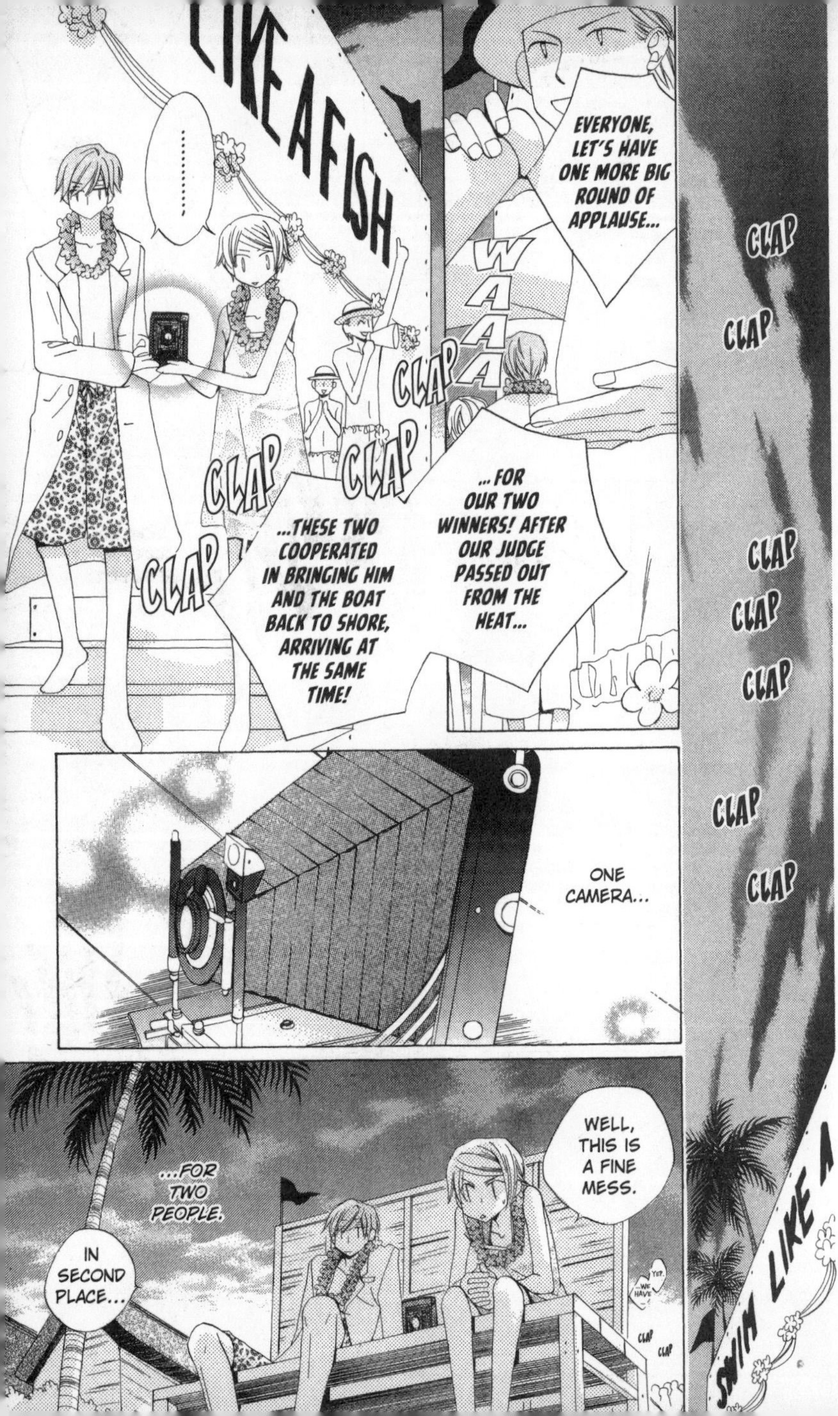
CLAP
CLAP
CLAP
CLAP
CLAP
CLAP
CLAP
SWIM LIKE A
EVERYONE, LET'S HAVE ONE MORE BIG ROUND OF APPLAUSE...
WAAAA
...FOR OUR TWO WINNERS! AFTER OUR JUDGE PASSED OUT FROM THE HEAT...
LIKE A FISH
......
CLAP
CLAP
CLAP
CLAP
...THESE TWO COOPERATED IN BRINGING HIM AND THE BOAT BACK TO SHORE, ARRIVING AT THE SAME TIME!
ONE CAMERA...
WELL, THIS IS A FINE MESS.
YEP.
...WE HAVE...
...FOR TWO PEOPLE.
IN SECOND PLACE...
CLAP
CLAP

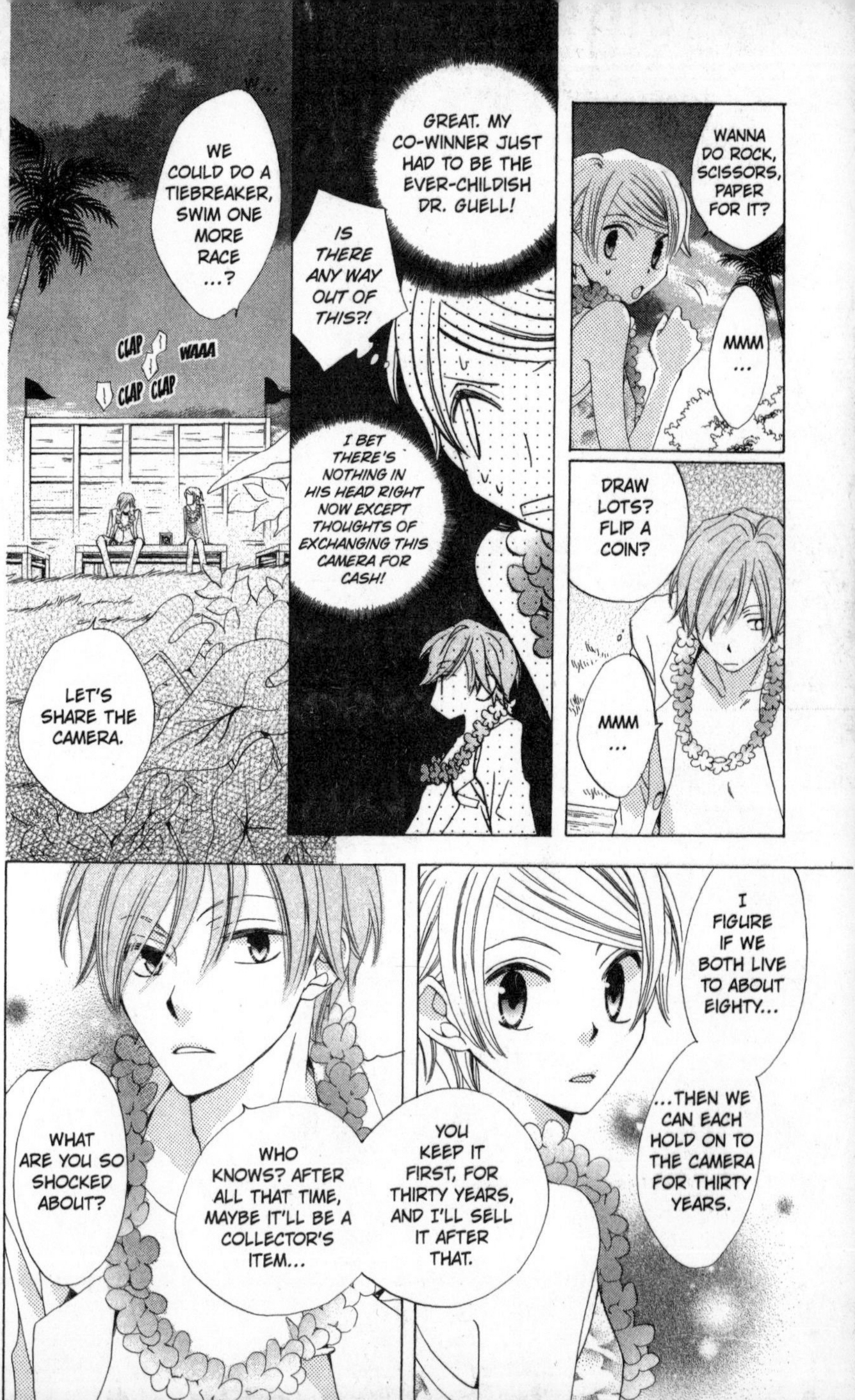
WANNA DO ROCK, SCISSORS, PAPER FOR IT?
MMM...
DRAW LOTS? FLIP A COIN?
MMM...
GREAT. MY CO-WINNER JUST HAD TO BE THE EVER-CHILDISH DR. GUELL!
IS THERE ANY WAY OUT OF THIS?!
I BET THERE'S NOTHING IN HIS HEAD RIGHT NOW EXCEPT THOUGHTS OF EXCHANGING THIS CAMERA FOR CASH!
WE COULD DO A TIEBREAKER, SWIM ONE MORE RACE ...?
CLAP
WAAA
CLAP CLAP
LET'S SHARE THE CAMERA.
I FIGURE IF WE BOTH LIVE TO ABOUT EIGHTY...
...THEN WE CAN EACH HOLD ON TO THE CAMERA FOR THIRTY YEARS.
YOU KEEP IT FIRST, FOR THIRTY YEARS, AND I'LL SELL IT AFTER THAT.
WHO KNOWS? AFTER ALL THAT TIME, MAYBE IT'LL BE A COLLECTOR'S ITEM...
WHAT ARE YOU SO SHOCKED ABOUT?

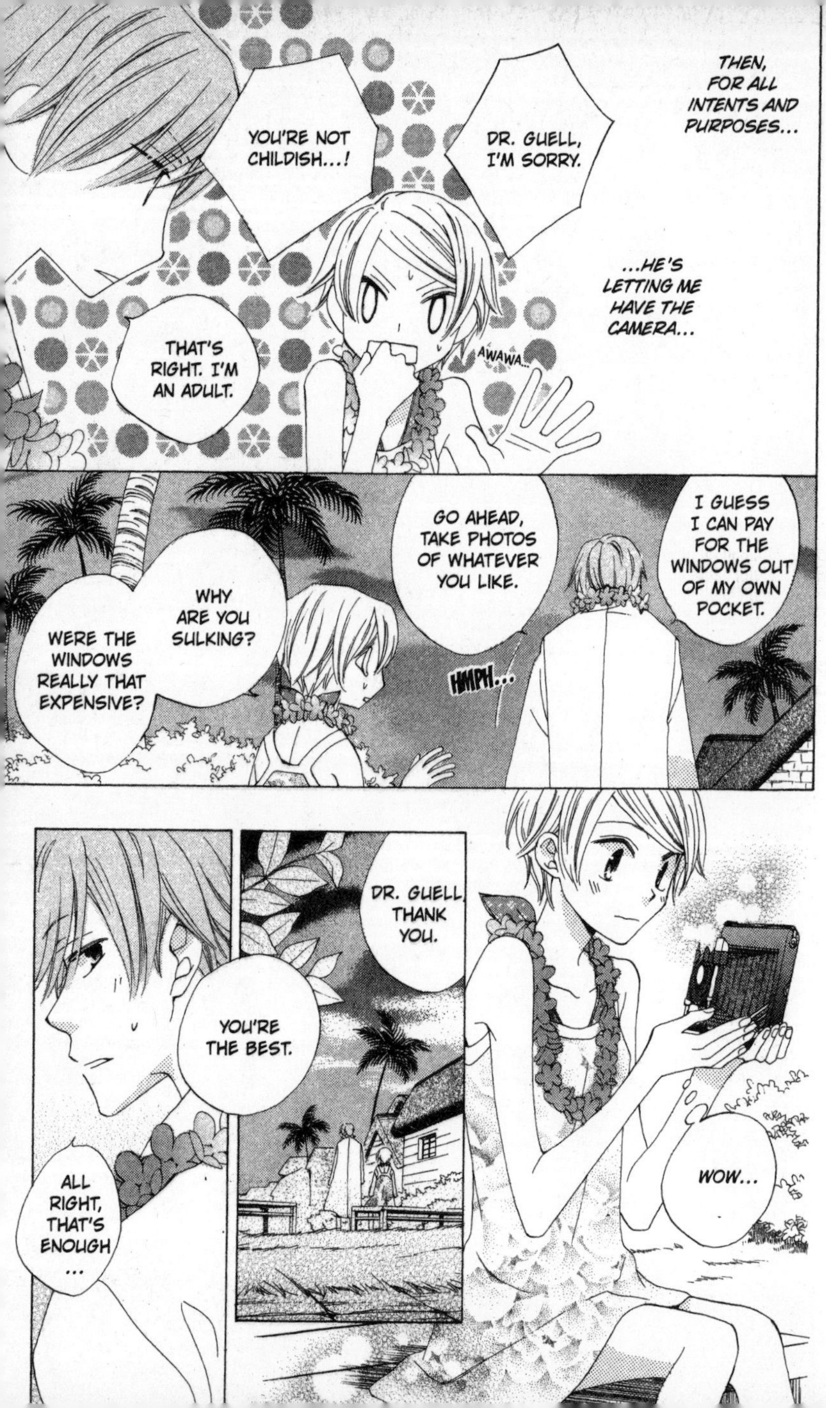
THEN, FOR ALL INTENTS AND PURPOSES...
DR. GUELL, I'M SORRY.
YOU'RE NOT CHILDISH...!
...HE'S LETTING ME HAVE THE CAMERA...
AWAWA...
THAT'S RIGHT. I'M AN ADULT.
I GUESS I CAN PAY FOR THE WINDOWS OUT OF MY OWN POCKET.
GO AHEAD, TAKE PHOTOS OF WHATEVER YOU LIKE.
HMPH...
WHY ARE YOU SULKING?
WERE THE WINDOWS REALLY THAT EXPENSIVE?
WOW...
DR. GUELL THANK YOU.
YOU'RE THE BEST.
ALL RIGHT, THAT'S ENOUGH...

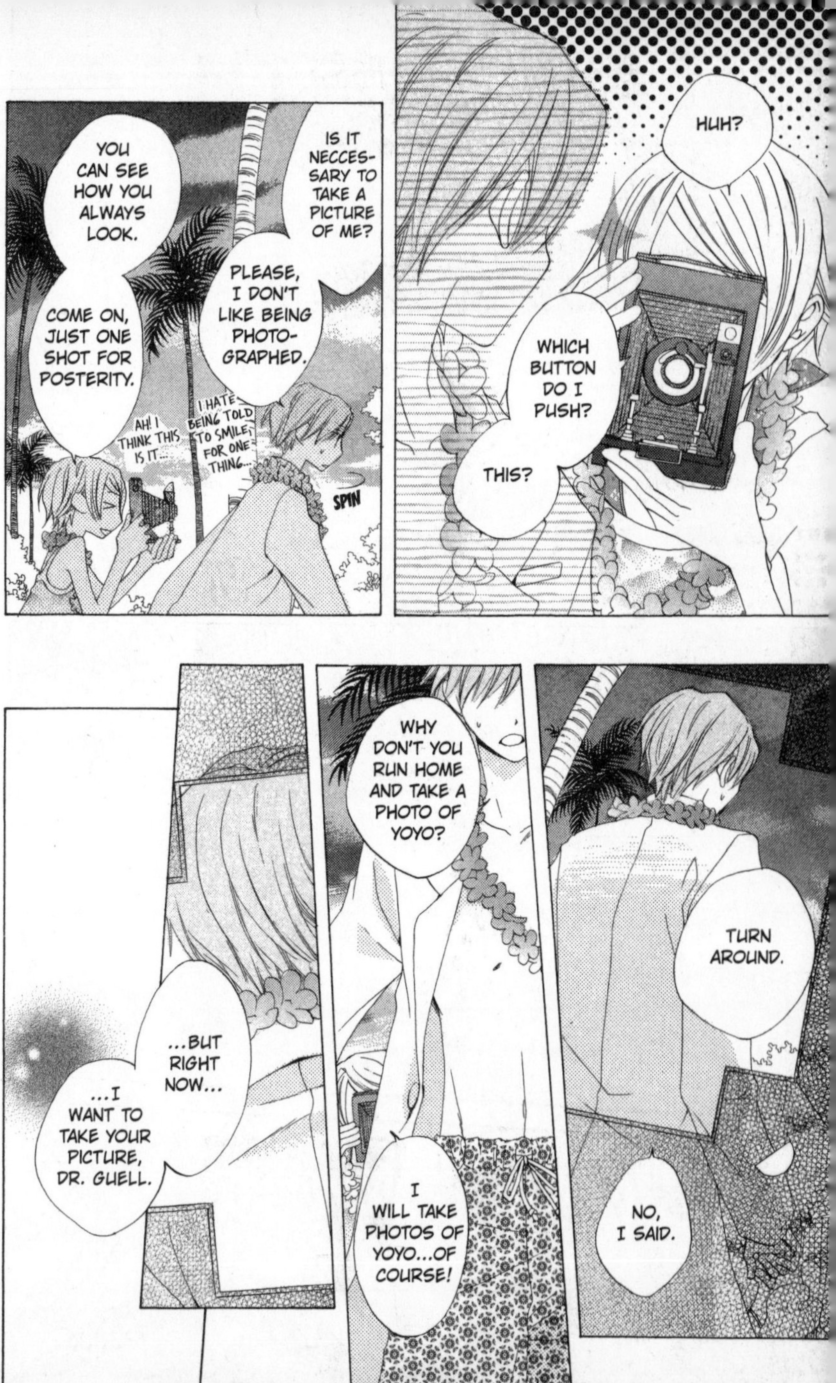
HUH?
WHICH BUTTON DO I PUSH?
THIS?
IS IT NECCES-SARY TO TAKE A PICTURE OF ME?
YOU CAN SEE HOW YOU ALWAYS LOOK.
PLEASE, I DON'T LIKE BEING PHOTO-GRAPHED.
COME ON, JUST ONE SHOT FOR POSTERITY.
I HATE BEING TOLD TO SMILE, FOR ONE THING...
SPIN
AH! I THINK THIS IS IT...
TURN AROUND.
NO, I SAID.
WHY DON'T YOU RUN HOME AND TAKE A PHOTO OF YOYO?
I WILL TAKE PHOTOS OF YOYO...OF COURSE!
...BUT RIGHT NOW...
...I WANT TO TAKE YOUR PICTURE, DR. GUELL.

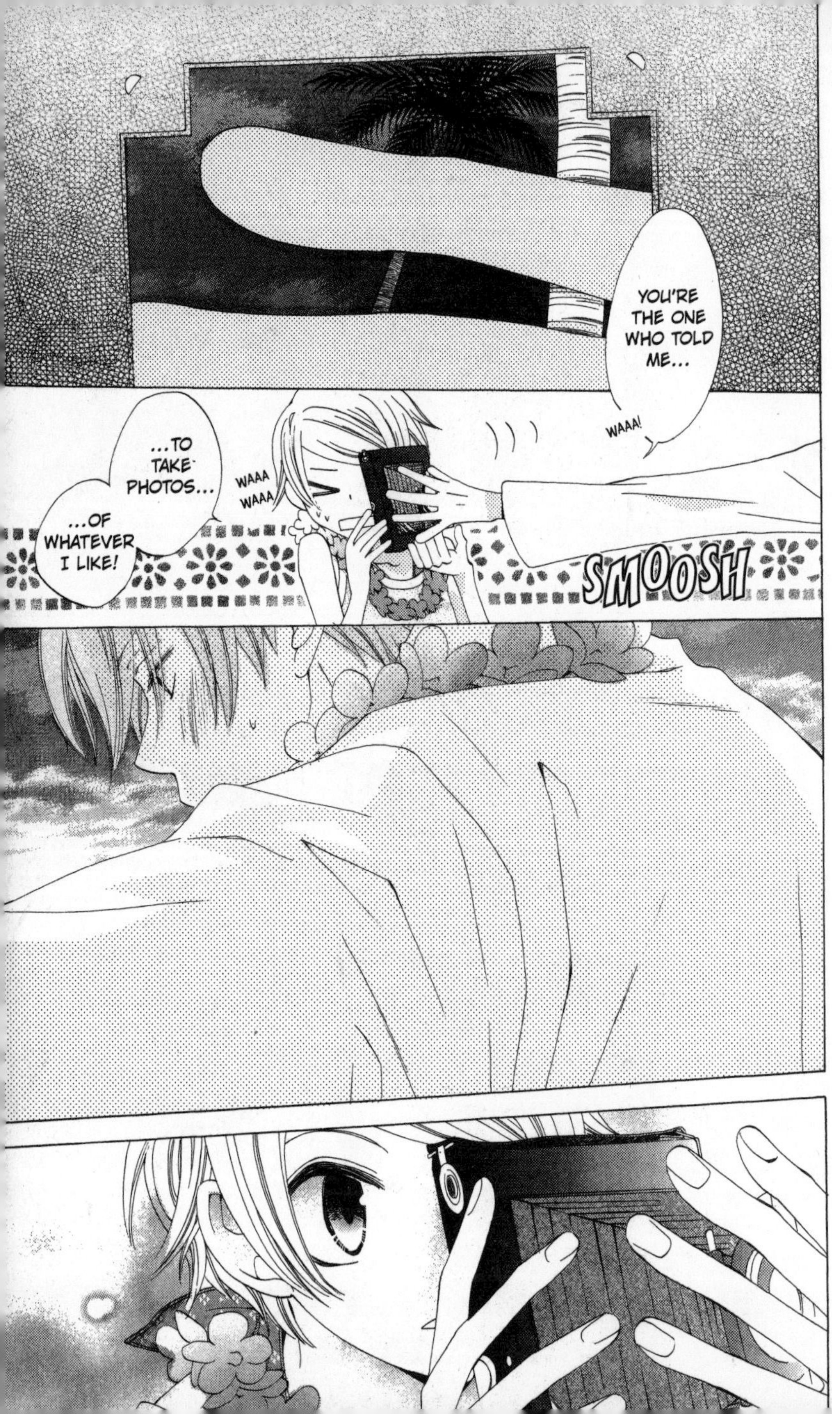
YOU'RE THE ONE WHO TOLD ME...
WAAA!
SMOOSH
WAAA WAAA
...TO TAKE PHOTOS...
...OF WHATEVER I LIKE!

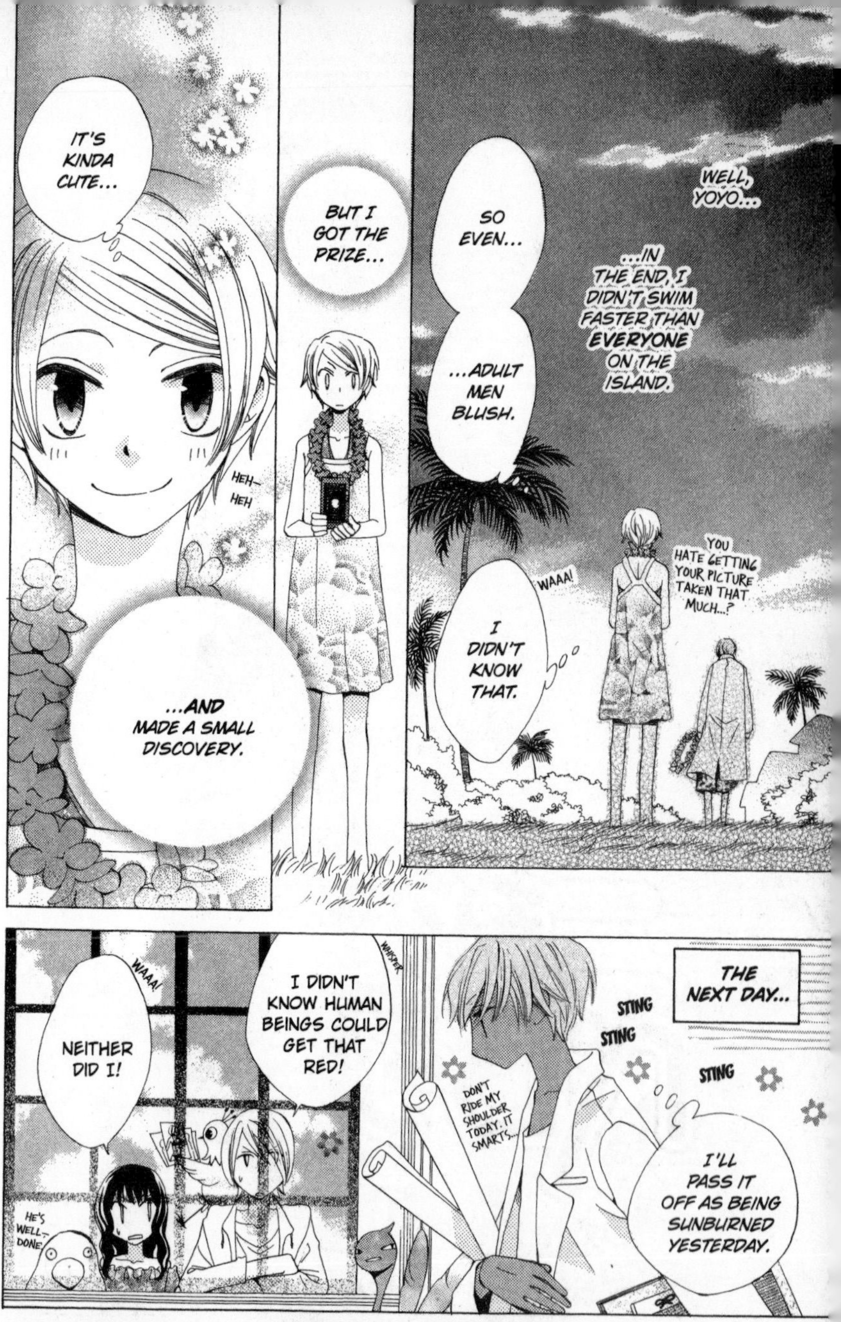
WELL, YOYO...
...IN THE END, I DIDN'T SWIM FASTER THAN EVERYONE ON THE ISLAND.
SO EVEN...
...ADULT MEN BLUSH.
YOU HATE GETTING YOUR PICTURE TAKEN THAT MUCH...?
WAAA!
I DIDN'T KNOW THAT.
BUT I GOT THE PRIZE...
IT'S KINDA CUTE...
HEH-HEH
...AND MADE A SMALL DISCOVERY.
THE NEXT DAY...
STING
STING
STING
I'LL PASS IT OFF AS BEING SUNBURNED YESTERDAY.
DON'T RIDE MY SHOULDER TODAY. IT SMARTS...
WHISPER
I DIDN'T KNOW HUMAN BEINGS COULD GET THAT RED!
WAAA!
NEITHER DID I!
HE'S WELL-DONE.

EPISODE 14: THE END

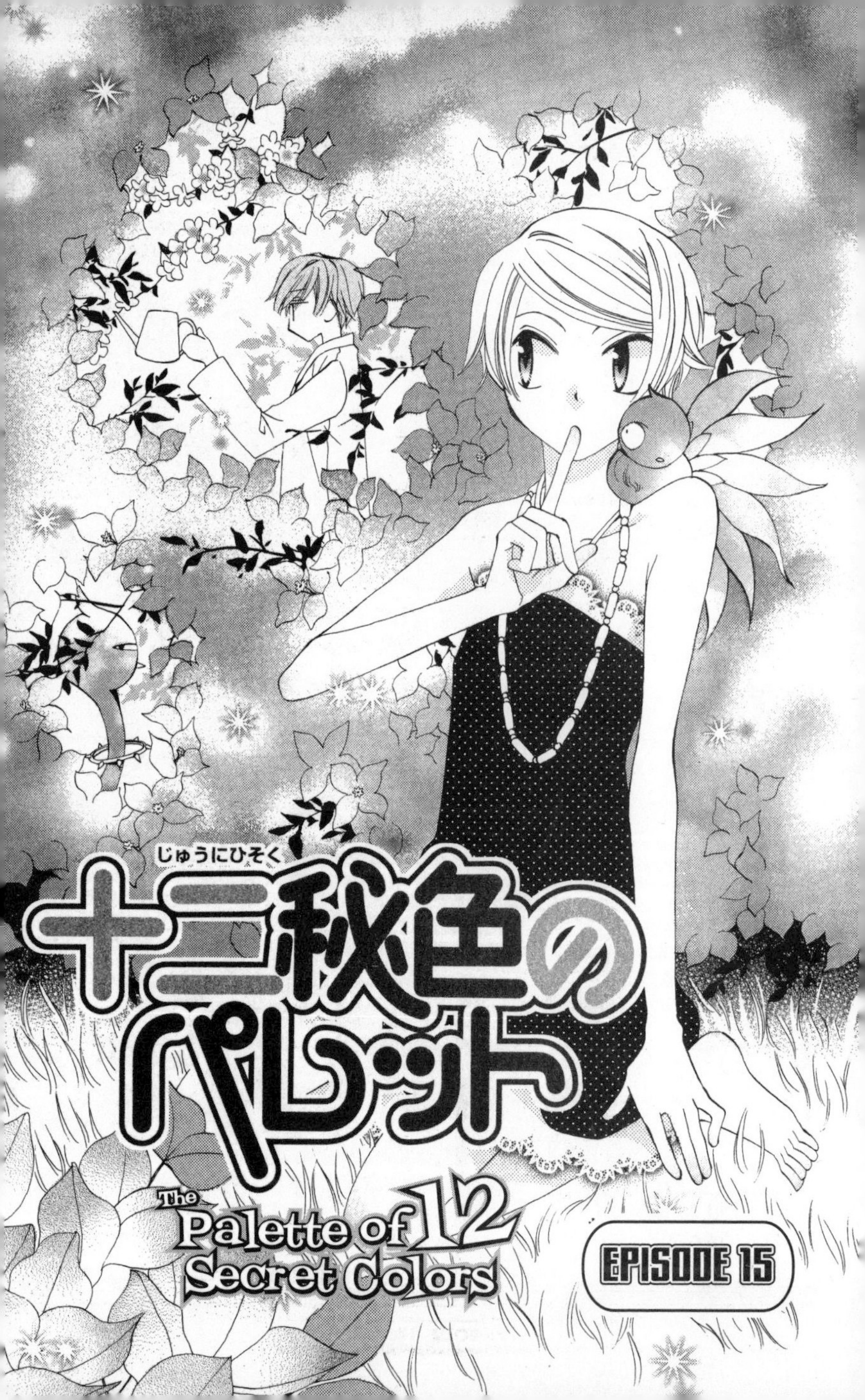
じゅうにひそく
十二秘色のパレット
The Palette of 12 Secret Colors
EPISODE 15

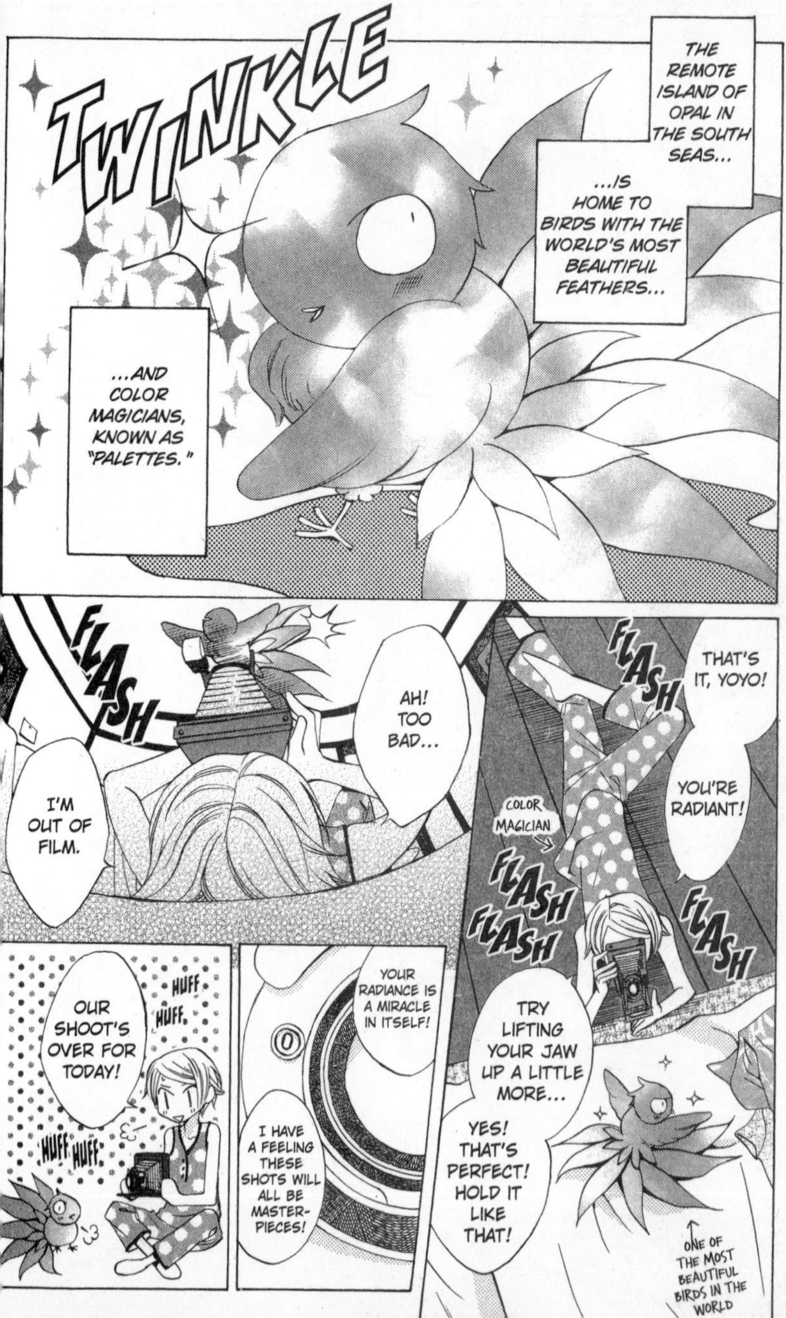
THE REMOTE ISLAND OF OPAL IN THE SOUTH SEAS...
...IS HOME TO BIRDS WITH THE WORLD'S MOST BEAUTIFUL FEATHERS...
TWINKLE
...AND COLOR MAGICIANS, KNOWN AS "PALETTES."
FLASH
THAT'S IT, YOYO!
YOU'RE RADIANT!
COLOR MAGICIAN
FLASH
FLASH
FLASH
TRY LIFTING YOUR JAW UP A LITTLE MORE...
YES! THAT'S PERFECT! HOLD IT LIKE THAT!
ONE OF THE MOST BEAUTIFUL BIRDS IN THE WORLD
FLASH
AH! TOO BAD...
I'M OUT OF FILM.
YOUR RADIANCE IS A MIRACLE IN ITSELF!
I HAVE A FEELING THESE SHOTS WILL ALL BE MASTER-PIECES!
HUFF HUFF
OUR SHOOT'S OVER FOR TODAY!
HUFF HUFF

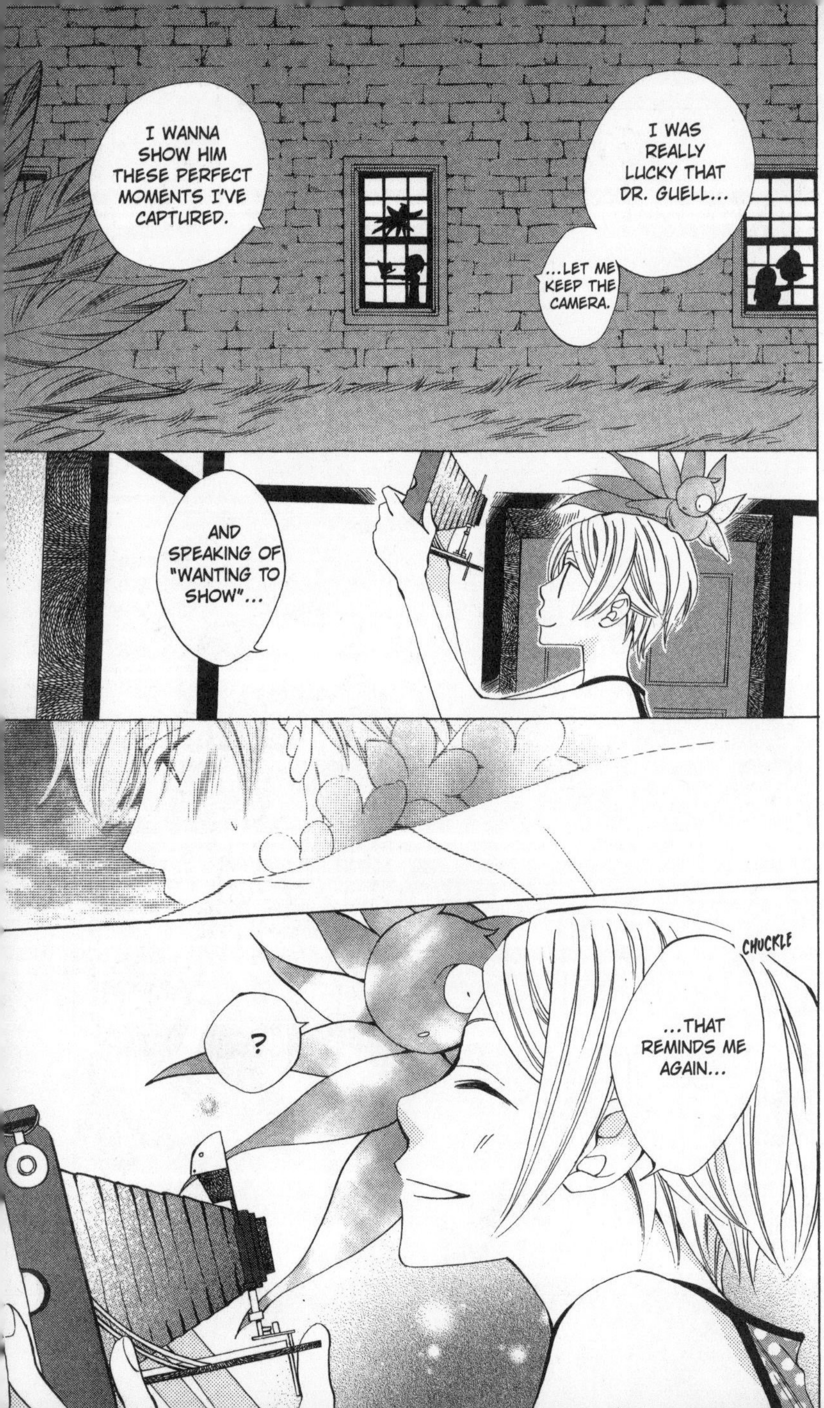
I WAS REALLY LUCKY THAT DR. GUELL...
...LET ME KEEP THE CAMERA.
I WANNA SHOW HIM THESE PERFECT MOMENTS I'VE CAPTURED.
AND SPEAKING OF "WANTING TO SHOW"...
CHUCKLE
...THAT REMINDS ME AGAIN...
?

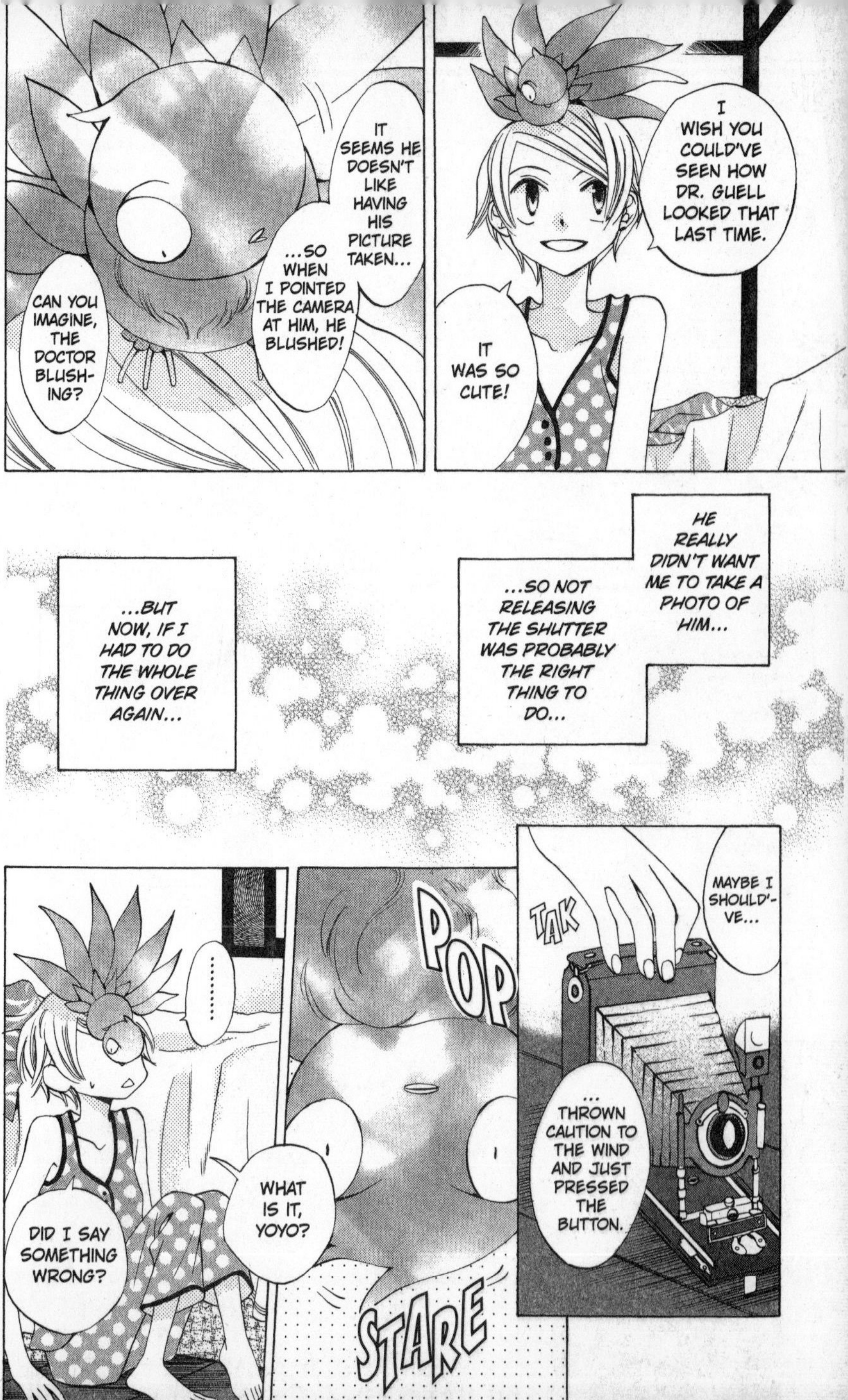
I WISH YOU COULD'VE SEEN HOW DR. GUELL LOOKED THAT LAST TIME.
IT WAS SO CUTE!
IT SEEMS HE DOESN'T LIKE HAVING HIS PICTURE TAKEN...
...SO WHEN I POINTED THE CAMERA AT HIM, HE BLUSHED!
CAN YOU IMAGINE, THE DOCTOR BLUSH-ING?
HE REALLY DIDN'T WANT ME TO TAKE A PHOTO OF HIM...
...SO NOT RELEASING THE SHUTTER WAS PROBABLY THE RIGHT THING TO DO...
...BUT NOW, IF I HAD TO DO THE WHOLE THING OVER AGAIN...
TAK
MAYBE I SHOULD'-VE...
...THROWN CAUTION TO THE WIND AND JUST PRESSED THE BUTTON.
POP
WHAT IS IT, YOYO?
STARE
......
DID I SAY SOMETHING WRONG?

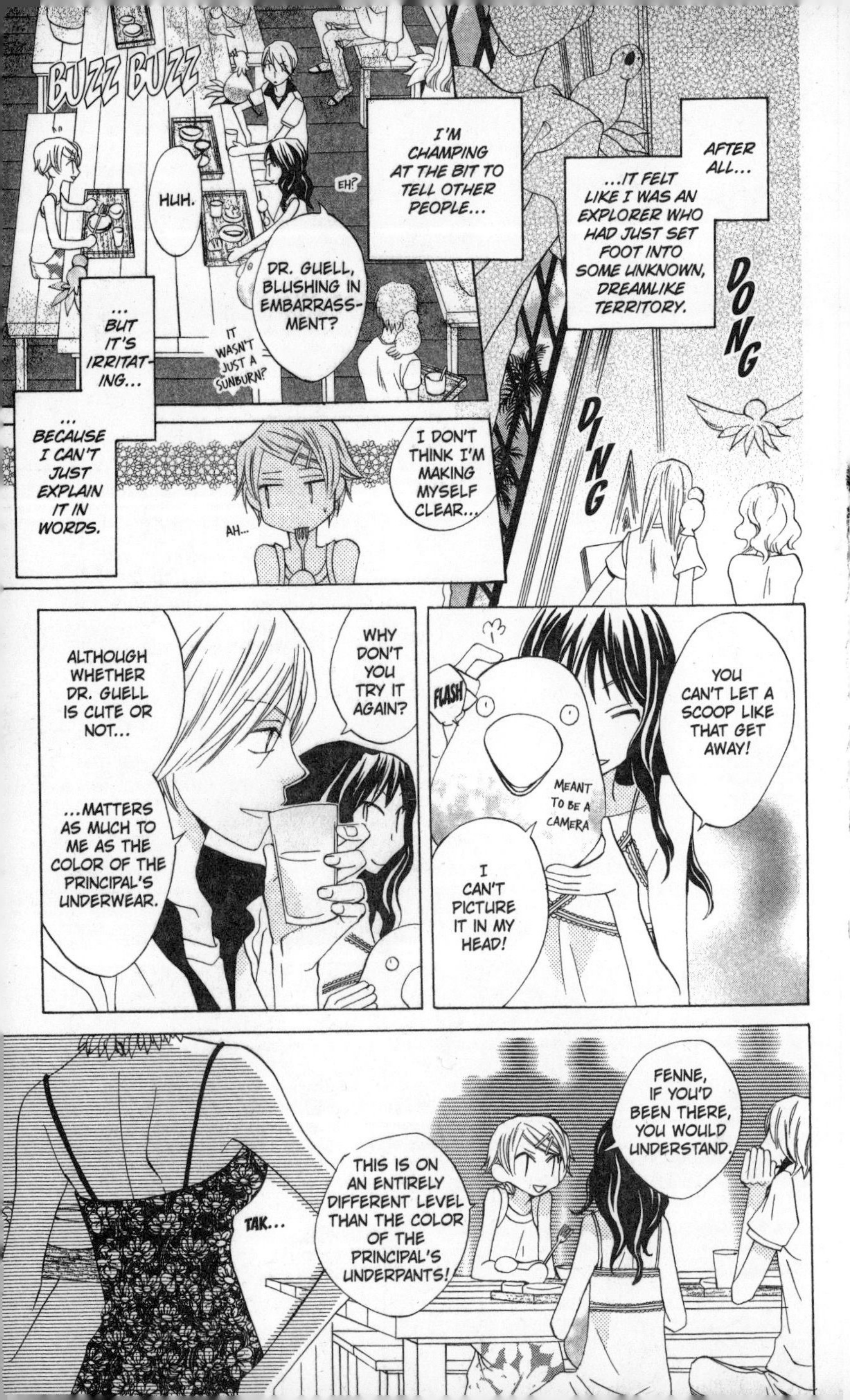
AFTER ALL...
...IT FELT LIKE I WAS AN EXPLORER WHO HAD JUST SET FOOT INTO SOME UNKNOWN, DREAMLIKE TERRITORY.
DING
DONG
I'M CHAMPING AT THE BIT TO TELL OTHER PEOPLE...
EH?
DR. GUELL, BLUSHING IN EMBARRASS-MENT?
HUH.
IT WASN'T JUST A SUNBURN?
BUZZ BUZZ
...BUT IT'S IRRITAT-ING...
...BECAUSE I CAN'T JUST EXPLAIN IT IN WORDS.
I DON'T THINK I'M MAKING MYSELF CLEAR...
AH...
YOU CAN'T LET A SCOOP LIKE THAT GET AWAY!
FLASH
MEANT TO BE A CAMERA
I CAN'T PICTURE IT IN MY HEAD!
WHY DON'T YOU TRY IT AGAIN?
ALTHOUGH WHETHER DR. GUELL IS CUTE OR NOT...
...MATTERS AS MUCH TO ME AS THE COLOR OF THE PRINCIPAL'S UNDERWEAR.
FENNE, IF YOU'D BEEN THERE, YOU WOULD UNDERSTAND.
THIS IS ON AN ENTIRELY DIFFERENT LEVEL THAN THE COLOR OF THE PRINCIPAL'S UNDERPANTS!
TAK...

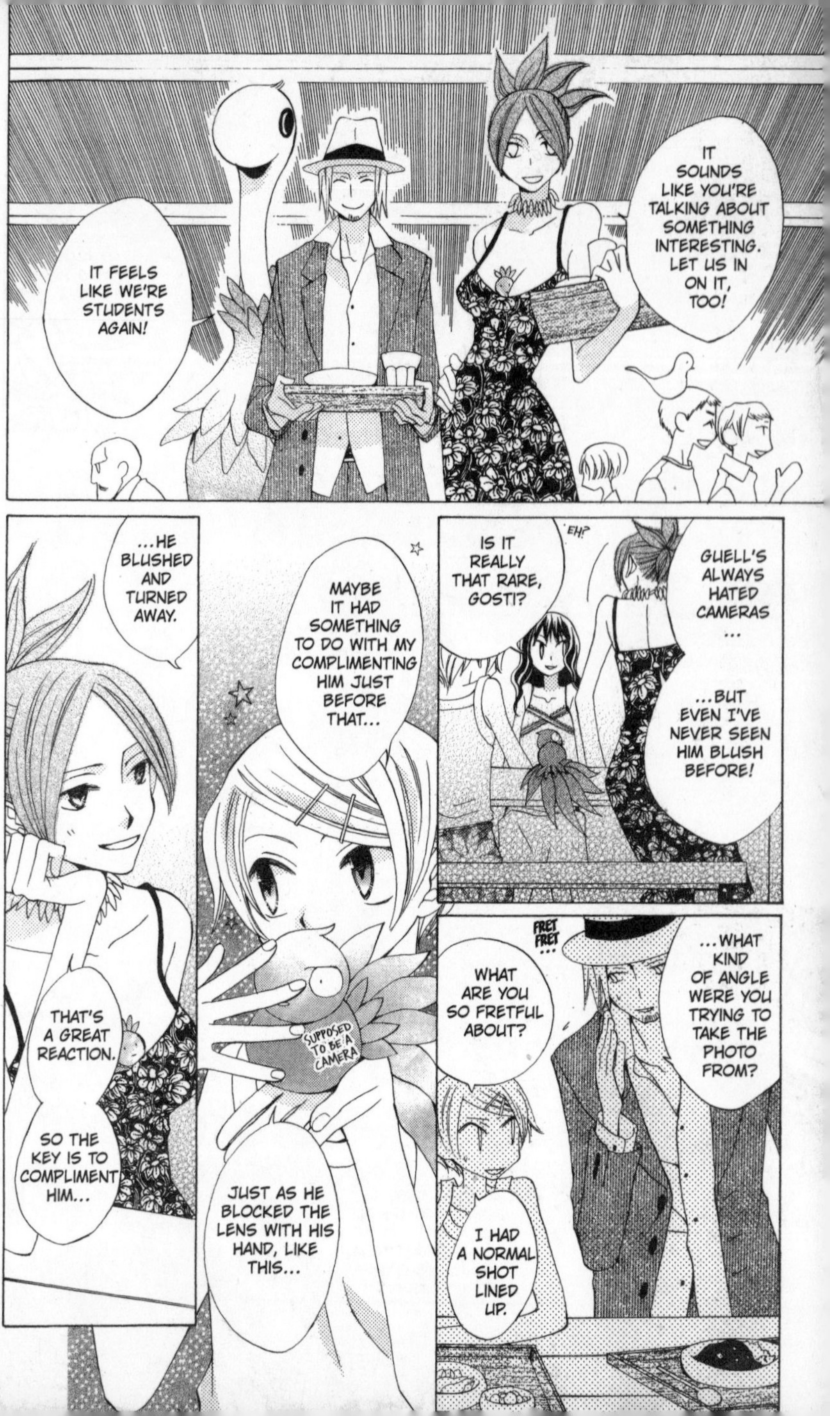
IT SOUNDS LIKE YOU'RE TALKING ABOUT SOMETHING INTERESTING. LET US IN ON IT, TOO!
IT FEELS LIKE WE'RE STUDENTS AGAIN!
GUELL'S ALWAYS HATED CAMERAS ...
...BUT EVEN I'VE NEVER SEEN HIM BLUSH BEFORE!
EH?
IS IT REALLY THAT RARE, GOSTI?
...WHAT KIND OF ANGLE WERE YOU TRYING TO TAKE THE PHOTO FROM?
FRET FRET ...
WHAT ARE YOU SO FRETFUL ABOUT?
I HAD A NORMAL SHOT LINED UP.
MAYBE IT HAD SOMETHING TO DO WITH MY COMPLIMENTING HIM JUST BEFORE THAT...
SUPPOSED TO BE A CAMERA
JUST AS HE BLOCKED THE LENS WITH HIS HAND, LIKE THIS...
...HE BLUSHED AND TURNED AWAY.
THAT'S A GREAT REACTION.
SO THE KEY IS TO COMPLIMENT HIM...

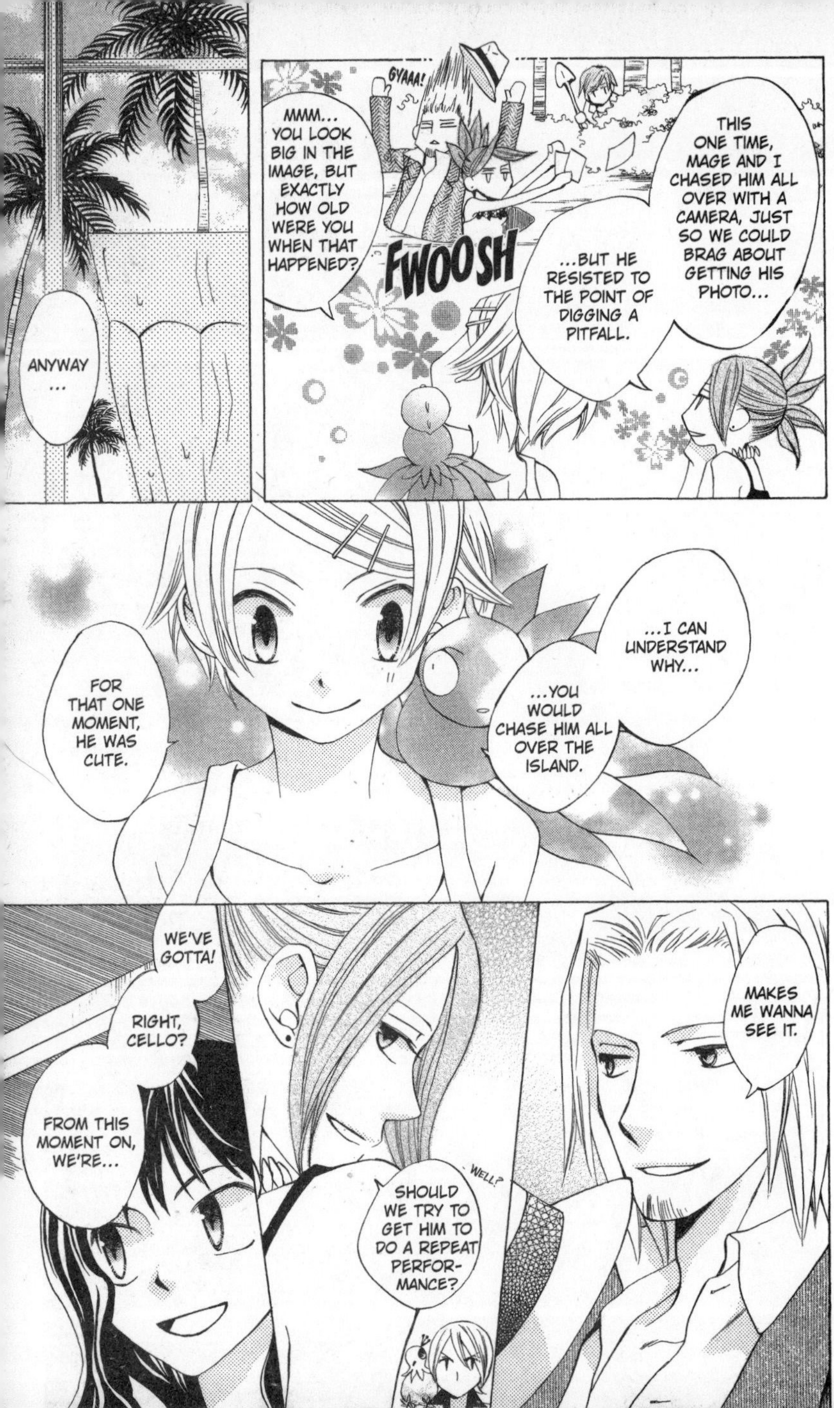
THIS ONE TIME, MAGE AND I CHASED HIM ALL OVER WITH A CAMERA, JUST SO WE COULD BRAG ABOUT GETTING HIS PHOTO...
GYAAA!
...BUT HE RESISTED TO THE POINT OF DIGGING A PITFALL.
MMM... YOU LOOK BIG IN THE IMAGE, BUT EXACTLY HOW OLD WERE YOU WHEN THAT HAPPENED?
FWOOSH
ANYWAY...
...I CAN UNDERSTAND WHY...
...YOU WOULD CHASE HIM ALL OVER THE ISLAND.
FOR THAT ONE MOMENT, HE WAS CUTE.
MAKES ME WANNA SEE IT.
WELL?
SHOULD WE TRY TO GET HIM TO DO A REPEAT PERFOR-MANCE?
WE'VE GOTTA!
RIGHT, CELLO?
FROM THIS MOMENT ON, WE'RE...

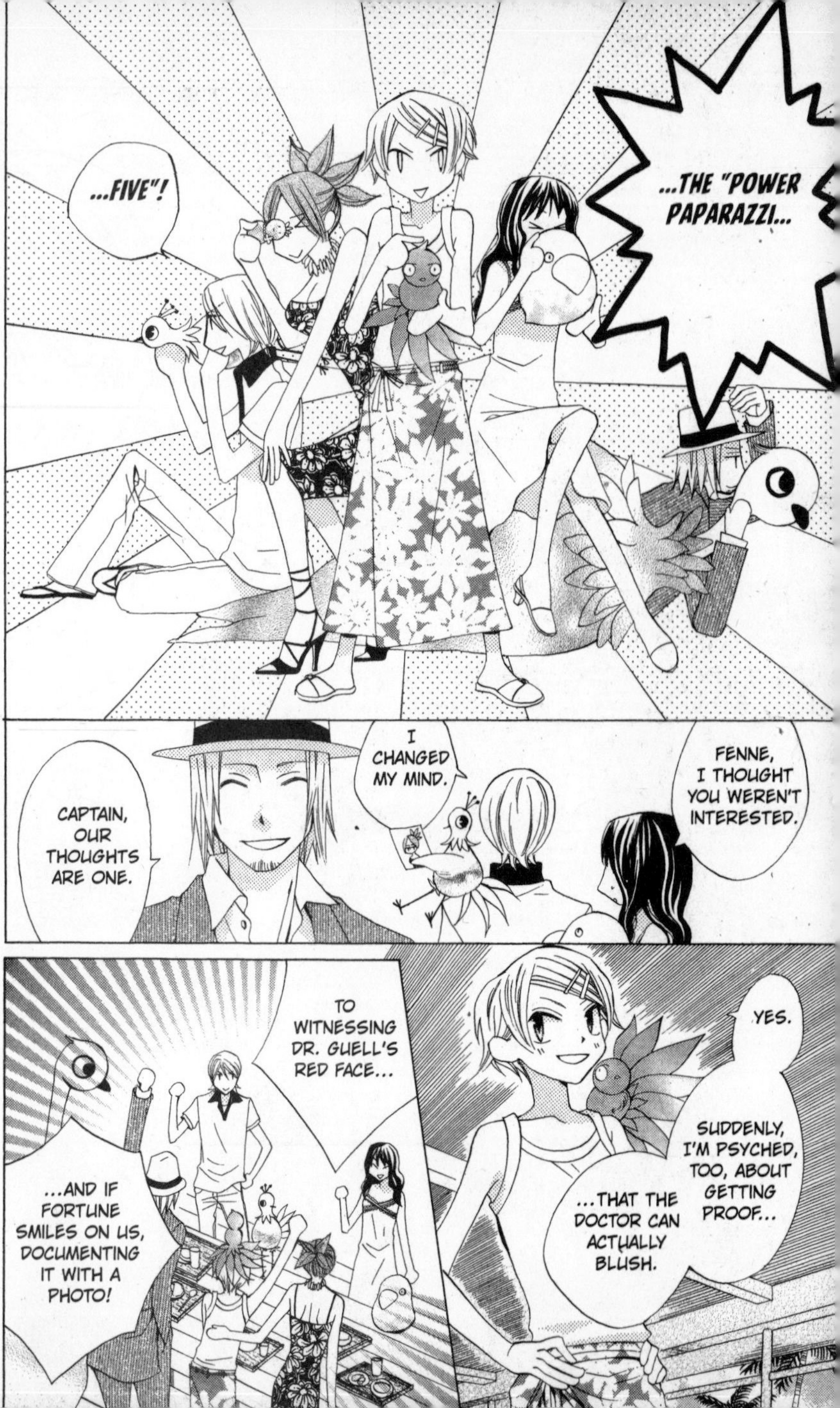
...THE "POWER PAPARAZZI...
...FIVE"!
FENNE, I THOUGHT YOU WEREN'T INTERESTED.
I CHANGED MY MIND.
CAPTAIN, OUR THOUGHTS ARE ONE.
YES.
SUDDENLY, I'M PSYCHED, TOO, ABOUT GETTING PROOF...
...THAT THE DOCTOR CAN ACTUALLY BLUSH.
TO WITNESSING DR. GUELL'S RED FACE...
...AND IF FORTUNE SMILES ON US, DOCUMENTING IT WITH A PHOTO!